Network Security Metrics

Lingyu Wang • Sushil Jajodia • Anoop Singhal

Network Security Metrics

Springer

Lingyu Wang
Concordia Institute for Information
Systems Engineering
Concordia University
Montreal, QC, Canada

Sushil Jajodia
Center for Secure Information Systems
George Mason University
Fairfax, VA, USA

Anoop Singhal
Computer Security Division, NIST
Gaithersburg, MD, USA

ISBN 978-3-319-88259-8   ISBN 978-3-319-66505-4   (eBook)
https://doi.org/10.1007/978-3-319-66505-4

Printed on acid-free paper

This Springer imprint is published by Springer Nature
The registered company is Springer International Publishing AG
The registered company address is: Gewerbestrasse 11, 6330 Cham, Switzerland

To my wife, Quan.
       – Lingyu

To my wife, Kamal, with love.
       – Sushil

To my wife, Radha, with love.
       – Anoop

Preface

Today's computer networks are playing the role of nerve systems in many critical infrastructures, governmental and military organizations, and enterprises. Protecting such a mission-critical network means more than just patching known vulnerabilities and deploying firewalls and IDSs. The network's robustness against potential zero day attacks exploiting unknown vulnerabilities is equally important. Many recent high-profile incidents, such as the worldwide WannaCry ransomware attack in May 2017, the attack on Ukrainian Kyivoblenergo Power Grid in December 2015, and the earlier Stuxnet infiltration of Iran's Natanz nuclear facility, have clearly demonstrated the real world significance of evaluating and improving the security of networks against both previously known attacks and unknown "zero day" attacks.

One of the most pertinent issues in securing mission-critical computing networks against security attacks is the lack of effective security metrics. Since "you cannot improve what you cannot measure," a network security metric is essential to evaluating the relative effectiveness of potential network security solutions. To that end, there have been plenty of recent works on different aspects of network security metrics and their applications. For example, as most existing solutions and standards on security metrics, such as CVSS and attack surface, typically focus on known vulnerabilities in individual software products or systems, many recent works focus on combining individual metric scores into an overall measure of network security. Also, some efforts are dedicated to develop network security metrics especially for dealing with zero day attacks, which imply little or no prior knowledge is present about the exploited vulnerabilities, and thus most existing approaches to security metrics will no longer be effective. Finally, some recent works apply security metric concepts to specific security applications, such as applying and visualizing a suite of network security metrics at the enterprise level, and measuring the operational effectiveness of a cybersecurity operations center. This book examines in detail those and other recent works on network security metrics.

There currently exists little effort on a systematic compilation of recent progresses in network security metrics research. This book will fill the gaps by providing a big picture about the topic to network security practitioners and security researchers alike. Security researchers who work on network security or security analytics-related areas seeking new research topics, as well as security practitioners including network administrators and security architects who are looking for state-of-the-art approaches to hardening their networks, will find this book useful as a reference. Advanced-level students studying computer science and engineering will also find this book useful as a secondary text.

More specifically, this book examines recent works on different aspects of network security metrics and their application to enterprise networks. First, the book starts by examining the limitations of existing solutions and standards on security metrics, such as CVSS and attack surface, which typically focus on known vulnerabilities in individual software products or systems. Chapters "Measuring the Overall Network Security by Combining CVSS Scores Based on Attack Graphs and Bayesian Networks", "Refining CVSS-Based Network Security Metrics by Examining the Base Scores" and "Security Risk Analysis of Enterprise Networks Using Probabilistic Attack Graphs" then describe different approaches to aggregating individual metric values obtained from CVSS scores into an overall measure of network security using attack graphs. Second, since CVSS scores are only available for previously known vulnerabilities, the threat of unknown attacks exploiting the so-called zero day vulnerabilities is not covered by CVSS scores. Therefore, chapters "k-Zero Day Safety: Evaluating the Resilience of Networks Against Unknown Attacks", "Using Bayesian Networks to Fuse Intrusion Evidences and Detect Zero-Day Attack Paths" and "Evaluating the Network Diversity of Networks Against Zero-Day Attacks" present several approaches to developing network security metrics in order to deal with zero day attacks exploiting unknown vulnerabilities. Finally, to address practical challenges in applying network security metrics to real world organization, chapter "Metrics Suite for Network Attack Graph Analytics" discusses several issues in defining and visualizing such metrics at the enterprise level, and chapter "A Novel Metric for Measuring Operational Effectiveness of a Cybersecurity Operations Center" demonstrates the need for novel metrics in measuring the operational effectiveness of a cybersecurity operations center.

Montreal, QC, Canada   Lingyu Wang
Fairfax, VA, USA   Sushil Jajodia
Gaithersburg, MD, USA   Anoop Singhal

Acknowledgements

Lingyu Wang was partially supported by Natural Sciences and Engineering Research Council of Canada under Discovery Grant N01035. Sushil Jajodia was partially supported by the Army Research Office grants W911NF-13-1-0421 and W911NF-15-1-0576, by the Office of Naval Research grant N00014-15-1-2007, National Institutes of Standard and Technology grant 60NANB16D287, and by the National Science Foundation grant IIP-1266147.

Contents

Measuring the Overall Network Security by Combining CVSS Scores Based on Attack Graphs and Bayesian Networks

Marcel Frigault, Lingyu Wang, Sushil Jajodia, and Anoop Singhal

Abstract Given the increasing dependence of our societies on networked information systems, the overall security of these systems should be measured and improved. This chapter examines several approaches to combining the CVSS scores of individual vulnerabilities into an overall measure for network security. First, we convert CVSS base scores into probabilities and then propagate such probabilities along attack paths in an attack graph in order to obtain an overall metric, while giving special considerations to cycles in the attack graph. Second, we show that the previous approach implicitly assumes the metric values of individual vulnerabilities to be independent, and we remove such an assumption by representing the attack graph and its assigned probabilities as a Bayesian network and then derive the overall metric value through Bayesian inferences. Finally, to address the evolving nature of vulnerabilities, we extend the previous model to dynamic Bayesian networks such that we can make inferences about the security of dynamically changing networks.

1 Introduction

Crucial to today's economy and national security, computer networks play a central role in most enterprises and critical infrastructures including power grids, financial data systems, and emergency communication systems. In protecting these networks against malicious intrusions, a standard way for measuring network security will bring together users, vendors, and labs in specifying, implementing, and evaluating

M. Frigault • L. Wang (✉)
Concordia Institute for Information Systems Engineering, Concordia University, Montreal, QC, Canada H3G 1M8
e-mail: wang@ciise.concordia.ca

S. Jajodia
Center for Secure Information Systems, George Mason University, Fairfax, VA 22030-4444, USA
e-mail: jajodia@gmu.edu

A. Singhal
Computer Security Division, NIST, Gaithersburg, MD 20899, USA
e-mail: anoop.singhal@nist.gov

© Springer International Publishing AG 2017
L. Wang et al., *Network Security Metrics*,
https://doi.org/10.1007/978-3-319-66505-4_1

network security products. Despite existing efforts in standardizing security metrics [4, 8], a widely-accepted network security metric is largely unavailable. At the research frontier, a qualitative and imprecise view toward the evaluation of network security is still dominant. Researchers are mostly concerned about issues with binary answers, such as whether a given critical resource is secure (vulnerability analysis) or whether an insecure network can be hardened (network hardening).

In particular, an important challenge in developing network security metrics is to compose measures of individual vulnerabilities, resources, and configurations into a global measure. A naive approach to such compositions may lead to misleading results. For example, less vulnerabilities are not necessarily more secure, considering a case where these vulnerabilities must all be exploited in order to compromise a critical resource. On the other hand, less vulnerabilities can indeed mean more security when exploiting any of these vulnerabilities is sufficient for compromising that resource. This example shows that to obtain correct compositions of individual measures, we need to first understand the interplay between different network components. For example, how an attacker may combine different vulnerabilities to advance an intrusion; how exploiting one vulnerability may reduce the difficulty of exploiting another vulnerability; how compromising one resource may affect the damage or risk of compromising another resource; how modifying one network parameter may affect the cost of modifying other parameters.

The study of composing individual measures of network security becomes feasible now due to recent advances in modeling network security with *attack graphs*, which may be automatically generated using mature tools, such as the Topological Vulnerability Analysis (TVA) system capable of handling tens of thousands of vulnerabilities taken from 24 information sources including X-Force, Bugtraq, CVE, CERT, Nessus, and Snort [2]. Attack graphs provide the missing information about relationships among network components and thus allow us to consider potential attacks and their consequences in a particular *context*. Such a context makes it possible to compose individual measures of vulnerabilities, resources, and configurations into a global measure of network security. The presence of such a powerful tool demonstrates the practicality of using attack graphs as the basis for measuring network security.

To that end, this chapter examines several approaches to combining the CVSS scores of individual vulnerabilities into an overall measure for network security. First, we convert CVSS base scores into probabilities and then propagate such probabilities along attack paths in an attack graph in order to obtain an overall metric, while giving special considerations to potential cycles in the attack graph. Second, we show that the previous approach implicitly assumes the metric values of individual vulnerabilities to be independent, and we remove such an assumption by representing the attack graph and its assigned probabilities as a Bayesian network and then derive the overall metric value through Bayesian inferences. Finally, to address the evolving nature of vulnerabilities, we extend the previous model to Dynamic Bayesian Networks such that we can make inferences about the security of dynamically changing networks.

2 Propagating Attack Probabilities Along Attack Paths

In practice, many vulnerabilities may still remain in a network after they are discovered, due to either environmental factors (such as latency in releasing software patches or hardware upgrades), cost factors (such as money and administrative efforts required for deploying patches and upgrades), or mission factors (such as organizational preferences for availability and usability over security). To remove such *residue vulnerabilities* in the most cost-efficient way, we need to evaluate and measure the likelihood that attackers may compromise critical resources through cleverly combining multiple vulnerabilities.

To that end, there already exist standard ways for assigning scores to vulnerabilities based on their relative severity. For example, the Common Vulnerability Scoring System (CVSS) measures the potential impact and environmental metrics in terms of each individual vulnerability [3]. The CVSS scores of most known vulnerabilities are readily available in public databases, such as the NVD [5]. However, such existing standards focus on the measurement of individual vulnerabilities, and how such vulnerabilities may interact with each other in a particular network is usually left for administrators to figure out. On the other hand, the causal relationships between vulnerabilities are well understood and usually encoded in the form of *attack graphs* [1, 7]. Attack graphs help to understand whether given critical resources can be compromised through multi-step attacks. However, as a qualitative model, attack graph still adopts a binary view towards security, that is, a network is either secure (critical resources are not reachable) or insecure.

Clearly, there is a gap between existing security metrics, which mostly focus on individual vulnerabilities, and qualitative models of vulnerabilities, which are usually limited to binary views of security. To fill this gap, this section describes a probabilistic metric for measuring network security. The metric draws strength from both existing security metrics and the attack graph model. More specifically, we combine the measurements of individual vulnerabilities obtained from existing metrics into an overall score of the network. This combination is based on the causal relationships between vulnerabilities encoded in an attack graph. The key challenge lies in handling complex attack graphs with cycles. We first define the basic metric without considering cycles. We provide an intuitive interpretation of the metric. Based on such an interpretation, we extend the definition to attack graphs with cycles.

2.1 Motivating Example

Attack graphs model how multiple vulnerabilities may be combined for advancing an intrusion. In an attack graph, security-related *conditions* represent the system state, and an *exploit* of vulnerabilities between connected hosts is modeled as a transition between system states. Figure 1 shows a toy example. The left side is the configuration of a network. Machine 1 is a file server behind the firewall that offers file transfer (ftp), secure shell (ssh), and remote shell (rsh) services. Machine 2 is an

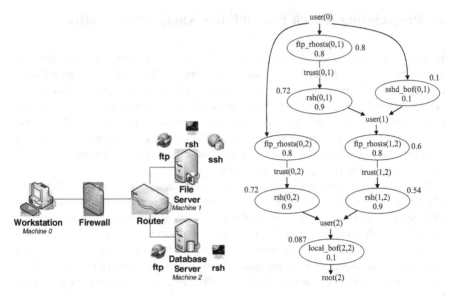

Fig. 1 An example of network configuration and attack graph

internal database server that offers ftp and rsh services. The firewall allows ftp, ssh, and rsh traffic to both servers and blocks all other incoming traffic.

The right-hand side of Fig. 1 shows the attack graph (the numerical values are not part of the attack graph and will be explained shortly), which is a directed graph with two kinds of vertices, namely, exploits shown as predicates inside ovals and conditions shown in plaintexts. For example, $rsh(0, 1)$ represents a remote shell login from machine 0 to machine 1, and $trust(0, 1)$ means a trust relationship is established from machine 0 to machine 1. A directed edge from a condition to an exploit means executing the exploit requires the condition to be satisfied, and that from an exploit to a condition means executing the exploit will satisfy the condition. We formalize the attack graph in Definition 1.

Definition 1 An attack graph G is a directed graph $G(E \cup C, R_r \cup R_i)$ where E is a set of exploits, C a set of conditions, and $R_r \subseteq C \times E$ and $R_i \subseteq E \times C$.

The attack graph in Fig. 1 depicts three *attack paths*. On the right, the attack path starts with an ssh buffer overflow exploit from machine 0 to machine 1, which gives the attacker the capability of executing arbitrary codes on machine 1 as a normal user. The attacker then exploits the ftp vulnerability on machine 2 to anonymously upload a list of trusted hosts. Such a trust relationship enables the attacker to remotely execute shell commands on machine 2 without providing a password. Consequently, a local buffer overflow exploit on machine 2 escalates the attacker's privilege to be the root of that machine. Details of the other two attack paths are similar and are omitted.

Informally, the numerical value inside each oval is an *attack probability* that indicates the relative likelihood of the corresponding exploit being executed by attackers when all the required conditions are already satisfied. This value thus only depends on each individual vulnerability, which is similar to many existing metrics, such as the CVSS [3]. On the other hand, we can clearly see the limitation of such metrics in assessing the impact, damage, or relevance of vulnerabilities, because such factors are rather determined by the combination of exploits. While we delay its definition and computation to later sections, the numerical value beside each oval represents the likelihood of reaching the corresponding exploit in this particular network. Clearly, a security administrator will be much happier to see the single score beside the last exploit (*localbof*(2, 2)) than looking at all the eight values inside ovals and wondering how those values may be related to each other.

2.2 Defining the Metric

We first assume acyclic attack graphs and delay the discussion of cycles to the next section. We associate each exploit e and condition c with two probabilities, namely, $p(e)$ and $p(c)$ for the *individual score*, and $P(e)$ and $P(c)$ for the *cumulative score*. The individual score $p(e)$ stands for the intrinsic likelihood of an exploit e being executed, given that all the conditions required for executing e in the given attack graph are already satisfied. On the other hand, the cumulative score $P(e)$ and $P(c)$ measures the overall likelihood that an attacker can successfully reach and execute the exploit e (or satisfy the condition c) in the given attack graph.

For exploits, we assume the individual score is assigned based on expert knowledge about the vulnerability being exploited. In practice, individual scores can be obtained by converting vulnerability scores provided by existing standards, such as dividing the CVSS base score by 10 [3], to probabilities. For conditions, we assume in this chapter that the individual score of every condition is always 1. Intuitively, a condition is either initially satisfied (for example, $user(0)$ in Fig. 1), or immediately satisfied after a successful exploit (in practice, we can easily remove such assumptions by assigning less-than-1 individual scores to conditions).

Unlike individual scores, the cumulative score takes into accounts the causal relationships between exploits and conditions. In an attack graph, such causal relationships may appear in two different forms. First, a conjunction exists between multiple conditions required for executing the same exploit. Second, a disjunction exists between multiple exploits that satisfy the same condition. The cumulative scores are defined in the two cases similar to the probability of the *intersection* and *union* of random events. That is, if the execution of e requires two conditions c_1 and c_2, then $P(e) = P(c_1) \cdot P(c_2) \cdot p(e)$; if a condition c can be satisfied by either e_1 or e_2 (or both), then $P(c) = p(c)(P(e_1) + P(e_2) - P(e_1) \cdot P(e_2))$. Definition 2 formalizes cumulative scores.

Definition 2 Given an acyclic attack graph $G(E \cup C, R_r \cup R_i)$, and any individual score assignment function $p : E \cup C \rightarrow [0, 1]$, the cumulative score function $P :$ $E \cup C \rightarrow [0, 1]$ is defined as

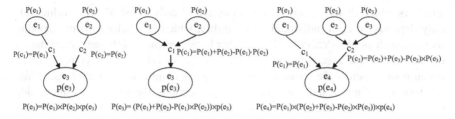

Fig. 2 Examples showing the need for cumulative scores of conditions

- $P(e) = p(e) \cdot \prod_{c \in R_r(e)} P(c)$
- $P(c) = p(c)$, if $R_i(c) = \phi$; otherwise, $P(c) = p(c) \cdot \oplus_{e \in R_i(c)} P(e)$ where the operator $\oplus$ is recursively defined as $\oplus P(e) = P(e)$ for any $e \in E$ and $\oplus(S_1 \cup S_2) = \oplus S_1 + \oplus S_2 - \oplus S_1 \cdot \oplus S_2$ for any disjoint and non-empty sets $S_1 \subseteq E$ and $S_2 \subseteq E$.

In Fig. 1, the cumulative scores of two exploits (shown as plaintexts besides corresponding exploits) can be calculated as follows.

1. $P(rsh(0, 1)) = P(trust(0, 1) \times p(rsh(0, 1)) = 0.8 \times 0.9 = 0.72$
2. $P(user(1)) = P(rsh(0, 1)) + P(sshdbof(0, 1)) - P(rsh(0, 1)) \times P(sshd bof(0, 1)) = 0.72 + 0.1 - 0.72 \times 0.1 = 0.748$

From the above example, the score of conditions may seem rather unnecessary (as a matter of fact, we do not show the score of conditions in Fig. 1). However, the attack graph shown in Fig. 1 is a special case where all the causal relationships between exploits happen to be disjunction only. In general, more complicated relationships may arise between exploits, and the cumulative score of conditions will be helpful in such cases. For example, Fig. 2 shows the calculation of cumulative scores when a conjunctive, disjunctive, and hybrid relationship exists between exploits, respectively. It would be cumbersome to explicitly deal with such different relationships in defining our metric. However, as long as we include conditions as an intermediate between exploits, we can safely ignore the difference between those cases.

Using probabilities for a security metric has been criticized as violating a basic design principle, that is, the value assignment should be specific and unambiguous rather than abstract and meaningless [6]. However, there is a simple interpretation for our metric. That is, the individual score $p(e)$ is the probability that any attacker can, and will execute e during an attack, given that all the preconditions are already satisfied. Equivalently, among all attackers that attempt to compromise the given network during any given time period, $p(e)$ is the fraction of attackers that can, and will execute e. This interpretation of individual scores also provides a natural semantics to the cumulative scores. That is, $P(e)$ or $P(c)$ stands for the likelihood, or the fraction of, attackers who will successfully exploit e or satisfy c in the given network. The cumulative score of a given goal condition thus indicates the likelihood that a corresponding resource will be compromised during an attack, or

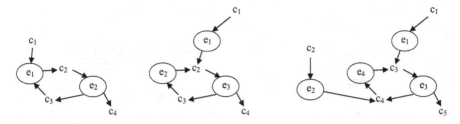

Fig. 3 Cycles in attack graphs

equivalently, among all attackers attacking the given network over a given time period, the average fraction of attackers who will successfully compromise the resource.

2.3 Handling Cycles in Attack Graphs

One complication in defining cumulative scores lies in the effect of cycles in attack graphs. Different types of cycles naturally exist in attack graphs, and they create different difficulties. Namely, some cycles can be completely removed; some cycles can be safely broken; some cycles, however, can neither be removed or broken.

Figure 3 shows an example for each type of such cycles. First, the left-hand side of Fig. 3 shows a cycle that can be completely removed because none of the exploits or conditions inside the cycle can ever be reached by attackers. More specifically, executing the exploit e_1 requires both c_1 and c_3 to be satisfied. However, c_3 can only be satisfied by the execution of e_2, which again requires e_1 to be executed first. Therefore, neither e_1 nor e_2 can ever be successfully executed, and thus conditions c_2 and c_3 can never be satisfied. Such a *removable* cycle can be completely ignored during calculating the cumulative scores. In another word, all exploits and conditions inside the cycle have a cumulative score of zero (notice that c_4 thus automatically receives a cumulative score of zero by definition).

Second, the middle case of Fig. 3 shows that some cycles cannot be removed because the exploits and conditions inside the cycle can indeed by reached. The condition c_2 can be satisfied by either e_1 or e_2. If c_2 is first satisfied by e_1, then both e_2 and e_3 can be successfully executed. Ignoring such a cycle will thus cause incorrect definition of the metric. Fortunately, this cycle can be easily broken by removing the directed edge from e_2 to c_2. Intuitively, c_2 is only satisfiable by e_1 even though later on it may be satisfied *again* by e_2 (we shall provide a clearer interpretation shortly). After we break the cycle in this way, the cumulative scores can then be easily calculated.

Third, the right-hand side of Fig. 3 shows a cycle that can be neither removed nor broken in the aforementioned manner. Both e_1 and e_2 can lead to exploits in the cycle to be executed. There are thus two different ways for breaking the cycle among

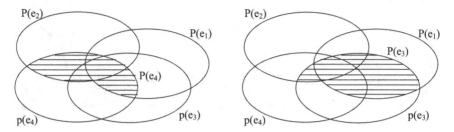

Fig. 4 Calculating cumulative scores in the presence of cycles

which we can only choose one. That is, we can either remove the edge from e_4 to c_3 by assuming c_3 is satisfied by e_1, or remove the edge from e_3 to c_4 by considering c_4 to be satisfied by e_2. However, there is no clear reason to prefer any of the two choices over the other. Moreover, removing both edges is clearly not a valid solution (the graph will be separated into two disjoint components). This example shows that removing or breaking a cycle is not a valid solution for all cases.

To find a meaningful solution, we revisit the aforementioned interpretation of the proposed metric. That is, an individual score represents the fraction of attackers who can (and will) execute an exploit or satisfy a condition (in the rest of the chapter, we shall refer to both as *reaching*), given that all preconditions are already satisfied; a cumulative score indicates the fraction of attackers who will reach an exploit or a condition. However, when cycles are present in an attack graph, an attacker may reach an exploit or a condition more than once. Clearly, extra caution must be taken in calculating cumulative scores to avoid counting any attacker twice.

Without the loss of generality, we consider the calculation of $P(e_4)$ on the right-hand side of Fig. 3. We illustrate those events using Venn diagrams in Fig. 4 (the shaded areas can be ignored for now). Notice that the figure depicts cumulative scores for e_1 and e_2 as they are not part of the cycle. Referring to the right-hand side of Fig. 3, we shall first calculate $P(e_4)$ by following the cycle clockwise from c_4, through e_4, c_3, e_3, and finally to c_4 again, as follows.

1. By abusing notations, denote $P(e_2)$ the set of attackers reaching e_2, represented as an oval in Fig. 4.
2. Among the attackers in $P(e_2)$, those who can execute e_4 form the intersection $P(e_2) \cap p(e_4)$.
3. The union of two sets of attackers, $P(e_2) \cap p(e_4) \cup P(e_1)$, will reach c_3.
4. The intersection of the above set with $p(e_3)$, that is, $(P(e_2) \cap p(e_4) \cup P(e_1)) \cap p(e_3)$ will reach e_3.
5. Among those who reach e_3, the attackers originally coming from the set $P(e_2)$ should not be counted again towards satisfying c_4. In another word, only those in $(P(e_2) \cap p(e_4) \cup P(e_1)) \cap p(e_3) \setminus P(e_2) = P(e_1) \cap p(e_3) \setminus P(e_2)$ should be counted.
6. Finally, the set of attackers that can reach e_4 is $(P(e_1) \cap p(e_3) \setminus P(e_2) \cup P(e_2)) \cap p(e_4) = (P(e_1) \cap p(e_3) \cup P(e_2)) \cap p(e_4)$

The shaded area in the left-hand side of Fig. 4 indicates the final result of $P(e_4)$. The right-hand side of Fig. 4 corresponds to $P(e_3)$, which can be calculated similarly. In the above calculation, we essentially break the cycle in the second to the last step, by disregarding those attackers who reach c_4 for the second time. This is reasonable because in measuring the fraction of attackers (or the likelihood of an attacker) reaching c_4, we should only count the fraction of distinct attackers. In another word, although an attacker can repeat an exploit for many times, this should not affect the metric.

Definition 3 formalizes cumulative scores for general attack graphs. In the definition, the first case corresponds to the exception where e is inside a removable cycle, so its cumulative score is defined (not computed) as zero. In the second case, the cumulative score is defined in $A(G, e)$ instead of G so to ensure that e is not inside any cycle and its cumulative score can thus be calculated based on Definition 2 (however, $A(G, e)$ is not guaranteed to be an acyclic attack graph so Definition 2 does not directly apply).

Definition 3 Given an attack graph $G(E \cup C, R_r \cup R_i)$, and any individual score assignment function $p : E \cup C \rightarrow [0, 1]$, we denote $A(G, e)$ (or $A(G, c)$) an attack graph obtained by removing from G all the outgoing edges at e (or c) and consequently removing all unreachable exploits and conditions from G. The cumulative score function $P : E \cup C \rightarrow [0, 1]$ is defined as

- If e (or c) does not appear in $A(G, e)$ (or $A(G, c)$), then $P(e) = 0$ (or $P(c) = 0$).
- Otherwise, $P(e)$ (or $P(c)$) is equal to its value calculated in $A(G, e)$ (or $A(G, c)$) based on Definition 2.

Definition 3 satisfies two desirable properties as stated in Proposition 1. The first property guarantees that the cumulative score is defined for all exploits and conditions in the given attack graph G. The second property ensures that the extended definition is still consistent with the aforementioned interpretation of the metric.

Proposition 1 *By Definition 3, for any exploit e (the result applies to a condition c in a similar way),*

- *$P(e)$ can be uniquely determined, and*
- *$P(e)$ represents the likelihood of an attacker (or fraction of attackers) reaching e for the first time in the given attack graph G.*

Proof We only discuss the case of an exploit e since a condition c is similar. First, e may be unreachable in G because it is inside a breakable cycle, such as the left-hand side of Fig. 3. In this case, removing all outgoing edges from e will essentially cause the cycle to be completely removed. We interpret this as $P(e) = 0$, which indicates that no attacker can reach e in G.

Suppose e is reachable. We prove the first claim through induction on the number k of exploits that can be reached before reaching e (we ignore those exploits that are not on any attack path that contains e so any exploit can either be reached before e, or after it). Clearly, for $k = 0$, $P(e) = p(e)$. Suppose the claim holds for any $k - 1$.

We consider an exploit e before which k others can be reached. Before any of those k exploits, at most $k - 1$ others can be reached (otherwise, there would be more than k exploits reachable before e), and hence the claim holds for the k exploits that can be reached before e. For exploits that can only be reached after reaching e at least once (notice those exploits could be within a cycle containing e), they will not appear in $A(G, e)$. The claim thus holds for e, because e is no longer in any cycle and the claim already holds for all the k remaining exploits in $A(G, e)$ (except e itself).

For the second claim, it suffices to show that any attacker can reach e for the first time in G iff it can do so in $A(G, e)$. The if part is true because any valid attack path in $A(G, e)$ will also exist in G. The only-if part holds because when we update the attack graph, only those exploits that can only be reached after reaching e are removed, so their removal will not affect any attack path from reaching e in $A(G, e)$, if such a path exists in G.   □

3   Bayesian Network-Based Attack Graph Model

This section describes a different approach for combining CVSS scores into an overall metric, using Bayesian networks (BNs). The new model takes as input the annotated attack graph and generates a special BN-based attack graph. The vertices of such an BN attack graph represent exploits and conditions derived from the attack graph. Each vertex is annotated with a probability derived from the CVSS score of the vulnerability, as shown in the previous section. Special conditional probabilities are assigned to represent the causal relationships among the exploits and conditions. Such a BN-based model enables making inferences about probabilities of an attacker reaching any condition using standard Bayesian inferences. In particular, the probability that the goal condition is satisfied given all initial conditions are, may be used as a metric for the overall security of the network. We first examine several concrete cases before presenting the general definition of the model.

3.1   Representing Attack Graphs Using BNs

Given an attack graph $G(E \cup C, R_r \cup R_i)$, we can construct an attack graph (AG) $B = (G, Q)$ where G is the directed graph corresponding to the AG in which the vertices now represent the binary variables of the system and the edges represent the conditional relationships among the variables; Q is the set of parameters that quantify the BN, i.e., conditional probabilities for the vertices. The key challenges are to encode in B both the CVSS scores of individual vulnerabilities, and the causal relationships among the exploits and conditions. Such encoding is possible through assigning special conditional probabilities. Specifically,

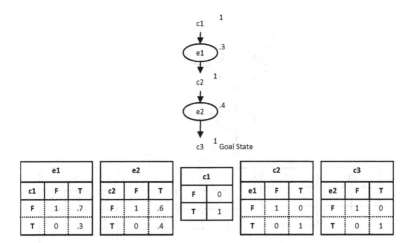

Fig. 5 Case 1: conjunction

1. We assign a probability of 1 to all the initial conditions in the attack graph since those conditions are satisfied initially.
2. We assign the CVSS score of corresponding vulnerability divided by 10 as the conditional probability of satisfying each exploit node given that all of its pre-conditions are already satisfied.
3. We assign 0 as the conditional probability of satisfying each exploit when at least one of its pre-conditions is not satisfied (since by definition of an exploit cannot be executed until all its pre-conditions are satisfied).
4. We assign 1 as the conditional probability of satisfying each condition if the condition is the post-condition of at least one satisfied exploit (since a post-condition can be satisfied by any exploit alone).

The following illustrates this methodology through several special cases.

1. Figure 5 depicts a simple AG with two exploits. Clearly, the AG indicates that one must execute both before reaching the goal condition c_3. Such a conjunctive relationship between the two exploits is encoded following the above methodology in the conditional probability tables (CPTs) shown in the figure. For example, c_1 is initially satisfied so assigned a value of 1; e_1 only depends on c_1, and its probability of being satisfied is 0 if c_1 is not true, whereas the probability is 0.3 otherwise (where 0.3 is the CVSS score of the vulnerability inside e_1 divided by 10). The overall security, i.e., the probability of satisfying c_3 given c_1 is satisfied may be calculated through Bayesian inferences as follows:

$$P(c3 = T) = \sum_{e2,c2,e1,c1 \in \{T,F\}} P(c3 = T, e2, c2, e1, c1)$$

$$= 0.12$$

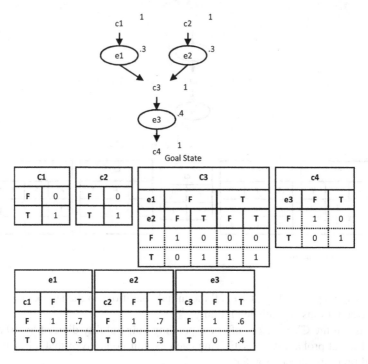

Fig. 6 Case 2: disjunction

2. Figure 6 depicts a case in which two exploits e_1 and e_2 are disjunctive in the
   sense that satisfying either is enough to proceed to e_3. It is interesting to note
   that the final score of this case is greater than that for the first case. This matches
   the intuition that as more paths to a goal state exist, the security of the network
   decreases.

$$P(c4 = T) = \sum_{e3,c3,e1,e2,c1,c2\epsilon\{T,F\}} P(c4 = T, e3, c3, e1, e2, c1, c2)$$

$$= 0.204$$

3. Figure 7 illustrates another case where we can obtain $P(c5 = T) = 0.036$.
   Obviously, the probability of achieving the goal state is significantly less than in
   the first two cases. Intuitively, this conjunction between more exploits restricts
   the number of potential attackers that can achieve the preconditions required to
   exploit $c5$.

4. Figure 8 depicts a case based on case 2. In case 2, exploits $e1$ and $e2$ are assumed
   to be independent, whereas in this case, we assume the likelihood of exploit B
   would increase upon successful exploitation of vulnerability A. This could be

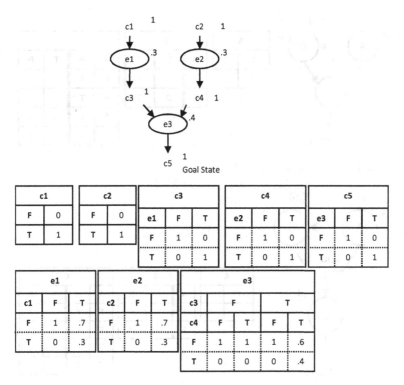

Fig. 7 Case 3: conjunction

the case where an attacker has gained knowledge following a successful exploit, e.g., if both exploits share the same or a similar vulnerability. In particular, we assume the likelihood of successfully exploiting vulnerability B without prior exploitation of vulnerability A is 0.3 (same as in case 2), and a successful exploitation of A would increase the likelihood of exploiting B to 0.5. The probability of achieving the goal state is the $P(C = T) = 0.204$, which is the same as in case 2. An interpretation of this result is that in order to exploit C we must have either a successful exploitation of A or B. In the event A is successfully exploited, the likelihood of B increases. However, the attacker can go directly to the attack phase on C without attempting to exploit B (in which case the adjusted score makes no difference) which is the same as in case 2.

5. Figure 9 shows a case similar to case 3 with the exception that a successful exploitation of A increases the likelihood of exploiting B. We can calculate $P(C = T) = 0.06$. Note that the result will always be the conjunction of the likelihood of A with the adjusted likelihood score for B. This is due to the fact that A must be exploited which in turn means that B will always have a likelihood equal to the adjusted value if C is exploited.

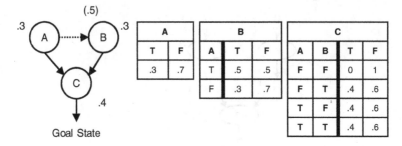

Fig. 8 Case 4: A increases likelihood of B

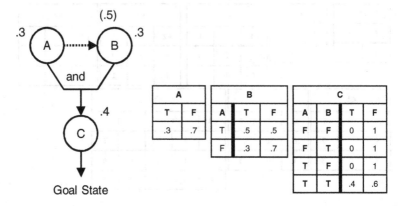

Fig. 9 Case 5: A increases likelihood of B

Now we are ready to formally define the Bayesian network-based attack graph as follows.

Definition 4 (Bayesian Network-Based Attack Graph) Given an attack graph $G(E \cup C, R_r \cup R_i)$, and a function $f()$ that maps each $e \in E$ to its CVSS score divided by 10, the Bayesian network-based attack graph is the Bayesian network $B = (G'(E \cup C, R_r \cup R_i), Q)$, where G' is obtained by annotating each $e \in E$ with $f(e)$, and regarding each node as a discrete random variable with two states T and F, and Q is the set of parameters of the Bayesian network given as follows.

1. $P(c = T) = 1$ for all the initial conditions $c \in C_I$.
2. $P(e \mid \exists c_{(c,e) \in R_r} = F) = 0$ (that is, an exploit cannot be executed until all of its pre-conditions are satisfied).
3. $P(c \mid \exists e_{(e,c) \in R_i} = T) = 1$ (that is, a post-condition can be satisfied by any exploit alone).
4. $P(e \mid \forall c_{(c,e) \in R_r \cup R_s} = T) = f(e)$ (that is, the probability of successfully executing an exploit when its pre-conditions have all been satisfied).

Fig. 10 Dependency among
exploit nodes

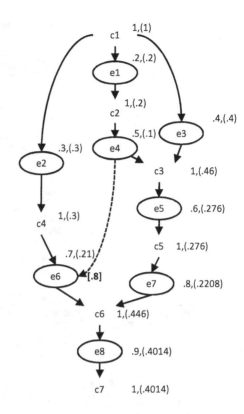

3.2 Comparing to the Previous Approach

The following demonstrates that the BN-based model we just presented may handle some cases which the previous approach introduced in Sect. 2 cannot. Consider the case depicted in Fig. 10 in which exploit $e6$ has an individual score of 0.7. However, if an attacker successfully exploits $e4$, they will gain knowledge that will make exploiting $e6$ easier and more likely. We represent this with the increased score for $e6$ to 0.8 shown in the square brackets. If we would follow the previous approach introduced in Sect. 2, we would face a problem in selecting a value for $e6$ between 0.7 and 0.8, since we do not know whether attacker would have already reached e_4 before reaching e_6, which would yield different scores for e_6. However, the BN-based approach can clearly handle such a case without the need for special considerations.

Figure 11 shows another interesting case using actual vulnerabilities and CVSS scores. For this case, the previous approach introduced in Sect. 2 will yield $P(CVE\text{-}2006\text{-}5302(1,2))=P(user(1)*P(trust2,1)*p(CVE\text{-}2006\text{-}5302(1,2))=.3433$. However, this calculation is to assume $trust(2,1)$ and $user(1)$ are independent in which case $P(trust(2,1)|user(1))=P(trust(2,1)=.5859$ which yields the value $P(CVE\text{-}2006\text{-}5302(1,2))=.3433$. However, the structure of the AG clearly shows that these

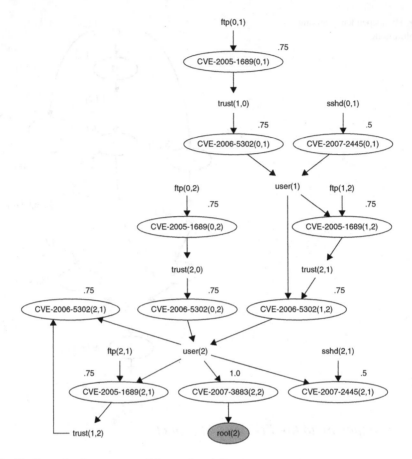

Fig. 11 Dependencies among conditions and exploits

exploits are not really independent, and the calculation using the BN-based model shows P(trust(2,1)|user(1))=.75 which yields P(CVE-2006-5302(1,2))=.4395, which is a different (valid) result. Therefore, in such cases, the previous approach would not be appropriate.

4 Dynamic Bayesian Network-Based Model

The previous two sections do not consider the evolving nature of networks and vulnerabilities. To this end, CVSS provides several temporal metric scores to model the time variant factors in determining the severity of a vulnerability, e.g., the availability of exploit code or patch for vulnerability. Such scores are, however, still intended for individual vulnerabilities instead of the overall security of a network.

The objective of this section is to extend the aforementioned BN-based model to a dynamic Bayesian network (DBN)-based model that can model the security of dynamically changing networks.

4.1 The General Model

To extend the BN-based model, temporal links between time slices of the DBN will be established between the unobservable variables of the model. With these links, the model will enable the inference of the unobserved variables based on the observed variables within the same time slice and those of the previous slice of the DBN. The model introduces three additional sets of vertices into the previous BN model, corresponding to the three temporal metrics defined in CVSS [3]. The first is the collection of E vertices that correspond to the *Exploitability* scores of the vulnerabilities. The second is the collection of RL vertices that correspond to the *Remediation Level* scores. Finally, the third is the collection of RC vertices that correspond to the *Report Confidence* scores.

The existing exploit vertices will then carry the final metric score—Temporal Score TS (instead of the base score in the static case), which has a similar role as the calculated scores in the case of the static BN-based model. However, in the static model, the final score for an exploit is calculated based on its base score and the causal relationship between this exploit and others, whereas in this model the final score of each exploit will depend on three factors: the temporal score, the causal relationship between this exploit and others within the same time slice, and the causal relationships with exploits in the previous time slice (this will become clearer later with discussions using concrete cases).

Definition 5 Given an attack graph G as a directed graph $G(E \cup C, R_r \cup R_i)$, we define E_E, E_{RL} and E_{RC} with the same cardinality as E to represent the set of E, RL and RC nodes and obtain an enriched set of nodes as $E' = E \cup E_E \cup E_{RL} \cup E_{RC}$. Let G' be the directed graph corresponding to E' in which the relations R_r and R_i remain the same; we can have one slice BN as a pair (G', Q) where Q represents the conditional probabilities assigned as before. We then define a DBN as a pair (B_0, B_d), where B_0 defines the prior $P(X_1)$, and B_d is a two-slice temporal Bayes net(2TBN) that defines $P(X_t|X_{t-1})$ by means of a DAG: $P(X_t|X_{t-1}) = \prod_{i=1}^{N} P(X_t^i|parents(X_t^i))$.

For B_0, conditional probabilities are assigned in a similar way as in the static model except that now the model uses the TS scores instead of the BS scores. More specifically, the TS scores are derived as the product of BS and TGS as specified in CVSS, and the derived TS scores are then assigned as conditional probabilities. For B_d, the assignment of interslice conditional probabilities will depend on specific requirements of applications, since different variables in a time slice may be regarded as unobservable, and the effect of a previous slice will depend on the semantics of the variables in question, as will be illustrated in following two cases.

4.2   Case 1: Inferring Exploit Node Values

In this case, we derive (infer) the probability values for the exploit nodes (their *TS* scores), which represents the probability of successful exploitation, from the base metric scores, temporal metric scores, and interslice dependencies. In this case, the security administrator can observe the *E*, *RL* and *RC* metric values for each exploit of the graph at all time slices (e.g., by consulting NVD). Based on these observed values, the security administrator can use the model to infer the evolving probability values for each of the exploit nodes, and in particular, the goal condition in order to evaluate the overall security of the network as it varies over time.

In this model, the interslice dependencies will be application dependent and thus be user defined values. The model introduces a variable τ, which we will refer to as the *Exploit Temporal Coefficient*, to adjust the TS score of an exploit in a time slice (t) based on whether or not the same exploit was successfully exploited in the previous time slice ($t - 1$) (if so τ will increase the TS score of the exploit for the present time slice). The value of τ is user defined and may be different for each exploit of the attack graph. The possible values for τ range from *1* in which the previous time slice has no effect on the present time slice to $max(BS * TGS)^{-1}$ for the exploit which will result in a TS value of *1* meaning that once an exploit has been successfully exploited in a previous time slice, it will always be considered exploited (which implies the notion that an attacker never relinquishes acquired knowledge or capabilities).

Definition 6 Given a DBN (B_0, B_d) that models an AG $G(E \cup C, R_r \cup R_i)$ where $E = (E_E \cup E_{RL} \cup E_{RC})$, we define τ to be the Exploit Temporal Coefficient such that $1 \leq \tau_{E_i} \leq min(BS_{E_i} * TGS_{E_i})^{-1}$. The Exploit Temporal Coefficient (τ) is a user-defined value which represents the factor by which a successful exploit of E_t is made more likely given the fact that E_{t-1} has been successfully exploited. The variable τ is defined such that it can adjust the transition parameter to a value (v) such that $TS_E \leq v \leq 1$. The transition parameter for any exploit node E in time slice $t - 1$ to the same exploit node in time slice t is defined as $P(E_t^i = T \mid E_{t-1}^i = T) = \tau_E * BS_{E^i} * TGS_{E^i}$ and $P(E_t^i = T \mid E_{t-1}^i = F) = BS_{E^i} \cdot TGS_{E^i}$, respectively.

Next we show an example application of this model. For this case, we consider only the *E* and *RL* temporal metrics. Figure 12 shows the DBN model in this case through a toy example of two exploits. In the model, the exploit vertices *addusrphp* and *sunvect* for this example are defined to be conditionally dependant on their respective *E* and *RL* vertex values as represented graphically in Fig. 12. Note that for simplicity we do not include a node representing the Base Score in this version of the model since it is a fixed value and is invariant throughout the time slices. The model does, however, use the value of the Base Score as input into the calculation of the TS score. In the example, vulnerability *addusrphp* must be exploited first in order for vulnerability *sunvect* to be exploited, and the goal state is the successful exploitation of vulnerability *sunvect*. To model the temporal dependencies, arcs linking the time slices are introduced between *addusrphp* and *sunvect* (unobserved parameters).

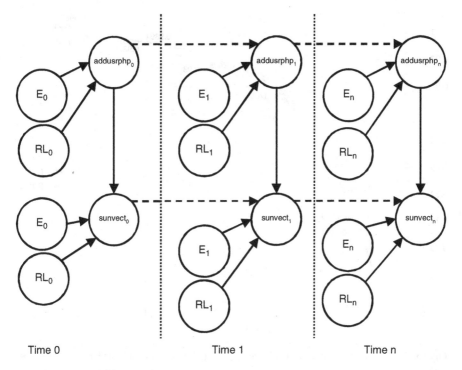

Fig. 12 DBN model for case 1

Suppose the objective is to calculate the probability value of an attacker successfully exploiting *sunvect* for any time slice. From NVD we obtain the BS for each vulnerability as follows: $BS(addusrphp) = 7.5$ and $BS(sunvect) = 10.0$. In this case study we consider only the E and RL temporal metrics from CVSS and we set them to their domain values E={U,POC,F,H} and RL={OF,TF,W,U}. To illustrate the model, we show the results for three example runs of the application. The resulting value for the probability of exploitation of *sunvect* for the first five time slices is shown in Fig. 13. The values used for each of these runs is shown in Fig. 14.

4.3 Case 2: Inferring TGS Node Values

In the second case, we assume the temporal metric scores of a vulnerability are of interest (for example, to security vendors who maintain these scores) and can be derived from base scores and the observed TS or exploit node scores (determined from reported security incidents involving that vulnerability). In this case, the DBN (B_0, B_d) will also be a two-slice temporal Bayes net(2TBN). However, the interslice arcs now link some or all of the temporal metric nodes (i.e., E or RL) depending

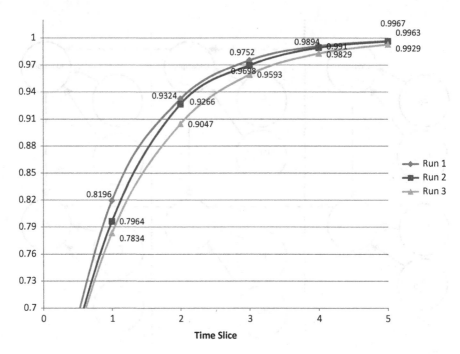

Fig. 13 $P(sunvect) = T$ at each time slice $\tau_{php} = (BS_{php} * TGS_{php})^{-1}$ and $\tau_{sun} = (BS_{sun} * TGS_{sun})^{-1}$

on the objective and upon which nodes are unobservable. The exploit nodes are observed at regular time intervals or time slices (i.e. by a security administrator monitoring the state of the network). Notice that the intraslice relationships remain unchanged and only the interslice arcs change. For simplicity we only consider the objective of inferring the E metric to illustrate our model. For each time slice, the value of each exploit node is observed to be either {T,F} (exploited or not), we then apply the DBN model to infer the values for the E metric as one of the following values E={U,POC,F,H}.

Figure 15 illustrates the DBN model for this case where only the unobservable E metric encoded in the TGS vertices are linked from one time slice to the next. The interpretation is that the value of the E metric in the previous time slice will have an impact on determining the likelihood of which state the E metric vertex will be in during the subsequent time slices.

The following discusses an example analysis using the model. Suppose reported security incidents show that *addusrphp* and *sunvect* have been observed to have the values indicated in Fig. 16 for five time slices. The DBN model can then infer the probabilistic scores for each of the E nodes. For example, in time slice 3, the model infers that $P(Esun_2 = U) = 0.612$ whereas $P(Esun_2 = H) = 0.062$ implying that it is ten times more likely that $Esun_3$ is in state U (Unproven) than in state H (High).

Case Study 1: Run 1						Case Study 1: Run 2				
Time Slice	Ephp	RLphp	Esun	RLsun	P(sun)=T	Time Slice	Ephp	RLphp	Esun	RLsun	P(sun)=T
0	U	U	U	U	0.5419	0	U	U	U	U	0.5419
1	U	U	U	U	0.8196	1	U	W	U	U	0.7964
2	U	U	U	U	0.9324	2	POC	W	U	U	0.9266
3	U	U	U	U	0.9752	3	POC	TF	U	U	0.9698
4	U	U	U	U	0.9910	4	F	TF	U	U	0.9894
5	U	U	U	U	0.9967	5	F	TF	U	U	0.9963
6	U	U	U	U	0.9988	6	H	TF	U	U	0.9989
7	U	U	U	U	0.9996	7	H	OF	U	U	0.9996
8	U	U	U	U	0.9998	8	H	OF	U	U	0.9998
9	U	U	U	U	0.9999	9	H	OF	U	U	0.9999

Case Study 1: Run 3					
Time Slice	Ephp	RLphp	Esun	RLsun	P(sun)=T
0	U	U	U	U	0.5419
1	POC	OF	POC	OF	0.7834
2	POC	OF	POC	OF	0.9047
3	POC	OF	POC	OF	0.9593
4	POC	OF	POC	OF	0.9829
5	POC	OF	POC	OF	0.9929
6	POC	OF	POC	OF	0.9971
7	POC	OF	POC	OF	0.9988
8	POC	OF	POC	OF	0.9994
9	POC	OF	POC	OF	0.9998

Fig. 14 Three sample runs $\tau_{php} = (BS_{php} * TGS_{php})^{-1}$ and $\tau_{sun} = (BS_{sun} * TGS_{sun})^{-1}$

5 Conclusion

To measure the overall risk of residue vulnerabilities in a network, we need to combine the CVSS scores of individual vulnerabilities into an overall measure for network security. This chapter has examined three different solutions. First, we converted CVSS base scores into probabilities and then propagated such probabilities along attack paths in an attack graph. Second, we have encoded attack graphs and assigned probabilities as a Bayesian network and then derived the overall metric value through Bayesian inferences. Finally, we extended the static BN-base model to dynamic Bayesian networks such that we can make inferences about the evolving security of networks. Those solutions provide practical ways for deriving meaningful indicators of network security based on CVSS scores. Moreover, they may allow us to apply existing theories and tools to network security, e.g., existing BN or DBN tools may be borrowed for inferring exploit node values or determining most probable explanations (MPE) for observed security incidents. However, those solutions also share many limitations, which will be addressed in later chapters of this book.

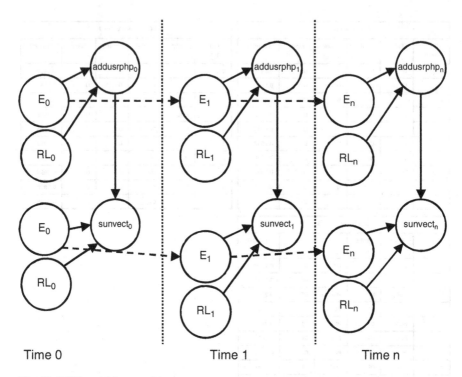

Time 0   Time 1   Time n

Fig. 15 DBN model for case 2

Time Slice	php,	RLphp,	sun,	RLsun,	TGSphp,				TGSsun,			
					U	POC	F	H	U	POC	F	H
0	F*	U*	F*	U*	0.736	0.099	0.088	0.077	0.814	0.083	0.063	0.040
1	F*	W*	F*	W*	0.581	0.157	0.166	0.096	0.705	0.135	0.111	0.049
2	T*	W*	F*	W*	0.441	0.185	0.239	0.134	0.612	0.174	0.152	0.062
3	T*	TF*	F*	TF*	0.341	0.192	0.285	0.183	0.509	0.203	0.202	0.086
4	T*	OF*	T*	OF*	0.268	0.186	0.312	0.234	0.40	0.212	0.258	0.130

Fig. 16 Case 2: inferred values of E metric when exploit and RL nodes observed. *Denotes observed value

Acknowledgements Authors with Concordia University were partially supported by the Natural Sciences and Engineering Research Council of Canada under Discovery Grant N01035. Sushil Jajodia was partially supported by the by Army Research Office grants W911NF-13-1-0421 and W911NF-15-1-0576, by the Office of Naval Research grant N00014-15-1-2007, National Institutes of Standard and Technology grant 60NANB16D287, and by the National Science Foundation grant IIP-1266147.

References

1. P. Ammann, D. Wijesekera, S. Kaushik, Scalable, graph-based network vulnerability analysis, in *Proceedings of ACM CCS'02* (2002)
2. S. Jajodia, S. Noel, B. O'Berry, Topological analysis of network attack vulnerability, in *Managing Cyber Threats: Issues, Approaches and Challenges*, ed. by V. Kumar, J. Srivastava, A. Lazarevic (Kluwer Academic Publisher, Dordrecht, 2003)
3. P. Mell, K. Scarfone, S. Romanosky, Common vulnerability scoring system. IEEE Secur. Priv. **4**(6), 85–89 (2006)
4. National Institute of Standards and Technology, Technology assessment: Methods for measuring the level of computer security. NIST Special Publication 500-133 (1985)
5. National vulnerability database. Available at: http://www.nvd.org, May 9, 2008
6. M.K. Reiter, S.G. Stubblebine, Authentication metric analysis and design. ACM Trans. Inf. Syst. Secur. **2**(2), 138–158 (1999)
7. O. Sheyner, J. Haines, S. Jha, R. Lippmann, J.M. Wing, Automated generation and analysis of attack graphs, in *Proceedings of the 2002 IEEE Symposium on Security and Privacy* (2002)
8. M. Swanson, N. Bartol, J. Sabato, J. Hash, L. Graffo, Security metrics guide for information technology systems. NIST Special Publication 800-55 (2003)

Refining CVSS-Based Network Security Metrics by Examining the Base Scores

Pengsu Cheng, Lingyu Wang, Sushil Jajodia, and Anoop Singhal

Abstract A network security metric enables the direct measurement of the effectiveness of network security solutions. Combining CVSS scores of individual vulnerabilities provides a measurement of the overall security of networks with respect to potential attacks. However, most existing approaches to combining such scores, either based on attack graphs or Bayesian networks, share two limitations. First, a dependency relationship between vulnerabilities will either be ignored, or modeled in an arbitrary way. Second, only one aspect of the scores, the probability of successful attacks, has been considered. In this chapter, we address those issues as follows. First, instead of taking each base score as an input, our approach works at the underlying base metric level where dependency relationships have well-defined semantics. Second, our approach interprets and combines scores in three different aspects, namely, probability, effort, and skill, which may broaden the scope of applications for CVSS and allow users to weigh different aspects of the score for their specific needs. Finally, we evaluate our approach through simulation.

1 Introduction

A network security metric is desirable since *you cannot improve what you cannot measure*. By applying a network security metric immediately before, and after, deploying potential security solutions, these solutions' relative effectiveness can be judged in a more direct and precise manner. Such a capability will render securing computer networks a science rather than an art. Standard techniques exist

P. Cheng • L. Wang (✉)
Concordia Institute for Information Systems Engineering, Concordia University, Montreal, QC, Canada H3G 1M8
e-mail: wang@ciise.concordia.ca

S. Jajodia
Center for Secure Information Systems, George Mason University, Fairfax, VA 22030-4444, USA
e-mail: jajodia@gmu.edu

A. Singhal
Computer Security Division, NIST, Gaithersburg, MD 20899, USA
e-mail: anoop.singhal@nist.gov

© Springer International Publishing AG 2017
L. Wang et al., *Network Security Metrics*,
https://doi.org/10.1007/978-3-319-66505-4_2

for measuring the relative severity of individual vulnerabilities, such as the Common Vulnerability Scoring System (CVSS) [7] scores which are readily available in vulnerability databases (for example, the NVD [8]).

The CVSS standard provides a solid foundation for developing network security metrics. On the other hand, CVSS is mainly intended to rank different vulnerabilities in the same network, and it does not directly provide a way for measuring the overall security of different network configurations. Naive ways for combining individual scores, such as taking the average or maximum value, may lead to misleading results, as we shall demonstrate shortly. The main reason is that such naive approaches do not take into consideration the causal relationships between vulnerabilities (that is, exploiting one vulnerability enables exploiting another). As we have seen in the previous chapter, several approaches exist to address this issue by combining CVSS scores based on attack graphs.

In this chapter, we first point out following two limitations shared by those existing approaches. First, a dependency relationship between vulnerabilities that is not captured in attack graphs may also affect the process of combining scores, which is either ignored, or handled in an arbitrary way, in existing approaches. Second, only one aspect of security metrics, namely, the probabilities of attacks, has been considered in most approaches, whereas other important aspects are being ignored. To address the above issues, we propose a novel multi-faceted approach to separately combine CVSS base metrics. Specifically, instead of taking the base score as a black box input, our approach breaks it down to the underlying base metrics. At the base metric level, dependency relationships between vulnerabilities have well-defined semantics and can thus be easily handled. Our approach also interprets CVSS scores in three different aspects, namely, probability, effort, and skill. We show that the scores need to be combined in different ways for different aspects. We evaluate our approach through simulations. The results confirm the advantages of our approach.

The contribution of this chapter is summarized in the following. First, we identify and demonstrate important limitations of existing approaches in defining or interpreting security metrics. Second, working at the base metric level, our approach brings out more semantics in combining CVSS scores and consequently produces metric results that may be more meaningful and adoptable to security practitioners. Third, the multi-faceted approach to interpreting CVSS scores may broaden the scope of applications for the standard and allow users to weigh different aspects of the score based on their specific needs.

The rest of this chapter is organized as follows. Section 2 reviews background knowledge necessary for understanding this chapter and demonstrates limitations of existing approaches as the motivation of our work. Section 3 presents our approaches to combining base metrics for handling dependencies between vulnerabilities and then extends this approach to further consider three different aspects of the metric scores. Section 4 presents the algorithms for combining skill and effort aspects and presents simulation results. Section 5 concludes the chapter.

2 Preliminaries

In this section, we first review two important concepts relevant to our further discussions, namely, attack graph and CVSS. We then motivate our discussions by demonstrating limitations of existing approaches through examples.

2.1 Attack Graph

Attack graph is a graphical representation of inter-dependent vulnerabilities found in networked hosts. An attack graph is a directed graph whose nodes are partitioned into two classes, namely, *exploits* and *security conditions* (or simply *conditions*). An exploit is typically represented as a predicate $v(h_s, h_d)$, where h_s and h_d represent two connected hosts and v a vulnerability on the destination host h_d. A security condition is a predicate $c(h)$, indicating the host h satisfies a condition c relevant to one or more exploits. The *require* relation R_r is a directed edge pointing from a condition to an exploit, which means the exploit cannot be executed unless the condition is satisfied. Second, the *imply* relation R_i pointing from an exploit to a condition means executing the exploit will satisfy the condition. These are more formally stated as Definition 1.

Definition 1 An attack graph G is a directed graph $G(E \cup C, R_r \cup R_i)$ where the set of nodes include E, a set of *exploits*, and C, a set of *conditions*, and the set of edges include the *require* relation $R_r \subseteq C \times E$ and the *imply* relation $R_i \subseteq E \times C$.

Figure 1 shows a simple example of attack graphs which depicts a simple scenario where a file server (host 1) offers the File Transfer Protocol (ftp), secure shell (ssh), and remote shell (rsh) services; a database server (host 2) offers ftp and rsh services. The firewall only allows ftp, ssh, and rsh traffic from a user workstation (host 0) to both servers. In the attack graph, exploits of vulnerabilities are depicted as predicates in ovals and conditions as predicates in clear texts. The two numbers inside parentheses denote the source and destination host, respectively. The attack graph represents three self-explanatory sequences of attacks (attack paths).

Two important semantics of attack graphs are as follows. First, the require relation is always *conjunctive* whereas the imply relation is always *disjunctive*. More specifically, an exploit cannot be realized until *all* of its required conditions have been satisfied, whereas a condition can be satisfied by any *one* of the realized exploits. Second, the conditions are further classified as *initial* conditions (the conditions not implied by any exploit) and *intermediate* conditions. An initial condition can be independently disabled to harden a network, whereas an intermediate condition usually cannot be.

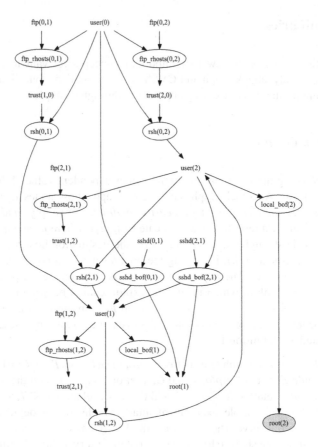

Fig. 1 An example of attack graph

2.2   Common Vulnerability Scoring System (CVSS)

Our discussions in subsequent sections will need metric scores assigned to individual vulnerabilities according to the Common Vulnerability Scoring System (CVSS) [7]. The CVSS is an open and free framework that provides a means for assigning quantitative values to vulnerabilities based on well defined metrics. In CVSS, each vulnerability is to be assigned a *base score (BS)* ranging from 0 to 10, on the basis of two groups of totally six *base metrics* [7]. The base metrics are intended to stay constant over time and across different user environments. Optionally, the base score can be further adjusted with temporal and environmental scores. We briefly review the CVSS standard in the following to make this chapter more self-contained.

The *Base Score* (BS) for each vulnerability quantifies its intrinsic and fundamental properties that are supposed to be constant over time and independent of user environments. The base score ranges from 0 to 10. The Base Score is calculated based on the following six metrics:

- *Access Vector—AV*: This indicates the types of accesses required for exploiting the vulnerability. Possible values are Local (numerical value 0.395), Adjacent Network (0.646), and Network (1.0), which are all self-explanatory.
- *Access Complexity—AC*: A quantitative measure of the attack complexity required to exploit the vulnerability. The range of values are: High (0.35), Medium (0.61) and Low (0.71).
- *Authentication—Au*: A measure of the number of times an attacker must authenticate to a target in order to exploit a vulnerability. The defined range of values are: Multiple (0.45), Single (0.56) and No (0.704).
- *Confidentiality—C*: A measure of the impact on confidentiality following a successful exploitation with the following defined range of values: None (0.0), Partial (0.275) and Complete (0.660).
- *Integrity—I*: A measure of the impact on integrity following a successful exploitation with the following defined range of values: None (0.0), Partial (0.275) and Complete (0.660).
- *Availability—A*: A measure of the impact on availability following a successful exploitation with the following defined range of values: None (0.0), Partial (0.275) and Complete (0.660).

The CVSS Framework imposes the use of a vector which encodes the metric score values used to compute the overall score for a vulnerability. The following is an example vector:

$$AV : N/AC : L/Au : N/C : N/I : C/A : C$$

from which we can derive the numerical scores as indicated above.

The Base Metric score (BS) is computed as follows,

$$BS = round\_to\_1\_decimal((0.6 * Impact + 0.4 * Exploitability$$
$$-1.5) * f(Impact))$$
$$Impact = 10.41 * (1 - (1 - ConfImpact) * (1 - IntegImpact)$$
$$*(1 - AvailImpact))$$
$$Exploitability = 20 * AccessVector * AccessComplexity * Authentication$$
$$f(Impact) = 0 \ \ if \ \ Impact = 0, \ 1.176 \ \ otherwise \tag{1}$$

Using the example vector, the following demonstrates how to compute the BS:

- *Exploitability* $= 20 * 1 * 0.71 * 0.704 == 9.9968$
- *Impact* $= 10.41 * (1 - (1 - 0) * (1 - 0.660) * (1 - 0.660) == 9.2066$
- $f(impact) = 1.176$
- *BaseScore* $= round\_to\_1\_decimal((0.6 * 9.2066) + (0.4 * 9.9968) - 1.5) * 1.176 == 9.4$

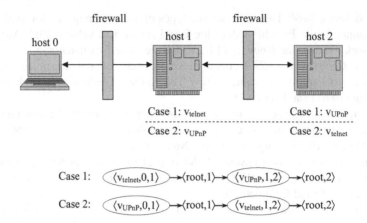

Fig. 2 An example network

Table 1 The CVSS base metrics and scores of two vulnerabilities

Metric group	Metric	Metric value of v_{telnet}	Metric value of v_{UPnP}
	Access vector	Network (1.00)	Adjacent network (0.646)
Exploitability	Access complexity	High (0.35)	High (0.35)
	Authentication	None (0.704)	None (0.704)
	Confidentiality	Complete (0.660)	Complete (0.660)
Impact	Integrity	Complete (0.660)	Complete (0.660)
	Availability	Complete (0.660)	Complete (0.660)
Base score (BS)		7.6	6.8

2.3   Existing Approaches and Their Limitations

To illustrate limitations of existing approaches to combining CVSS scores, we consider a toy example. Figure 2 depicts a network consisted of two hosts (host 1 and 2), and an attacker on host 0 in the Internet. We shall consider two cases based on the same network. In Case 1, we assume host 1 to be a UNIX server running a telnet service and host 2 a Windows XP workstation running the Universal Plug and Play (UPnP) service. In Case 2, we assume host 1 and 2 swap their OS (and hence the corresponding services). In both cases, the firewalls disallow any traffic except accesses to those services.

We assume the telnet service contains the vulnerability CVE-2007-0956 [8], denoted by v_{telnet}, which allows remote attackers to bypass authentication and gain system accesses via providing special usernames to the service. We also assume the UPnP service contains the vulnerability CVE-2007-1204 [8], denoted by v_{UPnP}, which is a stack overflow that allows attackers on the same subnet to execute arbitrary codes via sending specially crafted requests.

Table 1 shows the CVSS base metrics of those two vulnerabilities [8]. By applying Eq. (1), we can calculate the base score of vulnerability v_{telnet} to be

$BS = 7.6$. Similarly, we have $BS = 6.8$ for vulnerability v_{UPnP}. The difference in those base scores suggests that vulnerability v_{telnet} is relatively more severe then v_{UPnP}. This is sufficient for purposes like prioritizing vulnerabilities for removal. However, for other purposes, such as comparing the relative security of the two configurations of Case 1 and 2, we shall need to combine the base scores for judging the overall network security.

- *Average and Maximum* First, we consider two naive approaches to combining the CVSS scores, namely, by taking the average value (7.2 in both Case 1 and 2) and maximum value (7.6 in both cases), respectively. Although those approaches provide a rough sense of overall security, their limitations are also obvious. Since the average and maximum values are both defined over a set, they do not depend on where those vulnerabilities are located in a network and how they are related to each other. For example, if we assume the UNIX server in Fig. 2 is the only important network asset, then intuitively the overall network security is quite different between Case 1 (in which an attacker can directly attack the UNIX server on host 1) and Case 2 (in which the attacker must first compromise the Windows workstation on host 1 and use it as a stepping stone to attack host 2). Nonetheless, by taking the average or maximum base score, we cannot distinguish between the two cases.

- *Attack Graph-Based Approach* The above naive approaches lead to misleading results because they ignore causal relationships between vulnerabilities. Such causal relationships can be modeled in attack graphs, as illustrated in the lower portion of Fig. 2. Each triple $\langle v, h_1, h_2 \rangle$ inside an oval represents an exploit of vulnerability v on host h_2 from host h_1; each pair $\langle c, h \rangle$ represents a security-related condition c on host h; each arrow either points from a pre-condition to an exploit, or from an exploit to a post-condition.

  The attack graph-based approach [9] first converts each CVSS base score into a probability by dividing with its domain size, and then assigns the probability to exploits with the corresponding vulnerability. Each condition is also assigned a probability 1. The probabilities are then combined based on following causal relationships: An exploit is reachable only if all of its pre-conditions are satisfied (that is, a conjunction); a condition is satisfied as long as one reachable exploit has that condition as its post-condition (that is, a disjunction).

  In Case 1 of our example, we should assign $7.6/10 = 0.76$ to $\langle v_{telnet}, 0, 1 \rangle$, and $6.8/10 = 0.68$ to $\langle v_{UPnP}, 1, 2 \rangle$, and 1 to both conditions. We can then update $\langle root, 1 \rangle$ as a post-condition of $\langle v_{telnet}, 0, 1 \rangle$ to the new value 0.76; now by taking $\langle root, 1 \rangle$ again as a pre-condition of $\langle v_{UPnP}, 1, 2 \rangle$, we can then update $\langle v_{UPnP}, 1, 2 \rangle$ and $\langle root, 2 \rangle$ with the value $0.76 \times 0.68 = 0.52$. Similarly, we will obtain the same result for Case 2. At first glance, this is reasonable, since the attacker is exploiting the same two vulnerabilities in both cases.

  Unfortunately, upon more careful observation, we shall see this is not the case. First, we recall that the vulnerability v_{UPnP} (CVE-2007-1204) requires the attacker to be within the same subnet as the victim host. In Case 1, exploiting v_{telnet} on host 1 helps the attacker to gain accesses to local network, and hence

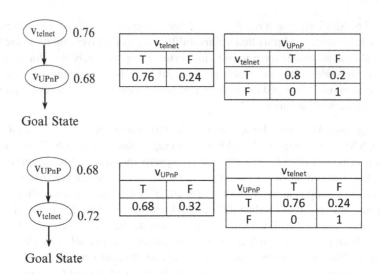

Fig. 3 Bayesian network-based approach [3]

makes it easier to exploit host 2. In another word, exploiting v_{telnet} has the effect of increasing the probability of successfully exploiting v_{UPnP}. In contrast, in Case 2, there is no such affect due to the reversed order of exploits. This difference between the two cases is apparently not captured by the identical result 0.52 produced by this approach.

- *Bayesian Network (BN)-Based Approach* Next we consider the Bayesian network-based approach [3]. The lower left-hand side of Fig. 3 shows the BN corresponding to Case 2 of our example. Similar to the previous approach, the CVSS base score is first converted into a conditional probability. For example, the conditional probability of successfully exploiting v_{UPnP}, given that all of its pre-conditions are satisfied, is assigned as 0.68. The lower right-hand side of Fig. 3 depicts the corresponding Conditional Probability Table (CPT) for each exploit in Case 2. The probability of reaching the goal state, which is assumed as exploiting both vulnerabilities in this example, can be calculated as $P(v_{telnet} = T) = \sum_{v_{UPnP} \in \{T,F\}} P(v_{telnet} = T, v_{UPnP}) = 0.52$.

  The upper left-hand side of Fig. 3 depicts the BN for Case 1. Since exploiting v_{telnet} on host 1 makes it easier to exploit v_{UPnP} on host 2, according to this approach, we should assign to $P(v_{UPnP} = T | v_{telnet} = T)$ a value higher than the one directly derived from the base score (that is, 0.68). If we assign, say, 0.8, then the possibility of achieving the goal state is $P(v_{UPnP} = T) = \sum_{v_{telnet} \in \{T,F\}} P(v_{UPnP} = T, v_{telnet}) = 0.61$. This result is more accurate since it reflects the dependency relationship between the two exploits. However, note that we have chosen an arbitrary value 0.8 because this approach does not provide means for determining that value, which is clearly a limitation.

3 Main Approach

In this section, we present our main approaches to dealing with dependencies between vulnerabilities by combining base metrics, and to combining metrics based on different aspects of the scores' semantics.

3.1 Combining Base Metrics

We first give an overview of our approach, which is followed by the formal framework and an example.

3.1.1 Overview

We first illustrate our approach by revisiting the example in Fig. 2. The key observation is that the existing approaches discussed in the previous section all take the CVSS base scores as their inputs. The base score is regarded as a black box, and the underlying base metrics are not involved in the process of combining scores. However, we notice that the dependency relationships between vulnerabilities are usually only visible at the level of base metrics, which makes it difficult for those approaches to properly handle such relationships.

Instead of working at the base score level, our approach handles potential dependency relationships between vulnerabilities at the base metric level. For the above example, the dependency relationship can be easily modeled at the base metric level as follows. When an attacker successfully exploits v_{telnet} on host 1, he/she gains accesses to the local network of host 2, which is required for exploiting v_{UPnP} on host 2. At the base metric level, this simply means the *AccessVector* metric of v_{UPnP}, which has the value *AdjacentNetwork*, should be replaced with *Network*, since the attacker is effectively accessing v_{UPnP} remotely (using host 1 as a stepping stone).

With this adjustment to the base metric *AccessVector*, we can apply Eq. (1) to recalculate a new *effective base score*, which is equal to 0.76 in this case. Clearly, the new result is also higher than the original value 0.68, but this result has well defined semantics, unlike the arbitrary value chosen by the previous approach [3]. The final score corresponding to Case 1 shown in Fig. 2 can now be calculated as $P(v_{UPnP} = T) = \sum_{v_{telnet} \in \{T,F\}} P(v_{UPnP} = T, v_{telnet}) = 0.58$. In Table 2, we summarize our discussions about the above example and compare the results produced by different approaches.

Table 2 Comparison of different approaches

Approaches	Case 1	Case 2	Summary
Average	7.2	7.2	Ignoring causal relationships
Maximum	7.6	7.6	(exploiting one vulnerability enables the other)
Attack graph-based approach [9]	0.52	0.52	Ignoring dependency relationships (exploiting one vulnerability makes the other easier)
BN-based approach [3]	0.61	0.52	Arbitrary adjustment for dependency relationships
Our approach	0.58	0.52	Adjustment with well-defined semantic

3.1.2 Formal Framework

We are now ready to formalize our approach. We assume an *attack graph* is given as a directed graph $G = \langle E \cup C, \{\langle x, y \rangle : (y \in E \wedge x \in pre(y)) \vee (x \in E \wedge y \in post(x))\} \rangle$ where E, C, $pre()$, and $post()$ denote a set of exploits (each of which is a triple $\langle v, h_s, h_d \rangle$ denoting an exploit of vulnerability v on host h_d from host h_s), a set of security-related conditions, a function that maps an exploit to the set of its pre-conditions, and a function that maps an exploit to the set of its post-conditions, respectively [6].

We call a condition *initial condition* if it is not the post-condition of any exploit. A sequence of exploits is called an *attack sequence* if for every exploit e in the sequence, all its pre-conditions are either initial conditions, or post-conditions of some exploits that appear before e in that sequence. We say an exploit e' is an *ancestor* of another exploit e, if e' appears before e in at least one minimal attack sequence (that is, an attack sequence of which no subsequence is a valid attack sequence).

We also assume the CVSS base metrics can be obtained for each exploit e as a vector bm of six numeric values each of which corresponds to a base metric [7]. We shall use the notation $bm[AV], bm[AC], \ldots, bm[A]$ to denote each corresponding element of the vector bm. Finally, we assume the dependency relationships between exploits are given using a function $adj()$ formalized in Definition 2. When a base metric m ($m \in \{AV, AC, Au, C, I, A\}$) of an exploit e is affected by another exploits e' due to dependency relationships, we assume $adj(e, e', m)$ is given. And we use $< e', e >$ to denote that exploit e can be affected by exploit due to dependency relationship.

Definition 2 Given an attack graph G with the set of exploits E, we define a function $adj() : E \times E \times \{AV, AC, Au, C, I, A\} \rightarrow [0, 1]$. We call $adj(e, e', m)$ the *adjusted value* for the metric m of exploit e due to e'.

Next, we formalize the concept of *effective base metric* and *effective base score* in Definition 3. For each exploit e, the effective base metric simply takes the original base metric if no adjusted value is given. Otherwise, the effective base metric will take the highest adjusted value defined over any ancestor of e (note that an exploit may be affected by many exploits in different ways, leading to more than one adjusted values), because a metric should always reflect the worst case scenario (that is, the highest value). The effective base score basically applies the same equation to effective base metrics instead of the original metrics. In the definition, both effective base metric and score can be defined with respect to a given subset of exploits, which will be necessary later in this section.

Definition 3 Given an attack graph G with the set of exploits E, the adjusted values given by function $adj()$, the CVSS base metric vector bm for each $e \in E$, and any $E' \subseteq E$ (E' will be omitted if $E' = E$), we define

- the *effective base metric* vector ebm of e with respect to E' as

  - $ebm[m] = bm[m]$ for each $m \in \{AV, AC, Au, C, I, A\}$, if $adj(e, e', m)$ is not defined for any ancestor e' of e in E'.
  - $ebm[m] = adj(e, e', m)$, if $adj(e, e', m)$ is the highest value defined over any ancestor e' of e in E'.

- the *effective base score* ebs of e as the base score calculated using Eq. (1) with the base metrics replaced with the corresponding effective base metrics.

Finally, Definition 4 formalizes a Bayesian network (BN)-based model for combining the effective base scores. The directed graph is directly obtained from the attack graph. The conditional probabilities are assigned according to the causal relationships between an exploit and its pre- and post-conditions. Since the dependency relationships between exploits are already reflected in our definition of effective base scores, the BN needs not to explicitly model them. With the BN model, we can easily calculate the probability of satisfying any given goal conditions (or equivalently, the probability of important network assets being compromised).

Definition 4 Given attack graph G with exploits E, and the effective base score ebs for each $e \in E$, we define a Bayesian network $B = \langle G, Q \rangle$ where

- G is the attack graph interpreted as a directed graph with each vertex representing a random variable taking either T (true) or F (false), and the edges representing the direct dependencies among those variables.
- Q is the collection of conditional probabilities assigned as the following.

  - $P(c = T | e = T) = 1$, for each $e \in E$ satisfying $c \in post(e)$.
  - $P(e = T | \bigwedge_{\forall c \in pre(e)} (c = T)) = ebs/10$.

3.1.3 An Example

We now illustrate our approach by applying it to the example shown on the left-hand side of Fig. 4. The figure shows a fictitious attack graph in which the dotted lines indicate dependency relationships, which will be explained shortly. On the

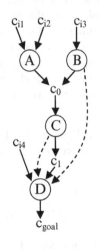

Adjusted Values:

$$adj(D,C,AV) = 1.0$$
$$adj(D,B,Au) = 0.704$$

Base Scores:

Exploits		AV	AC	Au	bs
A	Network	Low	None	9.43
B	Network	Medium	Single	7.95
C	Network	Medium	None	8.77
D	Local	Medium	Single	6

Effective base metric of D:
$$ebm_{D|C} = \langle Network, Medium, Single \rangle$$
$$ebm_{D|B,C} = \langle Network, Medium, None \rangle$$

Effective base score of D:
$$ebs_{D|C} = 7.95$$
$$ebs_{D|B,C} = 8.77$$

Fig. 4 An example attack graph (*left*) and the corresponding model (*right*)

right-hand side of Fig. 4, we give the corresponding model obtained by applying our formal framework as introduced above.

Specifically, we assume exploit C will give an attacker the local shell accesses to target host, which is required for exploiting D (since its base metric AV is *Local*), as indicated by the dotted line from C to D. This dependency relationship is modeled using the function $adj()$, as shown on the right-hand side of Fig. 4. Also, we assume that exploiting D requires the same authenticated account as B (both of their base score Au are *Single*). If attackers can exploit B, no additional accounts are required for exploiting D. This dependency relation is indicated by the dotted line from B to D, and modeled using the function $adj()$. Therefore, we can replace the base metric of exploit D with its effective base metrics for the two cases ($ebm_{D|C}$, $ebm_{D|B,C}$ as shown on the right-hand side of Fig. 4) in order to calculate its effective base scores (we assume the impact metrics of all exploits are *ConfImpact* = *Complete*, *IntegImpact* = *Complete*, and *AvailImpact* = *None*). Here we need consider two cases: $ebs_{D|C}$ when the attacker has already exploited C; and $ebs_{D|B,C}$ when the attacker has exploited B and C (we don't consider the case that B is already exploited while C is not, because from the semantics of this attack graph we can see that D cannot be exploited without C being exploited at first). We then calculate $P(D = T)$ using the BN model shown in Table 3 as $P(D = T) = \sum_{A,B,C\in\{T,F\}} P(D = T|B,C)P(C|A,B)P(A)P(B) = 0.27$.

Table 3 The BN model

A		C				D			
T	F	A	B	T	F	B	C	T	F
0.943	0.057	F	F	0	1	F	F	0	1
B		T	F	0.877	0.123	T	F	0	1
T	F	F	T	0.877	0.123	F	T	0.795	0.205
0.795	0.205	T	T	0.877	0.123	T	T	0.877	0.123

3.2 Considering Different Aspects of Scores

In this subsection, we first demonstrate the need for interpreting and combining base scores from different aspects. We then extend our approach accordingly to combine metric scores based on different aspects, and provide an example of our approach.

3.2.1 The Need for Considering Different Aspects

CVSS metrics and scores can be interpreted in different ways. In this chapter, we shall consider three aspects of the scores.

- First, as discussed in the previous section, the difference in scores may indicate different probabilities of attacks. For example, an *AccessVector* metric value of *AdjacentNetwork* corresponds to a lower numerical score than the value *Network*, which can be interpreted as that a vulnerability that requires accesses to local networks is less likely being exploited than one that is remotely accessible.
- Second, we can also interpret the difference in scores as the minimum amount of time and effort spent by any attacker. For example, if a vulnerability requires multiple authentications at both OS and applications, then it certainly will require more time and effort than one that requires no authentication at all.
- Third, the difference in scores can also indicate the minimum skill level of an attacker who can exploits that vulnerability. For example, exploiting a vulnerability with its *AccessComplexity* score as *High* will likely require more skills than exploiting one that has the value *Low* (note that each exploitability metric may potentially be interpreted in all three aspects).

Considering different aspects of CVSS scores will require different methods for combining such scores. We demonstrate this fact through an example. Figure 5 shows a network consisted of four hosts (host 1 through 4) and another host on the internet (host 0). We assume there are firewalls between the hosts that prevent any traffic except those indicated by lines shown in the figure. We also assume host 1 through 4 each has a vulnerability, denoted by a letter inside parentheses. Finally, we assume the base scores are partially ordered, that is, vulnerability *B* is more severe than all others, and *A* is more severe than *C* (for simplicity, we shall not consider

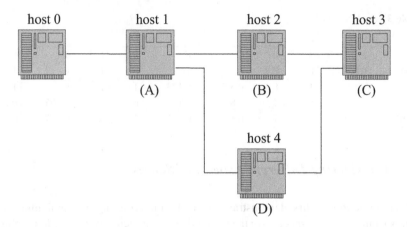

Fig. 5 An example of different aspects

effective base scores in this example). We now consider how the scores should be combined for each of the three aspects.

- First, suppose we have assigned probabilities P_A, P_B, P_C, and P_D to those four vulnerabilities based on the base scores. Also suppose the security of host 3 is our main concern. Clearly, the probability of host 3 being compromised can be calculated as $P = P_A * (P_B + P_D - P_B * P_C) * P_C$. Next, suppose we remove host 4 from the network. The probability will change to $P = P_A * P_B * P_C$, which is now smaller. This is reasonable since, by removing host 4, an attacker now has only one choice left, that is, to reach host 3 through host 2. Finally, suppose we further remove host 2 from the network, the probability now becomes $P = P_A * P_C$, which is larger. This is also reasonable since now an attacker only need to compromise host 1 before he/she can reach host 3.

- We show a different story by considering the effort aspect. First, suppose we have assigned some effort scores F_A, F_B, F_C, and F_D to the four vulnerabilities based on their base scores (we shall discuss how the effort score should be defined later). Without considering dependency relationships, the effort spent on exploiting vulnerabilities will accumulate.

  Therefore, addition is the natural way to combine the effort scores. However, there is one more complication. In this example, an attacker may compromise host 3 in two ways, either through host 2 or host 4. Since a metric should measure the worst case scenario, it should yield the minimum effort required to compromise host 3. That is, $F = F_A + F_B + F_C$ (note that F_B is less than F_D due to our assumption).

  If we remove host 4 from the network, we can easily see that the effort score will remain the same, $F = F_A + F_B + F_C$, instead of becoming smaller like in the case of attack probability. This is reasonable since vulnerability D is not on the minimum-effort attack sequence so its removal will not affect the effort score. If we further remove host 2 from the network, we can see that the effort score now reduces to $F = F_A + F_C$.

- Finally, we show yet another different story by considering the skill aspect. First, suppose we have assigned some effort scores S_A, S_B, S_C, and S_D to the four vulnerabilities based on their base scores. Based on our assumption, we have that S_B is the smallest among the four and S_A is less than S_C. It is now easy to see that to compromise host 3, the minimum level of skills required for any attacker is S_C regardless of which sequence of attacks is being followed. Also, whether we remove host 4 or host 2 (even host 1) from the network does not affect the skill score.

3.2.2 Combining Scores for Different Aspects

We now formalize our approach to combining scores for the effort and skill aspects. For both aspects, we shall only consider the exploitability metric group, that is, the first three elements of the effective base metric vector. The formula shown in Definition 5 basically converts the exploitability score (defined in CVSS as the multiplication of the three metrics) to the same domain as the CVSS base score. Note that the effective base metric vector of each exploit is now defined with respect to a given subsets of exploits. This is necessary since whether a base metric needs to be adjusted will depend on which attack sequence is involved.

Definition 5 Given an attack graph G with the set of exploits E and the effective base metric vector *ebm* for each $e \in E$ with respect to some $E' \subseteq E$, we define for e both the *effort score es(e)* and *skill score ss(e)* with respect to E' as $round\_to\_1\_decimal(frac0.6395ebm[AV] * ebm[AC] * ebm[Au] - 0.2793)$.

Although both scores are defined in the same way, they will need to be combined differently, as demonstrated in the previous section. Definition 6 formalizes the way we combine those scores. Roughly speaking, for combining effort score, we find an attack sequence whose summation of effort scores is the minimum among all attack sequences (although such an attack sequence is not necessarily unique, the minimum value is always unique); for combining skill scores, we find an attack sequence that whose maximum effort score is the minimum among all attack sequences. The range of the result of $es(e)$ and $ss(e)$ is within $[1, 10]$ so that we can follow the same range of CVSS Base score.

Definition 6 Given an attack graph G with the set of exploits E, and the effort score $es(e)$ and skill score $ss(e)$ for each $e \in E$, we define

- the *accumulative effort score* of e as $F(e) = min(\{\sum_{e' \in q} es(e') : q$ is an attacksequencewith e as its last element$\})$ (here $es(e')$ is defined with respect to q).
- the *accumulative skill score* of e as $S(e) = min(\{max(\{ss(e') : e' \in q\}) : q$ is an attack sequence with e as its last element$\})$ (here $ss(e')$ defined with respect to q).

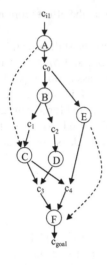

	AV	AC	Au	es, ss
v_A	Network	Low	None	1
v_B	Network	Medium	None	1.21
v_C	Local	Low	None	1 (w.r.t. q_1)
v_D	Local	Medium	None	3.49
v_E	Network	Medium	Single	1.59
v_F	Network	Medium	Single	1.59 (w.r.t. q_1) and 1.21 (w.r.t. q_2)

Attack Sequence	Effort $F(F)$	Skill $S(F)$
$q_1 : A \to B \to C \to F$	4.8	1.59
$q_2 : A \to B \to D \to E \to F$	8,5	3.49

Fig. 6 An example attack graph (*left*) and the effort and skill scores (*right*)

3.2.3 An Example

Now we demonstrate how our approach can be applied to calculate the accumulative effort and skill scores through a more elaborated example. On the left-hand side of Fig. 6 shows an example attack graph in which two attack sequences can both lead to the assumed goal condition. On the right-upper part of Fig. 6 we show CVSS metrics of the vulnerabilities. The dashed lines in the attack graph indicate dependency relationships between the exploits. Specifically, the adjusted *AccessVector* metric value of *C* should be *Network* and the adjusted *Authentication* metric value of *F* should be *None*.

The calculated cumulative effort scores and cumulative skill scores are shown on the right-lower part of Fig. 6. Note that in calculating the scores for each sequence, we need the effort and skill scores that are defined with respect to that sequence. In particular, exploit *F* has two different effort and skill scores, since its effective base metric *Authentication* is adjusted in sequence q_2 (due to exploit *E*) but not in sequence q_1.

4 Algorithm and Simulation

In this section, we first discuss algorithm design for implementing the proposed models, and then give simulation results that confirm the advantages of our approach.

Fig. 7 The virtual linkage
nodes

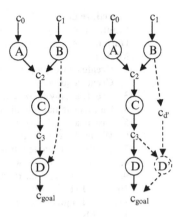

4.1 Algorithms

In order to capture the dependency relation in an attack graph, we will need to introduce new nodes and edges into an existing attack graph so to represent the semantics of dependency relations. More specifically, given a set of exploit nodes $S_k = \{e_i | <e_i, e_k>\}$, which contains all exploit nodes that have dependency relation with exploit node e_k, we add additional *virtual linkage nodes* and corresponding edges to represent the equivalent dependency relation in the attack graph model.

For example, on the left-hand side of Fig. 7 is an original attack graph with one dependency relation $< B, D >$. On the right-hand side, we add an virtual node D' and intermediate condition node $c_{d'}$ between node B and D to represent the scenario that, when B is exploited, the adjusted score for D is applied by D'. Note D and D' share the same set of pre-conditions and post-conditions so that D' keep the same relation in the attack graph, and meanwhile the intermediate condition node $c_{d'}$ is added to make sure that D' can be exploited when B is already exploited.

In Fig. 7, we have shown a simple example for adding such virtual linkage nodes. More generally, the procedure includes three steps shown as follows.

1. Given the original attack graph $G =< V, E >$ and a set $S_k = \{e_i | < e_i, e_k >\}$, for each $e_i \in S_k$, add intermediate condition node c'_i onto V with $post(e_i) = post(e_i) \cup \{c'_i\}$.
2. For each subset $T_k \subseteq S_k(T_k \neq \emptyset)$, add one node e_{T_k} onto V with $pre(e_{T_k}) = pre(e_k)$ and $post(e_{T_k}) = post(e_k)$. For each $e_i \in T_k$, append the corresponding intermediate condition node c'_i to $pre(e_{T_k})$.
3. For each e_{T_k}, assign $es(e_{T_k})$ and $ss(e_{T_k})$ as $es(e_k)$ and $ss(e_k)$ respectively, with respect to the corresponding T_k.

Before applying the following two algorithms, we first extend the original attack graph G by appending virtual linkage nodes for all dependency relations.

Procedure *CombineSkill*
Input: An attack graph G, a set of goal conditions C_{goal}
Output: A non-negative real number as combine skill score
Method:
1. **Create** new exploit e_{goal} with $pre(e_{goal}) = C_{goal}$, $post(e_{goal}) = \emptyset$
2. **Create** a queue Q
3. **Create** a array *score* to record the score of each condition
4. **Enqueue** initial conditions onto Q
5. **Create** a set $M = Q$, assign $s(c) = 0$ for each $c \in M$
6. **While** Q is not empty:
7.   **Dequeue** an item from Q to v
8.   **If** v is exploit node:
9.   **Let** $s(v) = max(\{s(u) : u \in pre(v)\} \cup \{ss(v)\})$
10.   **Let** $M = M \cup \{v\}$
11.   **Enqueue** each node $c' \in post(v)$ such that $\{e : c' \in post(e)\} \subseteq M$
12.   **Else** :
13.   **Let** $s(v) = min(\{s(u) : v \in post(u)\})$
14.   **Let** $M = M \cup \{v\}$
15.   **Enqueue** each node $e \in post(v)$ such that $pre(e) \subseteq M$
16. **Return** $s(e_{goal})$

Fig. 8 Combining the skill scores

4.1.1 Combining Skill Scores

In Fig. 8, we show formally the method for combining the *skillscore* of a given attack graph. Note that the input attack graph is the one after appending *virtual linkage nodes*.

In procedure *CombineSkill*, we first place all conditions to be achieved by attackers in a single set C_{goal}, and create a new exploit e_{goal} with pre-condition set $pre(e_{goal}) = C_{goal}$. Then, follow the aforementioned procedure, we add the corresponding *virtual linkage nodes* for each adjustable e_j with respect to the set S_j, which contains the exploits that can affect the skill score of node j due to dependency relationships. Then we conduct a *Breadth First Search (BFS)* to traverse the attack graph from initial conditions. At each step, we pick the minimal skill score of exploits that lead to condition v as the score of the condition v; for each exploit v, we assign the $ss(v)$ as the maximal of the scores of the pre-conditions of exploit v. In this way, we update the skill score of each exploit e as the accumulative skill score $S(e)$, up to the goal exploit e_{goal}.

The time complexity of this procedure can be derived from that of a BFS as $(O(|V| + |E|))$. The difference between our procedure and standard BFS is that, before a node is about to be enqueued, all of its predecessors will be checked (Line 11 in Fig. 8). The worst case is that each node has $|V| - 1$ predecessors. So the worst case time complexity of this procedure is $O(|E| \cdot |V| + |E|)$.

We now prove the correctness of procedure *CombineSkill* by induction. First, we extend the definition of $S(e)$ in Definition 6 to both exploit nodes and condition nodes. Specifically, if v is an exploit node, $S(v)$ still follow the definition in Definition 6. If v is a condition node, we let $S(v) = min(\{max(\{ss(e') : e' \in q\}) : q$ is an attack sequence with e' as its last element, and $v \in post(e')\})$. We need to show that $s(v) = S(v)$ is true for very node v at the end of the procedure, which shows that the procedure correctly computes the accumulative skill score of each exploit. We prove this by induction on $|M|$ with the induction hypothesis $\forall (v \in M)\ s(v) = S(v)$.

- Base case($M = \{c : c$ is initial condition$\}$): Since the initial conditions can be enabled without exploiting any exploits, $s(c) = 0 = S(c)$ for each $c \in M$.
- Inductive hypothesis: When a new node v to be added to M, $s(v) = S(v)$ for each $v \in M$.
- Inductive case: Here we only need to prove that the new node v satisfying $s(v) = S(v)$.

  - If v is an exploit: assume that $S(v) = s' < s(v)$. Let Q be the attack sequence ending with v such that $S(v) = max(\{ss(e) : e \in Q\}) = s'$. Since $v \in Q$, we have $ss(v) \leq s'$. By line 9 of the procedure *CombineSkill*, we have $s(v) = max(\{s(u) : u \in pre(v)\} \cup \{ss(v)\}) > s'$, so $s' < max(\{s(u) : u \in pre(v)\})$. Let's assume $c \in pre(v)$ such that $s' < s(c)$. And since $c \in M$, $S(c) = s(c) > s'$. However, since the attack sequence Q can reach the condition c, $S(c) \leq max(\{ss(e) : e \in Q\}) = s'$. So we come to a contradiction. Therefore we have $s(v) = S(V)$.
  - If v is a condition: assume that $S(v) = s' < s(v)$. Let Q be the attack sequence ending with e' such that $v \in post(e')$ and $S(e') = s' = S(v)$. By line 13 of the procedure *CombineSkill*, we have $s(v) = min(\{s(u) : v \in post(u)\}) \leq s(e')$, and $e' \in M$, because $v \in post(e')$. Then we have $s(e') = S(e') = S(v)$, so $s(v) \leq S(v)$, which contradicts with the assumption that $S(v) < s(v)$. Therefore $s(v) = S(v)$.

Since e_{goal} can be reached by at least one attack sequence, at last, $e_{goal} \in M$. According the previously proved claim, we have $S(e_{goal}) = s(e_{goal})$. Therefore the procedure *CombineSkill* is correct.

4.1.2 Combining Effort Scores

To calculate the combined effort score, we first create a goal exploit e_{goal} with respect to the set of goal conditions C_{goal}, and add *virtual linkage nodes* similar to the *CombineSkill* procedure. Then, starting from e_{goal}, we recursively call the *Min_Score* procedure to traverse though the attack graph G, and find the accumulative effort score of e_{goal} (Fig. 9).

More specifically, in line 4–7, we find the set C of further conditions needed to be enabled by exploiting more exploits, excepted for initial conditions. Line 8 and 9 deal with the base case of this recursion, where no more conditions needed to be enabled, and E contains a set of exploits which are necessary for an attack

Procedure *CombineEffort*
Input: A attack graph G, a set of goal conditions C_{goal}
Output: A non-negative real number *Score*
Method:
1. **Create** new exploit e_{goal} so that $pre(e_{goal}) = C_{goal}$
2. Let $Score = Min\_Score(\{e_{goal}\}, \emptyset)$
3. **Return** *Score*
Sub-Procedure *Min_Score*
Input: A set of exploits to be exploited E, a set exploits already exploited E_{path}
Output: A non-negative real number *MinScore*
Method:
4. **Let** $C = \{c : c \in pre(e'), e' \in E\}$
5. **For** each c in C
6.   **If** c is initial condition
7.   **Delete** c from C
8. **If** $C = \emptyset$
9.   **Return** $\sum_{e \in E} es(e)$
10. **Else**
11.   **Let** $E' = \{e' : c \in post(e'), c \in C\}$
12.   **Let** $MinScore = +\infty$
13.   **Let** $E_{path} = E_{path} \cup E$
14.   **For** each subset $E'' \subseteq E'$ satisfying $C \subseteq \bigcup_{e'' \in E''} post(e'')$
                and for any set $E''' \subset E'', C \cap \bigcup_{e''' \in E'''} post(e''') \neq C$
15.   **Let** $Score = Min\_Score(E'', E_{path})$
16.   **If** $Score < MinScore$
17.   **Let** $MinScore = Score$
18.   **Return** *MinScore*

Fig. 9 Combining the effort scores

sequence with e_{goal} as its last element. Line 10–17 deal with the recursive cases, where different attack sequences are explored. In line 14, we use some heuristic feature to avoid exploring attack sequences that cannot result in minimal combined effort scores. In line 15–17, potential attack sequences with minimal combined effort scores are explored by recursively call the *Min_Score* sub-procedure, and return the minimal combined effort scores among the different attack sequences.

The problem of combining effort score is NP-hard. This can be easily proved by considering a special case which is similar to the problem of computing k-zero day safety [10], which has been proven to be NP-hard. For example, when we assign $ss(e) = 1$ for each exploit e in the attack graph G, finding combined skill score is equivalent to finding k-zero day safety of G.

4.2   Simulation Results

We evaluate the proposed approaches through simulations that takes random attack graphs and simulated attackers as inputs and compares the distribution of resultant

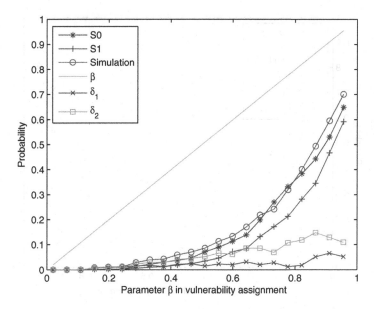

Fig. 10 The probability aspect (BRITE)

metric scores. To the best of our knowledge, there do not exist public datasets of real-world attack graphs that can be used for experiments. We employ the Boston university Representative Internet Topology gEnerator (BRITE) [2], and the Georgia Tech Internetwork Topology Models topology generator (GT-ITM) [5] to generate simulated network topologies. We then inject vulnerability information into the generated network topologies to obtain network configurations, and finally generate attack graphs from the configurations using the standard two-pass procedure [1]. All simulations are conducted on a computer equipped with a 3.0 GHz CPU and 8 GB memory.

The objective of the first two simulations is to evaluate our approach from the aspect of attack probability, as detailed in Sect. 3. For this purpose, we first randomly assign base metrics to each vulnerability and dependency relationships between pairs of vulnerabilities. We then apply both our approach and the existing approach by Marcel et al. [3] to calculate the probability of attacks with respect to a set of randomly chosen goal conditions. We also compare our result to the percentage of simulated attackers (each simulated attacker is modeled as a random subset of vulnerabilities that he/she can exploit) who can successfully reach the goal conditions.

In Fig. 10, we use the BRITE topology generator to create random network topology. The X-axis is the average effective base score of all vulnerabilities in each network divided by 10, denoted by β. The Y-axis is either the combined score of attack probability (for both our approach and the approach by Marcel et al.) or the percentage of successful attackers. Each result is the average of 500 simulations on

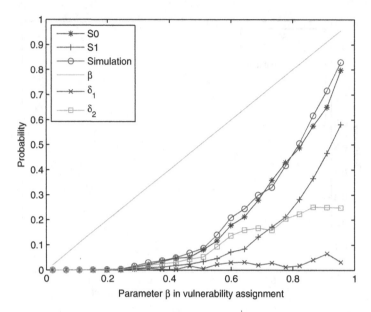

Fig. 11 Increased dependency relationships (BRITE)

different network configurations. The curve *Simulation* corresponds to the simulated attackers, which is used as a base line for comparison. The line β corresponds to the naive approach of taking the average base score among all vulnerabilities in a network, which is clearly inaccurate.

In Fig. 10, the curve S_0 corresponds to our approach and the curve S_1 the approach by Marcel et al. The curve δ_1 represents the absolute value of the difference between the probability result from our approach and the simulated attackers, and the curve δ_2 represents the absolute value of the difference between the probability result from the approach by Marcel et al. and the simulated attackers. Clearly, our result is closer to the simulated attackers than theirs. Also, our probability is always higher than theirs due to the proper handling of dependency relationships. In Fig. 10, we have assigned dependency relationships to n pairs of randomly chosen vulnerabilities where n is drawn from a uniform distribution on $[0, 3]$. Figure 11 shows a similar simulation, except that we increase the amount of dependency relationships to n pairs where n is now drawn from a (uniform distribution on $[0, 5]$. The results show that our approach is still very close to the simulated attackers, whereas Marcel's result further deviates from the baseline results. In Figs. 12 and 13, we present similar experiment result as Figs. 10 and 11 respectively, by using another topology generator GT-ITM.

In Fig. 14, we fix the distribution of CVSS score distribution based on [4]. We keep the uniform distribution of dependency number, but change the average number from 0 to 3 as shown on the X-axis. Similar to the aforementioned experiments, the Y-axis is either combined score of attack probability (by our approach and Marcel et al.), or the percentage of successful simulated attackers.

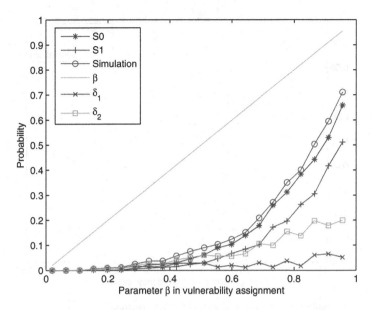

Fig. 12 The probability aspect (GT-ITM)

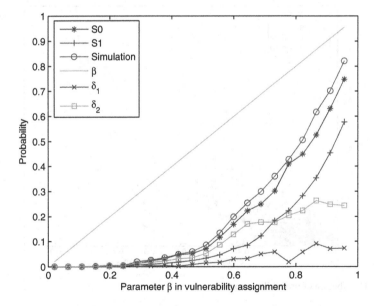

Fig. 13 Increased dependency relationships (GT-ITM)

The objective of the next simulation is to study the deviation of combined scores from the baseline of simulated attackers. For this purpose, Fig. 15 depicts the results computed on 800 different networks. The X-axis is the percentage of simulated attackers who can reach the goal conditions, and the Y-axis is the combined

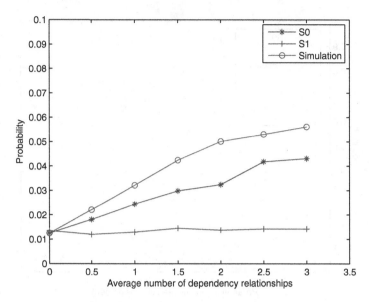

Fig. 14 The probability aspect using real world CVSS distribution

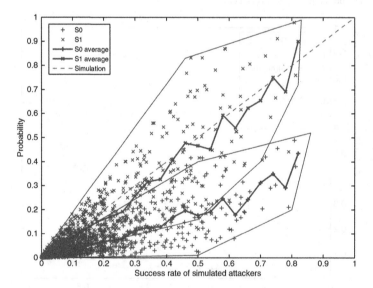

Fig. 15 Distribution of probability scores

probability score. The dots S_0 and S_1 correspond to the results of our approach
and Marcel's, respectively. The two solid lines labeled with S_0 and S_1 represent the
average probability score within each 0.05 interval of the X-axis. The two polygon
areas depict the distribution of combined scores produced by the two approaches. As

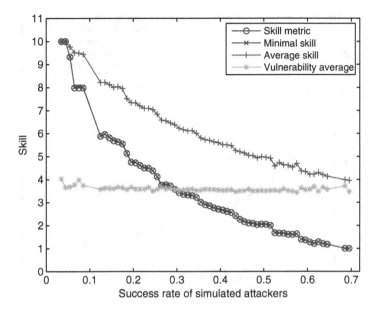

Fig. 16 The skill aspect

we can see from the figure, our results evenly spread around the simulated attackers' results, whereas Marcel's results are almost always lower than the baseline results.

The next simulation aims to evaluate our approach from the skill aspect. For this purpose, each simulated attacker is randomly assigned a skill level based on exponential distribution (significantly less attackers possess a higher level of skills). Each simulated attacker can only exploit those vulnerabilities whose skill scores (as defined in Sect. 3) are no greater than the attacker's assigned skill level. In Fig. 16, the X-axis is the percentage of successful simulated attackers, and the Y-axis is either the skill score produced by our approach or the skill level of simulated attackers. Each result is the average of 100 simulations. The curve *Skill metric* is the cumulative skill score of our approach; the curve *Minimal skill* corresponds to the lowest skill level of simulated attackers among those who can reach the goal conditions. We can see that those two curves almost overlap each other, indicating the accuracy of our approach. The curve *Average skill* shows the average skill level among successful simulated attackers, which has the same trend, but is always higher than our result. The curve *Vulnerability average* shows the average skill score of all vulnerabilities in each network, which is clearly not a valid metric for skill level.

The next simulation evaluates our approach from the effort aspect. For this purpose, each simulated attacker is randomly assigned an*effort threshold* based on exponential distribution (less attackers are willing to spend more effort). We assume each simulated attacker will only exploit those vulnerabilities whose effort scores (as defined in Sect. 3) are no greater than the attacker's assigned effort threshold. In

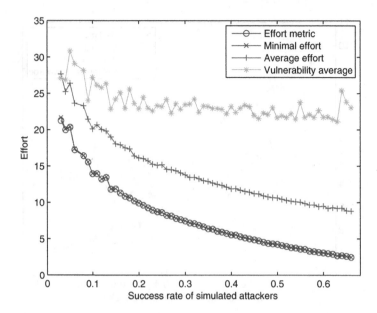

Fig. 17 The effort aspect

Fig. 17, the X-axis is the percentage of successful simulated attackers, and the Y-axis is either the effort score or the effort threshold (of simulated attackers). The curve *Effort metric* is the cumulative effort score of our approach; the curve *Minimal effort* and *Average effort* respectively correspond to the lowest and average effort threshold of those simulated attackers who successfully reach the goal conditions. Again, we can see our effort scores closely match the minimum required effort and follow the same trend as the average effort. The *Vulnerability average* curve shows the average skill score of all vulnerabilities is not as good a metric for measuring effort.

In Fig. 18, we demonstrate the comparison of computation time between *CombineEffort* and brute force algorithm for computing *Effort*. We tested four sets of cases. In each case, we generate random attack graphs of 90 instances. From this experiment shows that our heuristic algorithm *CombineEffort* reduces the computation time exponentially with respect to the size of attack graph.

5 Conclusion

In this chapter, we have addressed two important limitations of existing approaches to combining CVSS scores, namely, the lack of support for dependency relationships between vulnerabilities, and the lack of consideration for aspects other than attack probability. We have formally presented our approaches to removing both limitations. Specifically, we handled potential dependency relationships at the base metric level so the resulted adjustment in base scores had well-defined semantics. We have also extended our approach to interpret and combine CVSS metrics and scores in

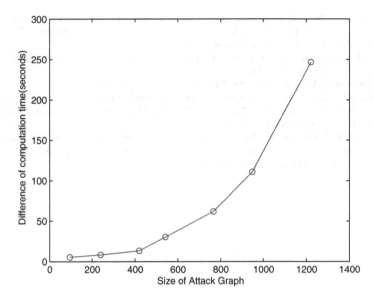

Fig. 18 Performance comparison for combining effort

the skill and effort aspects. The simulation results have confirmed the advantages of our approach. Future work will be directed to incorporating the temporal and environmental scores, the consideration of other aspects for interpreting the scores, and experiments with more realistic settings.

Acknowledgements Authors with Concordia University were partially supported by the Natural Sciences and Engineering Research Council of Canada under Discovery Grant N01035. Sushil Jajodia was partially supported by the by Army Research Office grants W911NF-13-1-0421 and W911NF-15-1-0576, by the Office of Naval Research grant N00014-15-1-2007, National Institutes of Standard and Technology grant 60NANB16D287, and by the National Science Foundation grant IIP-1266147.

References

1. P. Ammann, D. Wijesekera, S. Kaushik, Scalable, graph-based network vulnerability analysis, in *Proceedings of CCS'02* (2002)
2. Boston university representative internet topology generator. Available at http://www.cs.bu.edu/brite/
3. M. Frigault, L. Wang, A. Singhal, S. Jajodia, Measuring network security using dynamic Bayesian network, in *Proceedings of ACM workshop on Quality of protection* (2008)
4. L. Gallon, Vulnerability discrimination using CVSS framework, in *2011 4th IFIP International Conference on New Technologies, Mobility and Security (NTMS)*, Feb (2011), pp. 1–6
5. Georgia tech internetwork topology models topology generator. Available at http://www.cc.gatech.edu/projects/gtitm/

6. S. Jajodia, S. Noel, B. O'Berry, Topological analysis of network attack vulnerability, in *Managing Cyber Threats: Issues, Approaches and Challenges*, ed. by V. Kumar, J. Srivastava, A. Lazarevic (Kluwer Academic Publisher, 2003)
7. P. Mell, K. Scarfone, S. Romanosky, Common vulnerability scoring system. IEEE Secur. Privacy Mag. **4**(6), 85–89 (2006)
8. National vulnerability database. Available at: http://www.nvd.org,May9,2008
9. L. Wang, T. Islam, T. Long, A. Singhal, S. Jajodia, An attack graph-based probabilistic security metric, in *Proceedings of The 22nd Annual IFIP WG 11.3 Working Conference on Data and Applications Security (DBSec'08)* (2008)
10. L. Wang, S. Jajodia, A. Singhal, S. Noel, k-zero day safety: measuring the security risk of networks against unknown attacks, in *Proceedings of the 15th European Symposium on Research in Computer Security (ESORICS'10)* (2010)

Security Risk Analysis of Enterprise Networks Using Probabilistic Attack Graphs

Anoop Singhal and Xinming Ou

Abstract Today's information systems face sophisticated attackers who combine multiple vulnerabilities to penetrate networks with devastating impact. The overall security of an enterprise network cannot be determined by simply counting the number of vulnerabilities. To more accurately assess the security of enterprise systems, one must understand how vulnerabilities can be combined and exploited to stage an attack. Composition of vulnerabilities can be modeled using probabilistic attack graphs, which show all paths of attacks that allow incremental network penetration. Attack likelihoods are propagated through the attack graph, yielding a novel way to measure the security risk of enterprise systems. This metric for risk mitigation analysis is used to maximize the security of enterprise systems. This methodology based on probabilistic attack graphs can be used to evaluate and strengthen the overall security of enterprise networks.

1 Introduction

At present, computer networks constitute the core component of information technology infrastructures in areas such as power grids, financial data systems, and emergency communication systems. Protection of these networks from malicious intrusions is critical to the economy and security of any organization. Vulnerabilities are regularly discovered in software applications which are exploited to stage cyber attacks. Currently, management of security risk of an enterprise network is more an art than a science. System administrators operate by instinct and experience rather than relying on objective metrics to guide and justify decision making. In this report, we develop models and metrics that can be used to objectively assess the security risk in an enterprise network, and techniques on how to use such metrics to guide decision making in cyber defense.

A. Singhal (✉)
Computer Security Division, NIST, Gaithersburg, MD 20899, USA
e-mail: anoop.singhal@nist.gov

X. Ou
Department of Computer Science and Engineering, University of South Florida, Tampa, FL, USA

© Springer International Publishing AG 2017
L. Wang et al., *Network Security Metrics*,
https://doi.org/10.1007/978-3-319-66505-4_3

To improve the security of enterprise networks, it is necessary to measure the amount of security provided by different network configurations. The objective of our research was to develop a standard model for measuring security of computer networks. A standard model will enable us to answer questions such as "Are we more secure than yesterday?" or "How does the security of one network configuration compare with another?" Also, having a standard model to measure network security will bring together users, vendors, and researchers to evaluate methodologies and products for network security.

Some of the challenges for security risk analysis of enterprise networks are:

(a) *Security vulnerabilities are rampant*: CERT[1] reports about a hundred new security vulnerabilities each week. It becomes difficult to manage the security of an enterprise network (with hundreds of hosts and different operating systems and applications on each host) in the presence of software vulnerabilities that can be exploited.
(b) *Attackers launch complex multistep cyber attacks*: Cyber attackers can launch multistep and multi-host attacks that can incrementally penetrate the network with the goal of eventually compromising critical systems. It is a challenging task to protect the critical systems from such attacks.
(c) *Current attack detection methods cannot deal with the complexity of attacks*: Computer systems are increasingly under attack. When new vulnerabilities are reported, attack programs are available in a short amount of time. Traditional approaches to detecting attacks (using an Intrusion Detection System) have problems such as too many false positives, limited scalability, and limits on detecting attacks.

Good metrics should be measured consistently, inexpensive to collect, expressed numerically, have units of measure, and have specific context [1]. We meet this challenge by capturing vulnerability interdependencies and measuring security in the exact way that real attackers penetrate the network. We analyze all attack paths through a network, providing a metric of overall system risk. Through this metric, we analyze trade-offs between security costs and security benefits. Decision makers can therefore avoid over investing in security measures that do not pay off, or under investing and risk devastating consequences. Our metric is consistent, unambiguous, and provides context for understanding security risk of computer networks.

This report is organized as follows. Section 2 presents attack graphs and tools for generating attack graphs. Section 3 discusses past work in the area of security risk analysis. Section 4 discusses the Common Vulnerability Scoring System (CVSS). Section 5 discusses security risk analysis of enterprise networks using attack graphs. Section 6 presents some of the challenges for security risk analysis and, finally, Sect. 7 gives the conclusions.

---

[1]Computer Emergency Response Team, http://www.cert.org/.

2   Attack Graphs

Attack graphs model how multiple vulnerabilities may be combined for an attack. They represent system states using a collection of security-related conditions, such as the existence of vulnerability on a particular host or the connectivity between different hosts. Vulnerability exploitation is modeled as a transition between system states.

As an example, consider Fig. 1. The left side shows a network configuration, and the right side shows the attack graph for compromise of the database server by a malicious workstation user. In the network configuration, the firewall is intended to help protect the internal network. The internal file server offers file transfer (ftp), secure shell (ssh), and remote shell (rsh) services. The internal database server offers ftp and rsh services. The firewall allows ftp, ssh, and rsh traffic from a user workstation to both servers, and blocks all other traffic.

In the attack graph, attacker exploits are blue ovals, with edges for their preconditions and postconditions. The numbers inside parentheses denote source and destination hosts. Yellow boxes are initial network conditions, and the green triangle is the attacker's initial capability. Conditions induced by attacker exploits are plain text. The overall attack goal is a red octagon. The figure also shows the direct impact of blocking ssh or rsh traffic (to the fileserver) through the firewall, i.e., preventing certain exploits in the attack graph.

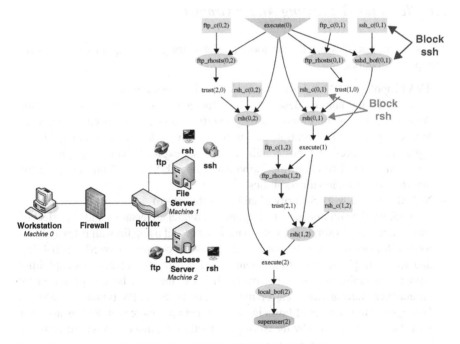

Fig. 1 Example network, attack graph, and network hardening choices

The attack graph includes these attack paths:

(a) *sshd_bof(0,1)* → *ftp_rhosts(1,2)* → *rsh(1,2)* → *local_bof(2)*
(b) *ftp_rhosts(0,1)* → *rsh(0,1)* → *ftp_rhosts(1,2)* → *rsh(1,2)* → *local_bof(2)*
(c) *ftp_rhosts(0,2)* → *rsh(0,2)* → *local_bof(2)*

The first attack path starts with *sshd_bof(0,1)*. This indicates a buffer overflow exploit executed from *Machine 0* (the workstation) against *Machine 1* (the file server), i.e., against its secure shell service. In a buffer overflow attack, a program is made to erroneously store data beyond a fixed-length buffer, overwriting adjacent memory that holds program control-flow data. The result of the *sshd_bof(0,1)* exploit is that the attacker can execute arbitrary code on the file server. The *ftp_rhosts(1,2)* exploit is now possible, meaning that the attacker exploits a particular ftp vulnerability to anonymously upload a list of trusted hosts from *Machine 1* (the file server) to *Machine 2* (the database server). The attacker can leverage this new trust to remotely execute shell commands on the database server, without providing a password, i.e., the *rsh(1,2)* exploit. This exploit establishes the attacker's control over the database server as a user with regular privileges. A local buffer overflow exploit is then possible on the database server, which runs in the context of a privileged process. The result is that the attacker can execute code on the database server with full privileges.

2.1 Tools for Generating Attack Graphs

This section describes briefly the tools available for generating attack graphs for enterprise networks.

- TVA (Topological Analysis of Network Attack Vulnerability)

     In [2–4], the authors describe a tool for generation of attack graphs. This approach assumes the monotonicity property of attacks, and it has polynomial time complexity. The central idea is to use an *exploit dependency graph* to represent the pre- and postconditions for an exploit. Then a graph search algorithm is used to chain the individual vulnerabilities and find attack paths that involve multiple vulnerabilities.
- NETSPA (A Network Security Planning Architecture)

     In [5, 6], the authors use attack graphs to model adversaries and the effect of simple counter measures. It creates a network model using firewall rules and network vulnerability scans. It then uses the model to compute network reachability and attack graphs representing potential attack paths for adversaries exploiting known vulnerabilities. This discovers all hosts that can be compromised by an attacker starting from one or more locations. NETSPA typically scales as O(nlogn) as the number of hosts in a typical network increases. Risk is assessed for different adversaries by measuring the total assets that can be captured by an attacker.

- MULVAL (Multihost, multistage, Vulnerability Analysis)

    In [7, 8], a network security analyzer based on Datalog is described. The information in vulnerability databases, the configuration information for each machine, and other relevant information are all encoded as Datalog facts. The reasoning engine captures the interaction among various components in the network. The reasoning engine in MULVAL scales well ($O(n^2)$) with the size of the network.

    In [9–12], some recent commercial tools for vulnerability analysis and attack graph generation are described. Skybox security [9] and Red Seal Systems [10] have developed a tool that can generate attack graphs. Risk is calculated using the probability of success of an attack path multiplied by the loss associated with the compromised target. Nessus [11] and Retina [12] are vulnerability management systems that can help organizations with vulnerability assessment, mitigation, and protection.

    All the tools for attack graph generation that are mentioned here are similar in capabilities. We will use the MULVAL tool in this document to illustrate our methodology of security risk analysis using attack graphs.

3 Past Work in Security Risk Analysis

Modelers generally think about security in terms of threats, risks, and losses [1]. Good models provide a rationale for measurements, and these models can be updated and calibrated as new data becomes available. A data model can also be used to automate security calculations. Some of the benefits of automating security metrics calculations are:

- *Accuracy*: Accuracy is required to trust the data that is collected and to develop consensus about the results.
- *Repeatability*: This is another important component of trust. If two measurements of a target can give the same consistent result, then the data can be trusted.
- *Reliability*: Automation of data collection will result in more reliability as it is not prone to human errors.
- *Transparency*: The steps used to derive the metrics are readily apparent, and they are accurately documented.

Security metrics have been suggested based on criteria compliance, intrusion detection, security policy, security incidents, and actuarial modeling. Statistical methods (Markov modeling, Bayesian networks, etc.) have been used in measuring network security. Complementary to our approach, measurements of attack resistance [13] and weakest successful adversary [14] have been proposed.

Early standardization efforts in the defense community evolved into the system security engineering capability maturity model (SSE-CMM) [15], although it does not assign quantitative measures. Lots of risk management work has been done at the National Institute of Standards and Technology (NIST) on risk identification, assessment and analysis. NIST Special Publication (SP) 800-55 [16] describes the security metrics implementation process. NIST SP 800-27 [17] describes the principles for establishing a security baseline. NIST SP 800-39 [18] is the document that describes information security standards and guidelines developed by NIST. The purpose of NIST SP 800-39 is to provide a guide for an organization-wide program for managing information security risk. NIST SP 800-55 (Revision 1) [19] provides performance measurement guide for information security. NIST SP 800-30 [20] presents a risk management guide for information technology systems. There are also standardization efforts for vulnerability scoring, such as the Common Vulnerability Scoring System (CVSS) [21], although these treat vulnerabilities in isolation, without considering attack interdependencies on target networks.

In early work in attack graph analysis, model checking was used to enumerate attack sequences linking initial and goal states [22, 23]. Because of explicit enumeration of attack states, these approaches scale exponentially with the size of the network. With a practical assumption of monotonic logic, attack graph complexity has been shown to be polynomial rather than exponential [24, 25]. Graph complexity has been further reduced, to worst-case quadratic in the number of hosts [2].

Further improvement is possible by grouping networks into protection domains, in which there is unrestricted connectivity among hosts within each domain [3]. With this representation, complexity is reduced to linear within each protection domain, and overall quadratic in the number of protection domains (which is typically much less than the number of hosts). Such attack graphs have been generated for tens of thousands of hosts (hundreds of domains) within a minute, excluding graph visualization [2]. A detailed description of this approach to attack graph analysis is given in [3, 26, 27].

Beyond improving attack graph complexity, frameworks have been proposed for expressing network attack models [28–30]. Capabilities for mapping multistep attacks have begun to appear in some commercial products [9, 10], although their limitations include not showing all possible attack paths simultaneously as needed for effective risk assessment. A more extensive review of attack graph research (as of 2005) is given in [31].

There have been some attempts at measuring network security risk by combining attack graphs with individual vulnerability metrics. Frigault et al. [32] proposes converting attack graphs and individual vulnerability score into Bayesian Network for computing the cumulative probability. Wang et al. [33] recognize the existence of cycles in an attack graph and present ideas about how to propagate probabilities over cycles. In [34], techniques for enterprise network security metrics are described. In [35], the concept of "Measuring the Attack Surface" is used to determine the security risk of software systems. In [36], a practical approach to quantifying security risk in enterprise networks is described.

In this chapter, we identify two layers in enterprise network security metrics: the *component metrics* and the *cumulative metrics*. The component metrics are about individual components' properties, which in many cases can be obtained from standard data sources like the National Vulnerability Database (NVD). The important feature of the component metrics is that they are only about individual components and do not consider interactions among components. As a result, they can be measured or computed separately. The cumulative security metrics account for both the baseline metrics of individual components and the interactions among components. We propose that the cumulative metrics shall be obtained by composing the component metrics through a *sound theoretical model with well-defined semantics*.

4 Common Vulnerability Scoring System (CVSS)

CVSS [21] is an industry standard for assessing the *severity* of computer system security vulnerabilities. It attempts to establish a measure of how much concern a vulnerability warrants, compared to other vulnerabilities, so efforts can be prioritized. It offers the following benefits:

- *Standardized vulnerability scores*: When an organization normalizes vulnerability scores across all of its software and hardware platforms, it can leverage a single vulnerability management policy.
- *Open framework*: Users can be confused when a vulnerability is assigned an arbitrary score. With CVSS, anyone can see the individual characteristics used to derive a score.
- *Prioritized risk*: When the environmental score is computed, the vulnerability now becomes contextual. That is, vulnerability scores are now representative of the actual risk to an organization.

CVSS is composed of three metric groups: *Base*, *Temporal*, and *Environmental*, each consisting of a set of metrics, as shown in Fig. 2.

These metric groups are described as follows:

- *Base*: representing "intrinsic and fundamental characteristics of a vulnerability that are constant over time and user environments"
- *Temporal*: representing "characteristics of a vulnerability that change over time but not among user environments"

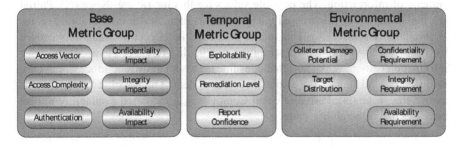

Fig. 2 CVSS metric groups

- *Environmental*: representing "characteristics of a vulnerability that are relevant and unique to a particular user's environment"

The base metric group captures the characteristics of a vulnerability that do not change with time and across user environment. The Access Vector, Access Complexity, and Authentication metrics capture how the vulnerability is accessed and whether or not extra conditions are required to exploit it. The three impact metrics measure how a vulnerability, if exploited, will directly effect the degree of loss of confidentiality, integrity, and availability. For example, a vulnerability could cause a partial loss of integrity and availability, but no loss of confidentiality. We briefly describe the metrics as follows.

Access vector (AV): This metric reflects how the vulnerability is exploited. The possible values for this metrics are: Local (L), Adjacent Network (A), and Network (N). The more remote an attacker can attack a host, the greater the vulnerability score.

Access complexity (AC): This metric measures the complexity of the attack required to exploit the vulnerability once an attacker has gained access to the target system. The possible values for this metric are: High (H), Medium (M), and Low (L). For example, consider a buffer overflow in an Internet service. Once the target system is located, the attacker can launch and exploit it at will. The lower the required complexity, the higher the vulnerability score.

Authentication (AU): This metric measures the number of times an attacker must authenticate in order to exploit a vulnerability. This metric does not gauge the strength complexity of the authentication process, but only that an attacker is required to provide credentials before an exploit is launched. The possible values for this metric are: Multiple (M), Single (S), and None (N). The fewer authentication instances that are required, the higher the vulnerability scores.

Confidentiality impact (C): This metric measures the impact on confidentiality of a successfully exploited vulnerability. Confidentiality refers to limiting information access and disclosure to only authorized users, as well as preventing access by, or disclosure to, unauthorized ones. The possible values for this metric are: None (N), Partial (P), and Complete (C). Increased confidentiality impact increases the vulnerability score.

Integrity impact (I): This metric measures the impact to integrity of a successfully exploited vulnerability. Integrity refers to the trustworthiness and guaranteed veracity of information. The possible values for this metric are: None (N), Partial (P), and Complete (C). Increased integrity impact increases the vulnerability score.

Availability impact (A): This metric measures the impact to availability caused by a successfully exploited vulnerability. Availability refers to the accessibility of information resources. Attacks that consume network bandwidth, processor cycles, or disk space all impact the availability of a system. The possible values for this metric are: None (N), Partial (P), and Complete (C). Increased availability impact increases the vulnerability score.

4.1 An Example

Consider CVE-2003-0062: Buffer Overflow in NOD32 Antivirus. NOD32 is an antivirus software application developed by Eset. In February 2003, a buffer overflow vulnerability was discovered in Linux and Unix versions prior to 1.013 that could allow local users to execute arbitrary code with the privileges of the user executing NOD32. To trigger the buffer overflow, the attacker must wait for (or coax) another user (possible root) to scan a directory path of excessive length.

Since the vulnerability is exploitable only to a user locally logged into the system, the Access Vector is "Local." The Access Complexity is "High" because this vulnerability can be exploited only under specialized access conditions. There is an additional layer of complexity because the attacker must wait for another user to run the virus-scanning software. Authentication is set to "None" because the attacker does not need to authenticate to any additional system. Together, these metrics produce a base score of 6.2.

The base vector for this vulnerability is: AV:L/AC:H/Au:N/C:C/I:C/A:C

Base metric	Evaluation	Score
Access vector	Local	0.395
Access complexity	High	0.35
Authentication	None	0.704
Confidentiality impact	Complete	0.66
Integrity impact	Complete	0.66
Availability impact	Complete	0.66
Formula		Base score
Impact $= 10.41 \times (1 - (0.34 \times 0.34 \times 0.34)) = 10.0$		
Exploitability $= 20 \times 0.35 \times 0.704 \times 0.395 = 1.9$		
f(Impact) $= 1.176$		
Base Score $= ((0.6 \times 10) + (0.4 \times 1.9) - 1.5) \times 1.176 = 6.2$		

Basically, for each metric group, an equation is used to weigh the corresponding metrics and produce a score (ranged from 0 to 10) based on a series of measurements and security experts' assessment, and the score 10 represents the most severe vulnerability. Specifically, when the base metrics are assigned values, the base equation calculates a score ranging from 0 to 10, and creates a vector. This vector is a text string that contains the values assigned to each metric. It is used to communicate exactly how the score for each vulnerability is derived, so that anyone can understand how the score was derived and, if desired, confirm the validity of each metric.

Optionally, the base score can be refined by assigning values to the temporal and environmental metrics. This is useful in order to provide additional context for a vulnerability by more accurately reflecting the risk posed by the vulnerability to a user's environment. Depending on one's purpose, the base score and vector may be sufficient. If a temporal score is needed, the temporal equation will combine the temporal metrics with the base score to produce a temporal score ranging from 0 to 10. Similarly, if an environmental score is needed, the environmental equation will combine the environmental metrics with the base score to produce an environmental score ranging from 0 to 10. More details on base, temporal, and environmental equations, and the calculations can be found in the CVSS standards guide [22].

5 Security Risk Analysis of Enterprise Networks Using Attack Graphs

In this section, we present our methodology for security risk analysis of Enterprise Networks using Attack Graphs. We will use the MULVAL tool for attack graph generation to illustrate our approach. We explain our methodology using three examples. Example one presents the methodology using a single vulnerability. Examples two and three present the methodology for a system containing multiple vulnerabilities.

Attack graphs provide the cumulative effect of attack steps to show how each of these steps can potentially enable an attacker to reach their goal. However, one limitation of an attack graph is that it assumes that a vulnerability can always be exploited. In reality, there is a wide range of probabilities that different steps can be exploited. It is dependent on the skill of the attacker and the difficulty of the exploit. Attack graphs show what is possible without any indication of what is likely. In this section, we present a methodology to estimate the security risk using the CVSS scores of individual vulnerabilities.

5.1 Example 1

In the simple example of Fig. 3, there is a firewall controlling network access from Internet to the DMZ subnet of an enterprise network. The Demilitarized Zone (DMZ) is typically used to place publicly accessible servers, in this case the web

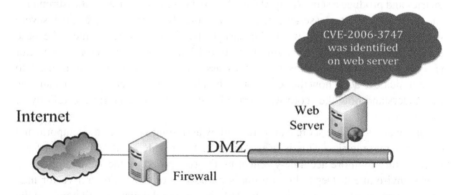

Fig. 3 Network for Example 1

server. The firewall protects the host in DMZ and only allows external access to ports necessary for the service. In this example, Internet is allowed to access the web server through TCP port 80, the standard HTTP protocol and port.

Suppose a vulnerability scan is performed on the web server, and a vulnerability is identified. The CVE ID of the discovered vulnerability is CVE-2006-3747. Using this ID as a key, one can query the National Vulnerability Database (NVD) and obtain a number of important properties of the vulnerability. Below is an excerpt from the information retrieved from NVD about CVE-2006-3747:

5.1.1 Overview

Off-by-one error in the ldap scheme handling in the Rewrite module (mod_rewrite) in Apache 1.3 from 1.3.28, 2.0.46 and other versions before 2.0.59, and 2.2, when RewriteEngine is enabled, allows remote attackers to cause a denial of service (application crash) and possibly execute arbitrary code via crafted URLs that are not properly handled using certain rewrite rules.

Impact
CVSS Severity (version 2.0):
CVSS v2 Base Score:7.6 (HIGH) (AV:N/AC:H/Au:N/C:C/I:C/A:C) (legend)
Impact Subscore: 10.0
Exploitability Subscore: 4.9
CVSS Version 2 Metrics:
Access Vector: Network exploitable
Access Complexity: High
Authentication: Not required to exploit
Impact Type: Provides administrator access, Allows complete confidentiality, integrity, and availability violation; Allows unauthorized disclosure of information; Allows disruption of service

The "Overview" section gives a number of key features of the vulnerability, including the relevant software modules and versions and what security impact the vulnerability poses to a system. The latter is further displayed in the "Impact" section. Most of the impact factors are expressed in the CVSS metric vector, which is "AV:N/AC:H/Au:N/C:C/I:C/A:C" in this case.

These CVSS metrics provide crucial information regarding the pre- and post-conditions for exploiting the vulnerability. Such information can then be used to construct an attack graph, which shows all possible attack paths in a network. The attack graph for this simple network is shown in Fig. 4.

The above graph is computed from the MulVAL network security analyzer [7, 8]. The square vertices represent configuration of the system, e.g., the existence of a software vulnerability on a machine (node 6), firewall rules that allow Internet to access the web server through the HTTP protocol and port (node 1), and services running on a host (node 5). The diamond vertices represent potential privileges an attacker could gain in the system, e.g., code execution privilege on web server

Fig. 4 Attack Graph for
Example 1

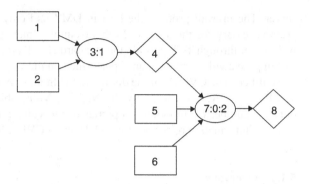

(node 8). The elliptical vertices are "attack nodes" which link preconditions to postconditions of an attack. For example, node 7 represents the attack "remote exploit of a server program." Its preconditions are: the attacker has network access to the target machine for the specific protocol and port (node 4), the service on that port is running (node 5), and the service is vulnerable (node 6). The postcondition of the attack is that the attacker gains the specific privilege on the machine (node 8).

An attack graph can help a system administrator understand what could happen in their network, through analyzing the configuration of an enterprise network system. When the size of the system increases, it becomes increasingly difficulty for a human to keep track of and correlate all relevant information. An automatic attack-graph generator has its unique advantage in that it can identify non-obvious attack possibilities arising from intricate security interactions within an enterprise network, which can be easily missed by a human analyst. It achieves this through building up a knowledge base (KB) about generic security knowledge independent of any specific scenarios. For example, the KB rule that generated part of the attack graph in Fig. 4 is shown below.

```
execCode(H, Perm)  :-
    vulExists(H, VulID, Software, remote, privEscalation),
    networkServiceInfo(H, Software, Protocol, Port, Perm),
    netAccess(H, Protocol, Port).
```

This is a generic Datalog rule for how to reason about remote exploit of a service program. It is easy to see that the three subgoals correspond to the three predecessors of node 7, and the head of the rule corresponds to its successor. The variables (in upper case-led identifiers) are automatically instantiated with the concrete values from a system's configuration tuples. There are many other rules like the one above in the knowledge base. All the rules form a Datalog program, and a Prolog system can efficiently evaluate such a program against thousands of input tuples. The evaluation process will find out *all* consequences arising from these rules. Complex multistep, multi-host attack paths are naturally captured in this logical reasoning process, even though each rule itself only describes a specific type of attacks.

An attack graph is often perceived to have a deterministic semantics: as long as all the preconditions of an attack can be achieved, the attack can always succeed resulting in the attacker obtaining the postcondition privilege. In reality, it is often not that clear. The "possibly execute arbitrary code" in the vulnerability's overview highlights the uncertainty in the true consequence of exploiting a vulnerability. Depending on the difficulty level of the exploit, the attacker's skills and resources, and how hard it is to get to it, a vulnerability may or may not pose a high risk to the system. Since all security hardening measures (e.g., patching) inevitably incur cost in terms of human labor, increased inconvenience, or degraded performance, security administration is an art of balancing risk and cost. A quantitative model for risk assessment is indispensable to make this effort a more scientific process.

Deriving Security Risk from Attack Graphs Since all the attack nodes in an attack graph do not always guarantee success, we can attach a *component metric* to each attack node. The component metric is a numeric measure indicating the conditional probability of attack success when all the preconditions are met. Such component metrics can be derived from CVSS metric vector. For example, we can map the AC metric to probability such that higher AC metric value is mapped to a lower value in probability. Then we can aggregate the probabilities over the attack-graph structure to provide a *cumulative metric*, which indicates the absolute probability of attack success in the specific system. The cumulative metrics are not only affected by the individual vulnerabilities' properties, but are also to a large extent affected by how the security interactions may happen in the specific system which affects the way an attacker can move from one step to another. By combining the component metrics with the attack-graph structure, one can obtain a security metric that is tailored to the specific environment, instead of a generic metric such as the CVSS Base Score.

In the example attack graph of Fig. 4, node 7 is attached a component metric 0.2 which is derived from the vulnerability's AC metric based on the mapping High→0.2, Medium→ 0.6, Low → 0.9. Node 3 has a component metric 1 since it represents network access semantics, not a real attack step and thus without an uncertainty in its success. Since this attack graph is very simple, we can easily see that the cumulative metric for node 8 (compromise of the web server) is also 0.2.

5.2 Example 2

In the example shown in Fig. 5, a new subnet Internal is added, which hosts the database server. The access to the Internal subnet is mediated by an internal firewall. Only the web server can access the database server, which also has a remote vulnerability in the MySQL DB service (CVE-2009-2446). The attack graph for this network is shown in Fig. 6.

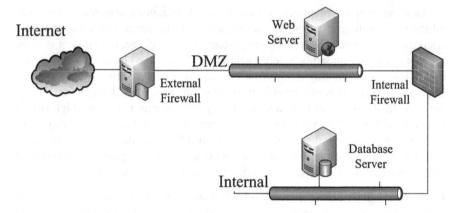

Fig. 5 Network for Example 2

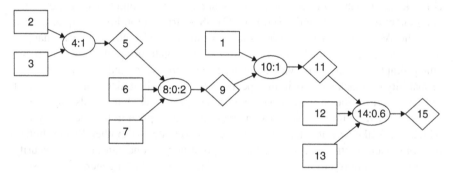

Fig. 6 Attack Graph for Example 2

This attack graph shows a two-stage attack. The attacker can first compromise the web server (node 8). Then they can use the web server as a stepping stone to further compromise the database server (node 14). The component metric for node 2 is 0.6, since the MySQL vulnerability is easier to exploit than the Apache vulnerability. In this attack graph, since there is only one path to reach the compromise of the database sever (node 15), it is easy to see that the cumulative metric for node 1 is the multiplication of the two component metrics on the path: 0.2×0.6=0.12. This is intuitive since the longer the attack path, the lower the risk.

This example highlights the need to account for security interactions in the specific network to fully understand the risk a vulnerability brings to a system. Although the vulnerability on the database server has a high CVSS score (8.5 in this case), the cumulative risk contributed by the vulnerability to the specific system may be marginal, since it is located at a place hard to get to by an attacker.

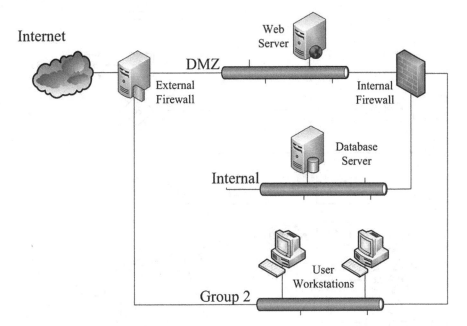

Fig. 7 Network for Example 3

5.3 Example 3

Example 3 adds another subnet to the network, called "Group 2", as shown in Fig. 7. This subnet contains the user desktop machines used by the company's employees. These machines run the Windows operating system and Internet Explorer (IE) browser. Vulnerability CVE-2009-1918 was identified in IE that would enable execution of arbitrary code on the victim's machine. To exploit this vulnerability, an attacker must trick a user into visiting a maliciously crafted web page. The vulnerability is not a highly complex one to exploit, i.e., once a user visits the malicious page, it is highly likely that their machine will be compromised. The other two vulnerabilities discussed above also exist on the web server and database server in this example. The attack graph for this network is shown in Fig. 8.

In even such a small network, how security on one machine can affect another can be manifold and non-obvious. A careful examination of the attack graph reveals a number of potential intrusion paths leading to the compromise of the various hosts. An attacker could first compromise the web server and use it as a stepping stone to further attack the database server (3, 17, 18, 21, 22, 23, 26, 29, 30). Or they could first gain control on a user workstation by tricking a user into clicking a malicious link, and launch attacks against the database server from the workstation (3, 7, 10, 13, 14, 25, 26, 29, 30). There are many other attack paths. In general, if we enumerate all possible attack paths in a system, the number could be exponential.

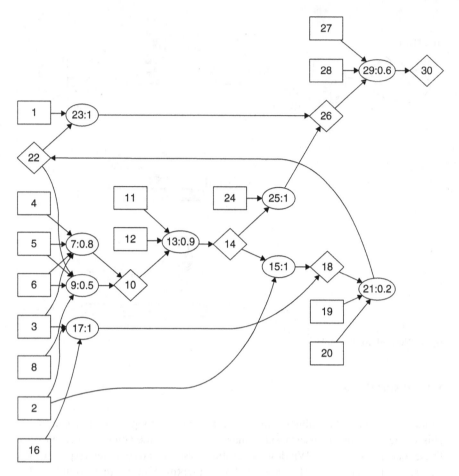

Fig. 8 Attack Graph for Example

However, the privileges and attacks on all these paths are interdependent on each other, and the number of pair-wise inter-dependencies is quadratic to the size of the network. Instead of enumerating all attack paths, a logical attack graph like MulVAL enumerates the interdependencies among the attacks and privileges. This provides an efficient polynomial-time algorithm for computing a compact representation of *all* attack paths in a system.

There are a number of attack nodes in this graph. Nodes 21 and 29 are the exploit against the web server and database server respectively, which have been explained before. An interesting node is 13, which is about the exploit of the IE vulnerability. The component metric 0.9 indicates that this exploit has a high success rate when all the preconditions are met. Of the three preconditions, one of them is that the user (secretary) must access malicious input through the IE program on the host (node

10). This precondition is further calculated by two rules. Node 7 is the instantiation of the following rule:

```
accessMaliciousInput(H, Victim, Software) :-
    inCompetent(Victim),
    isClient(Software),
    hacl(H, MaliciousMachine, httpProtocol, httpPort),
    attackerLocated(MaliciousMachine).
```

The predicate "inCompetent" indicates that somebody is not trustworthy for using computers carefully and may fall victim of social-engineering attacks, e.g., clicking a malicious url. The predicate "isClient" indicates that a piece of software is a client software and as a result, the exploit of the vulnerability will need user assistance. This type of information can be obtained from the NVD data as well. Intuitively, the clause specifies that if someone is not careful, and their machine can access a malicious host controlled by an attacker, they may access malicious input provided by the attacker. The component metric assigned to this likelihood is 0.8 as shown in the graph. Basically, this number will need to be provided by the user of the risk analysis tool. Node 9 captures another scenario for the user to access malicious input: they may browse to a compromised web site. This could happen in this network since the attacker could compromise the corporate web server (node 22), and the firewall allows the user workstation to access the corporate web server (node 2). The component metric for node 9 is 0.5, again input by the users. The component metrics like those for nodes 7 and 9 are different from those associated with vulnerabilities. They are affected by the security awareness of users of the enterprise system and are thus context-specific. To provide these metric values, the risk analysis tool can conduct an initial survey asking multiple-choice questions like "How likely will the user of workstations visit a malicious web site?" Based on the answers provided by the system administrator, a set of component metrics representing the above likelihood can be derived and used in subsequent analyses.

It is less obvious how to calculate in this attack graph the likelihood that an attacker can obtain a privilege (e.g., node 30, code-execution privilege on the database server). The complexity comes from shared dependencies and cycles that exist in this attack graph. A number of methods have been developed to handle such complexities and to calculate attack success likelihood in arbitrary attack graphs [33, 36]. We will use this example to illustrate how to use such calculated metrics to aid in security administration.

5.4 Using Metrics to Prioritize Risk Mitigation

When considering improvements in network security, a network administrator can be constrained by a variety of factors including money and time. For example, some changes, though preferable, may not be feasible because of the time necessary to make the change and the system downtime that would occur while the change was made. Considering the network topology in Example 3, it is not immediately clear

Table 1 Probabilities of compromise for hosts in Fig. 7 (columns reflect different scenarios)

Host	Initial scenario	Patch web server	Patch db server	Patch workstations	Change network access
Database server	0.47	0.43	0	0.12	0.12
Web server	0.2	0	0.2	0.2	0.2
Workstations	0.74	0.74	0.74	0	0.74

which of the vulnerabilities should be patched first, assuming that a fix is available for each of the three.

Table 1 shows the metric calculation results based on the method of Homer et al. [36]. Column 2 shows the risk metrics for Example 3. Columns 3–6 show the new risk assessment values based on various mitigation options: patching different vulnerabilities or changing the firewall rules so that the user workstations cannot access the database server. We try to give intuitive reasons to justify the security risk scores for each of the options.

Patching the vulnerability on the web server would eliminate the known risk of compromise for the web server, but would have little effect on the other two hosts. The web server does not contain sensitive information, so protecting this host may not be the best choice. Even if the web server vulnerability gets patched, there are other attack paths. For example, an attacker can first gain control of a user workstation and then launch attacks against the database server from the workstation.

Patching the vulnerability on the database server would eliminate the known risk of compromise for the database server, but have no effect on the risk in the other two hosts, since privileges on the database server do not enable new attacks on the other hosts. This option would secure the sensitive data on the database server, which may be most desirable, but at the cost of having a period of downtime on the database server which may affect business revenues.

Patching the vulnerability on the user workstations would eliminate the risk on itself, as well as significantly reducing the risk in the database server, though the risk in the web server is unchanged. This option secures the workstations and makes the database server more secure, which may be a better solution.

Network configuration changes can also have drastic effects on the security risk. The final column in the table shows the effect of blocking network access from the workstations to the database server. This option eliminates an attack path to the database server that depends on privileges on the workstations, lowering the risk of compromise for the database server, but leaving the web server and workstations vulnerable. Depending on other resource constraints and asset valuations, this may also be a viable solution. There may not be a single "best" option for all organizations. Indeed, different administrators could easily make different choices in this same situation, based on the perceived importance of the hosts and the expected time necessary to carry out a mediation, as well as human resources available. The quantitative risk metrics make clear the effects emerging from each of these possible changes, providing a network administrator with objective data beneficial for judging the relative value of each option.

6   Challenges

There are many challenges for security risk analysis of enterprise networks using attack graphs.

- Enterprise networks can contain hundreds of hosts, with each host running several applications. We need to determine if the current techniques for attack graph generation can scale well for networks containing hundreds of hosts and several applications.
- Obtaining detailed information about exploits is a manual problem. Some of the information about each exploit is available in NVD and CVSS. However, gathering detailed information about an exploit requires human effort that can be large. New techniques are needed to automatically get the exploit information for doing security analysis of enterprise networks.
- Attack graphs for networks with several hosts can contain cycles. These cycles need to be treated properly in security risk analysis. In [33, 36], some preliminary work on how to detect and handle such cycles has been done. Assuming monotonicity in the acquisition of network privileges, such cycles should be excluded in doing the security risk analysis using attack graphs. Handling cycles correctly is a key challenge in this work.
- CVSS scores do not have a fine granularity. Currently the scores are coarse-grained in terms of High, Medium, and Low. A more precise scoring system will improve the overall results of security risk analysis.
- New techniques are needed to model zero-day vulnerabilities about which we have no prior knowledge or experience. New techniques need to be developed for security risk analysis of networks against potential zero-day attacks. We have some preliminary results on modeling zero day attacks [37].

7   Conclusions

This chapter addresses the system administrator's problem of how to analyze the security risk of enterprise networks and how to select the security hardening measures from a given set of security mechanisms so as to minimize the risk to enterprise systems from network attacks. We have presented a model and a methodology for security risk analysis of enterprise networks using probabilistic attack graphs. This model annotates the attack graph with known vulnerabilities and their likelihoods of exploitation. By propagating the exploit likelihoods through the attack graph, a metric is computed that quantifies the overall security risk of enterprise networks. This methodology can be applied to evaluate and improve the security risk of enterprise systems. The experiments discussed in this report show the effectiveness of our approach and how it can be used by the system administrators to decide among the different risk mitigation options.

References

1. A. Jaquith, *Security Metrics: Replacing Fear, Uncertainty, and Doubt* (Addison Wesley, Upper Saddle River, 2007)
2. S. Noel, J. Jajodia, Understanding complex network attack graphs through clustered adjacency matrices, in *Proceedings of the 21st Annual Computer Security Applications Conference* (2005)
3. S. Noel, S. Jajodia, Managing attack graph complexity through visual hierarchical aggregation, in *Proceedings of the ACM CCS Workshop on Visualization and Data Mining for Computer Security* (2004)
4. S. Jajodia, S. Noel, B. O'Berry, Topological analysis of network attack vulnerability, in *Managing Cyber Threats: Issues, Approaches and Challenges*, ed. by V. Kumar, J. Srivastava, A. Lazarevic (Springer, New York, 2005)
5. K. Ingols, R. Lippmann, K. Piwowarski, Practical attack graph generation for network defense, in *Proceedings of ACSAC Conference* (2006)
6. K. Ingols, M. Chu, R. Lippmann, S. Webster, S. Boyer, Modeling modern network attacks and countermeasures using attack graphs, in *Proceedings of ACSAC Conference* (2009)
7. X. Ou, W.F. Boyer, M.A. McQueen, A scalable approach to attack graph generation, in *Proceedings of 13th ACM CCS Conference* (2006), pp. 336–345
8. X. Ou, S. Govindavajhala, A.W. Apple, MULVAL: a logic based network security analyzer, in *14th USENIX Security Symposium* (2005)
9. Skybox Security, http://www.skyboxsecurity.com/
10. RedSeal Systems, http://www.redseal.net/
11. Nessus Vulnerability Scanner, http://www.nessus.org
12. Retina Security Scanner, http://www.eeye.com/
13. L. Wang, A. Singhal, S. Jajodia, Measuring the overall security of network configurations using attack graphs, in *Proceedings of the 21st IFIP WG 11.3 Working Conference on Data and Applications Security* (Springer-Verlag, 2007)
14. J. Pamula, S. Jajodia, P. Ammann, V. Swarup, A weakest-adversary security metric for network configuration security analysis, in *Proceedings of the 2nd ACM Workshop on Quality of Protection* (ACM Press, 2006)
15. The Systems Security Engineering Capability Maturity Model, http://www.sse-cmm.org/index.html
16. M. Swanson, N. Bartol, J. Sabato, J. Hash, L. Graffo, *Security Metrics Guide for Information Technology Systems*, Special Publication 800-55 (National Institute of Standards and Technology, 2003)
17. G. Stoneburner, C. Hayden, A. Feringa, *Engineering Principles for Information Technology Security*, Special Publication 800-27 (Rev A) (National Institute of Standards and Technology, 2004)
18. Joint Task Force Transformation Initiative, *NIST Special Publication 800-39, Managing Information Security Risk, Organization, Mission and Information System Review* (2011)
19. E. Chew, M. Swanson, K. Stine, N. Bartol, A. Brown, W. Robinson, *NIST Special Publication 800-55 Revision 1, Performance Measurement Guide for Information Security* (2008)

20. G. Stoneburner, A. Goguen, A. Feringa, *NIST Special Publication 800-30, Risk Management Guide for Information Technology Systems* (2001)
21. P. Mell, K. Scarforne, S. Romanosky, *A Complete Guide to the Common Vulnerability Scoring System (CVSS) Version 2.0*, http://www.first.org/cvss/cvss-guide.html
22. R. Ritchey, P. Ammann, Using model checking to analyze network vulnerabilities, in *Proceedings of the IEEE Symposium on Security and Privacy* (2000)
23. O. Sheyner, J. Haines, S. Jha, R. Lippmann, J. Wing, Automated generation and analysis of attack graphs, in *Proceedings of the IEEE Symposium on Security and Privacy* (2002)
24. P. Ammann, D. Wijesekera, S. Kaushik, Scalable, graph-based network vulnerability analysis, in *Proceedings of the ACM Conference on Computer and Communications Security* (2002)
25. R. Lippmann, K. Ingols, C. Scott, K. Piwowarski, K. Kratkiewicz, M. Artz, R. Cunningham, Validating and restoring defense in depth using attack graphs, in *MILCOM Military Communications Conference* (2006)
26. S. Noel, S. Jajodia, Advanced vulnerability analysis and intrusion detection through predictive attack graphs, in *Critical Issues in C4I, Armed Forces Communications and Electronics Association (AFCEA) Solutions Series* (2009)
27. S. Noel, S. Jajodia, Proactive intrusion prevention and response via attack graphs, in *Practical Intrusion Detection*, ed. by R. Trost Addison-Wesley Professional, (2009)
28. F. Cuppens, R. Ortalo, LAMBDA: a language to model a database for detection of attacks, in *Proceedings of the Workshop on Recent Advances in Intrusion Detection* (2000)
29. S. Templeton, K. Levitt, A requires/provides model for computer attacks, in *Proceedings of the New Security Paradigms Workshop* (2000)
30. R. Ritchey, B. O'Berry, S. Noel, Representing TCP/IP connectivity for topological analysis of network security, in *Proceedings of the 18th Annual Computer Security Applications Conference* (2002)
31. R. Lippmann, K. Ingols, *An Annotated Review of Past Papers on Attack Graphs*, Lincoln Laboratory Technical Report ESC-TR-2005-054 (2005)
32. M. Frigault, L. Wang, A. Singhal, S. Jajodia, Measuring network security using dynamic bayesian network, in *2008 ACM Workshop on Quality of Protection*, October 2008
33. L. Wang, T. Islam, T. Long, A. Singhal, S. Jajodia, An attack graph based probabilistic security metrics, in *Proceedings of 22nd IFIP WG 11.3 Working Conference on Data and Application Security (DBSEC 2008)*, London, UK, July 2008
34. A. Singhal, S. Xou, Techniques for enterprise network security metrics, in *Proceedings of 2009 Cyber Security and Information Intelligence Research Workshop*, Oakridge National Labs, Oakridge, April 2009
35. P. Manadhata, J. Wing, M. Flynn, M. McQueen, Measuring the attack surface of two FTP daemons, in *Proceedings of 2nd ACM Workshop on Quality of Protection* (2006)
36. J. Homer, X. Ou, D. Schmidt, *A Sound and Practical Approach to Quantifying Security Risk in Enterprise Networks*," Technical report, Kansas State University, Computing and Information Sciences Department (2009)
37. J. Wang, N. Singhal, K Zero day safety: measuring the security of networks against unknown attacks, in *European Symposium on Research in Computer Security (ESORICS)*, September 2010

k-Zero Day Safety: Evaluating the Resilience of Networks Against Unknown Attacks

Lingyu Wang, Sushil Jajodia, Anoop Singhal, Pengsu Cheng, and Steven Noel

Abstract By enabling a direct comparison of different security solutions with respect to their relative effectiveness, a network security metric may provide quantifiable evidences to assist security practitioners in securing computer networks. However, the security risk of unknown vulnerabilities is usually considered as something unmeasurable due to the less predictable nature of software flaws. This leads to a challenge for security metrics, because a more secure configuration would be of little value if it were equally susceptible to zero day attacks. In this chapter, we describe a novel security metric, *k-zero day safety*, to address this issue. Instead of attempting to rank unknown vulnerabilities, the metric counts how many such vulnerabilities would be required for compromising network assets; a larger count implies more security since the likelihood of having more unknown vulnerabilities available, applicable, and exploitable all at the same time will be significantly lower.

1 Introduction

One of the main difficulties in securing computer networks is the lack of means for directly measuring the relative effectiveness of different security solutions in a given network, since "you cannot improve what you cannot measure". Indirect measurements, such as the false positive and negative rates of an intrusion detection

L. Wang (✉) • P. Cheng
Concordia Institute for Information Systems Engineering, Concordia University, Montreal, QC, Canada H3G 1M8
e-mail: wang@ciise.concordia.ca

S. Jajodia
Center for Secure Information Systems, George Mason University, Fairfax, VA 22030-4444, USA
e-mail: jajodia@gmu.edu

A. Singhal
Computer Security Division, NIST, Gaithersburg, MD 20899, USA
e-mail: anoop.singhal@nist.gov

S. Noel
The MITRE Corporation, McLean, VA, USA
e-mail: snoel@mitre.org

© Springer International Publishing AG 2017
L. Wang et al., *Network Security Metrics*,
https://doi.org/10.1007/978-3-319-66505-4_4

system or firewall, may sometimes be obtained through laboratory testing, but they typically say very little about the actual effectiveness of the solution when it is deployed in a real world network which may be very different from the testing environment. In practice, choosing and deploying a security solution still heavily rely on human experts' experiences following a trial-and-error approach, which renders those tasks an art, instead of a science.

In such a context, a network security metric is desirable because it would enable a direct measurement and comparison of the amounts of security provided by different security solutions. Existing efforts on network security metrics typically assign numeric scores to vulnerabilities based on known facts about vulnerabilities. However, such a methodology is no longer applicable when we consider zero day attacks. In fact, a popular criticism of past efforts on security metrics is that they cannot deal with unknown vulnerabilities, which are generally believed to be unmeasurable [4]. Unfortunately, without considering unknown vulnerabilities, a security metric will only have questionable value at best, since it may determine a network configuration to be more secure while that configuration is in fact equally susceptible to zero day attacks. We thus fall into the agnosticism that security is not quantifiable until we can fix all potential security flaws but by then we certainly do not need security metric at all [4].

In this chapter, we describe a novel network security metric, *k-zero day safety*, to address this issue. Roughly speaking, instead of attempting to measure *which* unknown vulnerabilities are more likely to exist, we start with the worst case assumption that this is not measurable. The metric then simply counts *how many* zero day vulnerabilities are required to compromise a network asset. A larger count will indicate a relatively more secure network, since the likelihood of having more unknown vulnerabilities all available at the same time, applicable to the same network, and exploitable by the same attacker, will be lower. We will formally define the metric model and design heuristic algorithms for computing the metric value. We demonstrate the usefulness of the metric by extending it to sub-metrics and applying it to network hardening through a series of case studies.

The remainder of this chapter is organized as follows. The rest of this section first builds intuitions through a running example. We then present our model and define the metric in Sect. 3, apply the metric to network hardening in Sect. 4, describe a series of case studies in Sect. 5, and finally conclude the chapter in Sect. 6.

2 Motivating Example

In Fig. 1, host 1 and 2 comprise the internal network in which the firewall allows all outbound connection requests but blocks inbound requests to host 2. Assume the main security concern here is whether any attacker on host 0 can obtain the root privilege on host 2. Clearly, if we assume all the services to be free of known vulnerabilities, then a vulnerability scanner or attack graph will both draw the same

Fig. 1 An example network

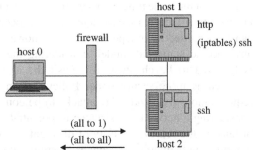

Fig. 2 Sequences of zero day attacks

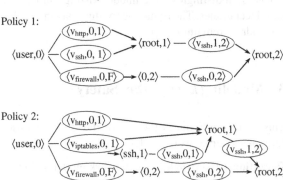

conclusion that this network is secure (attackers on host 0 cannot obtain the root privilege on host 2.

Now consider the following two iptables policies. *Policy 1*: The iptables rules are left in a default configuration that accepts all requests. *Policy 2*: The iptables rules are configured to only allow specific IPs, excluding host 0, to access the ssh service. Clearly, since the network is already secure, policy 1 will be preferable due to its simplicity (no special iptables rules need to be configured by the administrator) and functionality (any external host may connect to the ssh service on host 1).

Next, we compare the two policies with respect to the network's resistance to potential zero-day vulnerabilities. Specifically, Under Policy 1, the upper diagram in Fig. 2 (where each triple indicates an exploit ⟨vulnerability, source host, destination host⟩ and a pair indicates a condition ⟨condition, host⟩) illustrates three possible ways for compromising host 2. The first and third paths require two different zero-day vulnerabilities, whereas the second only requires one zero-day vulnerability (in the secure shell service). Therefore, the network can be compromised with at least one zero-day attack under Policy 1. On the other hand, under Policy 2, only the second case is different, as illustrated in the lower diagram in Fig. 2. However, all three cases now require two different zero-day vulnerabilities. The network can thus be compromised with at least two zero-day attacks under Policy 2.

Considering the fact that each zero-day attack has only a limited lifetime (before the vulnerability is disclosed and fixed), it is reasonable to assume that the likelihood of having a larger number of distinct zero-day vulnerabilities all available at the same time in this particular network will be significantly smaller (the probability will decrease exponentially if the occurrences of different vulnerabilities can be regarded as independent events; however, our metric will not depend on any specific statistical model, considering the process of finding vulnerabilities is believed to be chaotic). To revisit the above example, the network can be regarded as more secure under Policy 2 than under Policy 1 since the former requires more (two) zero-day attacks to be compromised. The key observation is, considering a network's resistance to potential zero-day vulnerabilities may assist in ranking the relative security of different network configurations, which may be otherwise indistinguishable under existing vulnerability analysis or attack graph-based techniques. The remainder of this chapter will build upon this key observation and address remaining issues.

3   Modeling k-Zero Day Safety

This section introduces the k-zero day safety metric model. First, the following formalizes our network model.

Definition 1 (Network)   The network model includes:

– the sets of hosts H, services S, and privileges P.
– the mappings from hosts to sets of services $serv(.) : H \rightarrow 2^S$ and privileges $priv(.) : H \rightarrow 2^P$.
– the relation of connectivity $conn \subseteq H \times H$.

The main design rationale here is to hide internal details of hosts while focusing on the interfaces (services and connectivity) and essential security properties (privileges). A few subtleties are as follows. First, hosts are meant to include not only computers but all networking devices potentially vulnerable to zero-day attacks (e.g., firewalls). Second, a currently disabled connectivity (e.g., $\langle 0, 2 \rangle$ in the above example) still needs to be considered since it may potentially be re-enabled through zero-day attacks (e.g., on firewalls). Third, only *remote services* (those remotely accessible over the network), and *security services* (those used for regulating accesses to remote services) are considered. Modeling local services or applications is not always feasible (e.g., attackers may install their own applications after obtaining initial accesses to a host). Instead, we will model the effect of compromising such applications through privilege escalation. For this purpose, privileges under which services are running, and those that can be potentially obtained through a privilege escalation, will both be considered.

Next, we model zero day exploits. The very notion of *unknown* vulnerability means that we cannot assume any vulnerability-specific property, such as exploitability or impact. Instead, our model is based on generic properties of existing vulnerabilities. Specifically, we define two types of zero-day vulnerabilities. First, a zero-day vulnerability in services are those whose details are unknown except that

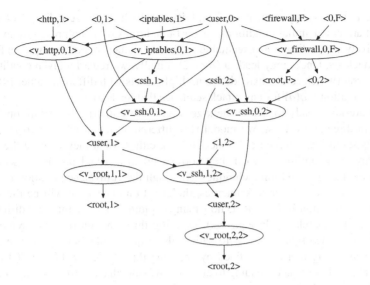

Fig. 3 An example zero day attack graph

their exploitation requires a network connection between the source and destination hosts, a remotely accessible service on the destination host, and existing privilege on the source host. In addition, exploiting such a vulnerability can potentially yield any privilege on the destination host. Those assumptions are formalized as the first type of zero-day exploits in Definition 2. The second type of zero-day exploits in the definition represent privilege escalation following the exploitation of services.

Definition 2 (Zero-Day Exploit) Given a network,

- for each remote service s, we define a zero-day vulnerability v_s such that the zero-day exploit $\langle v_s, h, h' \rangle$ has three pre-conditions, $\langle s, h' \rangle$ (existence of service), $\langle h, h' \rangle$ (connectivity), and $\langle p, h \rangle$ (attacker's existing privilege); it has one post-condition $\langle p_s, h' \rangle$ where p_s is the privilege of service s on h'.
- for each privilege p, we define a zero day vulnerability v_p such that the pre-conditions of the zero-day exploit $\langle v_p, h, h \rangle$ include the privileges of remote services on h, and the post-condition is $\langle p, h \rangle$.

Now that we have defined zero-day exploits, it is straightforward to extend a traditional attack graph with zero-day exploits. Specifically, a *zero-day attack graph* is simply a directed graph composed of both zero-day and known exploits, with edges pointing from pre-conditions to corresponding exploits and from exploits to their post-conditions. For example, Fig. 3 shows the zero day attack graph (in this special case, all exploits are zero day).

In a zero-day attack graph, we use the notion of *initial condition* for conditions that are not post-conditions of any exploit (e.g., initially satisfied conditions, or those as the result of insider attacks or user mistakes). We also need the notion of *attack sequence*, that is, any sequence of exploits in which the pre-conditions of every exploit are either initial conditions, or post-conditions of some preceding exploits (intuitively, this indicates an executable sequence of attacks). For example, in Fig. 3, four attack sequences may lead to $\langle root, 2\rangle$. Finally, we regard a given condition a as the *asset* (which can be extended to multiple assets with different values [9]) and use the notation $seq(a)$ for any attack sequence that leads to a.

We are now ready to define the k-zero day safety metric. In Definition 3, we do so in three steps. First, we model two different cases in which two zero day exploits should be counted only once, that is, either when they involve the same zero day vulnerability or when they correspond to a trivial privilege escalation due to the lack of isolation techniques. Although the equivalence relation in those two cases has very different semantics, the effect on our metric will be the same. The metric function $k0d(.)$ counts how many exploits in their symmetric difference are distinct (not related through $\equiv_v$). Defining this function over the symmetric difference of two sets allows it to satisfy the required algebraic properties. The k-zero day safety metric is defined by applying the metric function $k0d(.)$ to the minimal attack sequences leading to an asset. We note that $k0d(a)$ is always unique even though multiple attack sequences may lead to the same asset. The empty set in the definition can be interpreted as the conjunction of all initial conditions (which are initially satisfied).

Definition 3 (*k-Zero Day Safety*) Given the set of zero-day exploits E_0, we define

- a relation $\equiv_v \subseteq E_0 \times E_0$ such that $e \equiv_v e'$ indicates either e and e' involve the same zero day vulnerability, or $e = \langle v_s, h_1, h_2\rangle$ and $e' = \langle v_p, h_2, h_2\rangle$ are true, and exploiting s yields p. e and e' are said distinct if $e \not\equiv_v e'$.
- a function $k0d(.) : 2^{E_0} \times 2^{E_0} \rightarrow [0, \infty]$ as $k0d(F, F') = max(\{ |F''| : F'' \subseteq (F \triangle F'), (\forall e_1, e_2 \in F'') (e_1 \not\equiv_v e_2)\})$ where $|F''|$ denotes the cardinality, $max(.)$ the maximum value, and $F \triangle F'$ the symmetric difference $(F \setminus F') \cup (F' \setminus F)$.
- for an asset a, we use $k = k0d(a)$ for $min(\{k0d(q \cap E_0, \phi) : q \in seq(a)\})$ where $min(.)$ denotes the minimum value. For any $k' \in [0, k)$, we say a is k'-zero day safe (we may also say a is k-zero day safe when the meaning is clear from the context).

Example 1 For the running example, suppose all exploits of services involve distinct vulnerabilities except $\langle v_{ssh}, 0, 1\rangle$, $\langle v_{ssh}, 1, 2\rangle$, and $\langle v_{ssh}, 0, 2\rangle$. Assume *ssh* and *http* are not protected by isolation but *iptables* is protected. Then, the relation $\equiv_v$ is shown in Table 1 where 1 indicates two exploits are related and 0 the opposite. Clearly, if we assume $A = \{\langle root, 2\rangle\}$ then we have $k0d(A) = 2$, and the network is 0 or 1-zero day safe (we may also say it is 2-zero day safe when the meaning is clear from the context).

Table 1 An example of relation $\equiv_v$

	$\langle v_{iptables}, 0, 1\rangle$	$\langle v_{http}, 0, 1\rangle$	$\langle v_{ssh}, 0, 1\rangle$	$\langle v_{root}, 1, 1\rangle$	$\langle v_{ssh}, 1, 2\rangle$	$\langle v_{firewall}, 0, F\rangle$	$\langle v_{ssh}, 0, 2\rangle$	$\langle v_{root}, 2, 2\rangle$
$\langle v_{iptables}, 0, 1\rangle$	1	0	0	0	0	0	0	0
$\langle v_{http}, 0, 1\rangle$	0	1	0	1	0	0	0	0
$\langle v_{ssh}, 0, 1\rangle$	0	0	1	1	1	0	1	0
$\langle v_{root}, 1, 1\rangle$	0	1	1	1	0	0	0	0
$\langle v_{ssh}, 1, 2\rangle$	0	0	1	0	1	0	1	1
$\langle v_{firewall}, 0, F\rangle$	0	0	0	0	0	1	0	0
$\langle v_{ssh}, 0, 2\rangle$	0	0	1	0	1	0	1	1
$\langle v_{root}, 2, 2\rangle$	0	0	0	0	1	0	1	1

4 Applying k-Zero Day Safety

In this section, we first demonstrate the power of our metric through applying it to network hardening. We then discuss practical issues in instantiating the model from given networks.

4.1 Redefining Network Hardening

Network hardening is to improve the security of existing networks through deploying security solutions or making configuration changes. In most existing work, network hardening is defined as a reachability problem in attack graphs, that is, finding a set of security conditions, disabling which will render goal conditions (assets) not reachable from initial conditions [3, 6, 8]. Since the reachability is a binary property, such a definition is qualitative in nature. Each network hardening solution is either valid or invalid, and all valid solutions will be deemed as equally good in terms of security (although those solutions may be ranked from other aspects, such as their costs [8]).

Based on the proposed k-zero day safety metric, we can now redefine network hardening as *rendering a network k-zero day safe for a larger k*. Clearly, such a concept generalizes the above qualitative approaches. Specifically, under our model, those qualitative approaches essentially achieve $k > 0$, meaning that attacks are no longer possible with known vulnerabilities only. In contrast to those qualitative approaches, our definition can rank network hardening solutions based on the relative degree of security guarantee provided by those solutions. Such a ranking would enable us to model network hardening as various forms of optimization problems, either with k as the objective function and cost as constraints (that is, to maximize security) or vice versa.

Moreover, the metric also provides insights to specific hardening options, since any means for increasing k would now become a potential hardening option. For clarify purposes, we unfold k based on our model in Eqs. (1)–(4). Based on those equations, we can see that k may be increased in many ways, including:

$$k = k0d(A) = \sum_{a \in A}(k0d(a) \cdot v(a))/\sum_{a \in A} v(a) \tag{1}$$

$$k0d(a) = min(\{k0d(q \cap E_0, \phi) : q \in seq(a)\}) \tag{2}$$

$$k0d(q \cap E_0, \phi) = max(\{\ |F| : F \subseteq q \cap E_0, (\forall e_1, e_2 \in F)\ (e_1 \not\equiv_v e_2)\}) \tag{3}$$

$$seq(a) = \{e_1, e_2, \ldots, e_j : a \text{ is implied by } \cup_j post(e_j),$$

$$(\forall i \in [1, j])\ (\forall c \in pre(e_i))\ (c \in C_I) \vee (\exists x \in [1, i-1]\ c \in post(e_x))\} \tag{4}$$

- *Increasing Diversity* Increasing the diversity of services will enable stronger assumptions about distinct zero day exploits (less exploits related by $\equiv_v$) in Eq. (3), and consequently likely (but not necessarily, which is exactly why a metric is needed) increase k.
- *Strengthening Isolation* Strengthening isolation around services will provide a similar effect as the above option.
- *Disabling Services* Disabling or uninstalling unnecessary services will disable corresponding initial conditions and therefore yield longer attack sequences in Eq. (4) and consequently a larger k.
- *Firewalls* Blocking unnecessary connectivity will provide a similar effect as the above option since connectivity is a special type of initial conditions.
- *Stricter Access Control* Enforcing stricter policies may improve user security and lessen the risk of insider attacks or unintentional user mistakes and thus disable existing initial conditions in Eq. (4) and lead to a larger k.
- *Asset Backup* Asset backup will lead to more conjunctive clauses of conditions in the definitions of assets, and consequently longer attack sequences and a larger k.
- *Detection and Prevention* Protecting services and assets with intrusion detection and prevention efforts will lead to negation of conditions in the definition of assets and consequently a similar effect as the above option.
- *Security Services* Introducing more security services to restrict accesses to remote services may also disable initial conditions and consequently lead to longer attack sequences and a larger k.
- *Patching Known Vulnerabilities* Since known vulnerabilities may serve as short-cuts for bypassing zero day exploits, patching them will likely yield longer attack sequences and a larger k.
- *Prioritizing Hardening Options* The hardening options maybe prioritized based on the asset values in Eq. (1) and shortest attack sequences in Eq. (2) such that an option is given higher priority if it can lead to more significant reduction in k.

The above hardening options closely match current practices, such as the so-called *layered defense, defense in depth, security through virtualization,* and *security through diversity* approaches, and so on. This confirms the practical relevance of the proposed metric. Note that none of those hardening options can always guarantee improved security (that is, a hardening option does not always increase the value of k, as will be illustrated in Sect. 5). With the proposed metric, the relative effectiveness of potential network hardening options can now be directly compared in a simple, intuitive manner. Their cost can also be more easily justified, not based upon speculation or good will, but simply with a larger k.

4.2   Instantiating the Model

This section describes input information that need to be collected for instantiating the proposed metric model from a given network and discusses the practicality and scalability.

To instantiate the network model (Sect. 3), we need to collect information about hosts (e.g., computers, routers, switches, firewalls, etc.), connectivity between hosts, and for each host, its remotely accessible services, security mechanisms and services, and privileges. Such information is typically already available to administrators in the form of a network map or configuration database. A network scanning will assist in collecting or verifying information about hosts, connectivity, and services. Nonetheless, a close examination of host configurations (including firewall rules) is still necessary since network maps and network scanning will usually not reveal hidden or disabled services or connectivity (which may be re-enabled through zero day attacks and thus must be correctly modeled), and privileges are often best identified by examining the host configuration. Collecting and maintaining such information for a large network certainly involves substantial time and efforts. However, we note that a key advantage of our model is its exclusion of local applications and services (modeling which would be infeasible for most networks). Focusing on remote services allows our model to stay manageable and scalable, considering the fact that most hosts typically only have a few open ports (but many more local applications).

To instantiate the zero day attack graph model, we need to collect both zero day exploits, and exploits of known vulnerabilities. The former can be directly composed based on the network model since all zero day exploits have hard-coded conditions (Sect. 3). Known vulnerabilities may be discovered through various vulnerability scanners, and their pre- and post-conditions may be obtained from public vulnerability databases. These may also be directly available from existing attack graphs of known vulnerabilities. One subtlety here is that the exploits not reachable from the asset can no longer be omitted since they may now be reachable from the asset with the help of zero day exploits. Traditional attack graphs are practical for realistic applications, with efficient implementations (e.g., the MulVAL project [5]) and commercial tools (e.g., the CAULDRON tool [2]) available. A zero day attack graph would have comparable complexity as traditional attack graphs, because the number of added zero day exploits is comparable to that of known vulnerabilities.

To instantiate the k-zero day safety metric model, we need to collect initial conditions (initially satisfied conditions), an asset condition (or, in a more general form, logic clauses of multiple conditions [9]), and the equivalence relation $\equiv_v$ (Sect. 3). In our model, the notion of initial condition may refer to either a fact (e.g., existence of a service or connectivity) or an assumption (e.g., attackers' existing privilege on a host due to insider attack or user mistakes). In the former case, initial conditions are already part of the network model. In the latter case, determining initial conditions will require examining facts (e.g., access control policies and users' relative experiences) and then estimating potential risk (e.g., attackers are less likely to have initial privilege on a well guarded server than on a desktop shared by many inexperienced users). The asset condition(s) needs to be determined base on the relative value or importance of hosts. Finally, instantiating the equivalence relation between zero day exploits of two remote services requires examining the similarity between such services (and underlying OS and applications), and instantiating the relation between zero day exploits of a remote service and a privilege requires examining the existence and strength of isolation techniques around that service.

We note that the above subtleties in determining initial conditions and equivalence relations arise mainly because those concepts are designed as a means for handling uncertain information (e.g., the human factor). There exists an inherent trade-off between the effort required for collecting and estimating such information, and the accuracy and quality of the resultant model. While the model can still be applied even when drastic approaches are taken toward such information (e.g., simply assuming insider attack or user mistakes to be absent), the instantiated model will not be as accurate as it can be with more refined and accurate input information (which also demands more effort). In an extreme case, an overly conservative assumption may lead to a trivial result (e.g., no network is 1-zero day safe, if every host is considered to have insider attacks). While such an assumption may be the safest and easiest choice, it is also the least helpful in terms of improving the security (since nothing can be done).

5 Case Study

In this section, we illustrate through a series of case studies that our metric can reveal interesting and sometimes surprising results, which are not always obvious even for a small network; for larger and more realistic networks, the systematic approach to security evaluation using the metric and algorithms will thus become even more important.

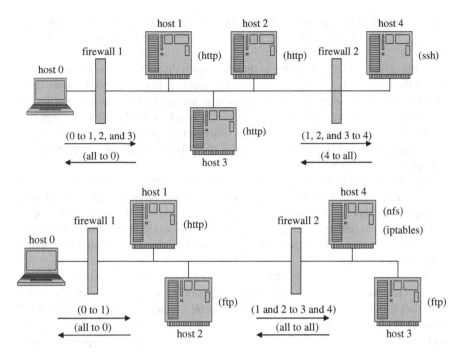

Fig. 4 Case study: security by diversity

5.1 Diversity

It is a common belief that greater diversity in software and services may help to improve networks' security. However, there lacks a precise approach to actually determining when, and how, diversity will help security. In this case study, we show that diversity does not always mean more security through applying the proposed metric.

The upper half of Fig. 4 shows a small network in which services running on each host are marked beside that host and firewall rules are depicted below each firewall. Unless explicitly stated otherwise, we will assume different services or firewalls involve different zero day vulnerabilities. We also assume that none of the services, except *iptables* and *tcpwrapper*, are protected by sufficient isolation. No known vulnerabilities are assumed in the services. Finally, suppose our main security concern is over host 4's root privilege.

Now, suppose the three Web servers (host 1 through 3) are providing the *http* service using the same software such that their corresponding zero day vulnerabilities are related by the $\equiv_v$ relation. This lack of diversity seems to result in poor security since one zero day vulnerability will compromise all three servers. However, by applying the *k*-zero day safety metric, we can see that *k* would remain the same regardless of the degree of diversity in these *http* services, because any shortest attack sequence will only involve one of these three services (e.g., $\langle v_{http}, 0, 1 \rangle, \langle v_{ssh}, 1, 4 \rangle$). Therefore, increasing diversity will not increase k in this case.

In the above case, one may argue that the reason diversity does not help security is that the three Web servers are, intuitively speaking, in parallel to the asset (host 4). However, such informal observations will not lead to a general solution, as illustrated by the lower half of Fig. 4. In this network (with the same assumptions as above), we are concerned with the diversity in the *ftp* services on host 2 and 3, which are clearly not in parallel to the asset (host 4), so the above observation will not apply to this second case.

Assume the *iptables* services on host 4 only accept requests from host 2 and 3. Given that host 2 and 3 are directly accessible from each other, compromising host 2 through a zero day vulnerability will also compromise host 3. It thus seems tempting to prevent this situation by diversifying the *ftp* services on host 2 and 3. However, by applying the k-zero day safety metric, we will find that such a hardening option actually does not help.

Suppose we use ftp_x and ftp_y to indicate two different ways for providing the *ftp* service on host 2 and 3 such that their corresponding zero day vulnerabilities are not related by $\equiv_v$. We can then find that the shortest attack sequences of the original network (before diversifying the *ftp* services) are $\langle v_{http}, 0, 1 \rangle, \langle v_{ftp_x}, 1, 2 \rangle, \langle v_{nfs}, 2, 4 \rangle$ and $\langle v_{http}, 0, 1 \rangle, \langle v_{ftp_y}, 1, 3 \rangle, \langle v_{nfs}, 3, 4 \rangle$; the shortest attack sequences after diversifying the *ftp* services become $\langle v_{http}, 0, 1 \rangle, \langle v_{ftp_x}, 1, 2 \rangle, \langle v_{nfs}, 2, 4 \rangle$ and $\langle v_{http}, 0, 1 \rangle, \langle v_{ftp_y}, 1, 3 \rangle, \langle v_{nfs}, 3, 4 \rangle$. That is, diversifying the *ftp* services does not help increasing k.

This case study indicates that increasing diversity in hosts and services does not always help improving a network's security. More importantly, the way diversity affects security is not always straightforward even for a small network as depicted above, and intuitive observations or estimations may easily lead to incorrect and misleading results, which will certainly be exasperated in larger and more complex networks. On the other hand, the proposed k-zero day safety model and algorithms will automate such a daunting task and provide a meaningful evaluation about how diversity affects security in any reasonably large networks.

5.2 Known Vulnerability and Unnecessary Service

In this case study, we show how the existence of known vulnerabilities and unnecessary services, which may seem innocent enough at first glance, may actually affect the k-zero day safety of a network. The case study will also demonstrate that patching known vulnerabilities does not always improve the network's resistance to zero day attacks; a formal approach thus becomes necessary to evaluate the effectiveness of, and to prioritize, such patching tasks.

In the upper half of Fig. 5, assume no known vulnerabilities and we are mainly concerned by the root privilege on host 5. Assume host 4 is an administration client,

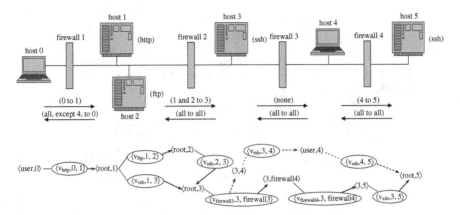

Fig. 5 Case study: removing unnecessary services and known vulnerabilities

and consider the effect of leaving an unnecessary *rsh* service running on host 4 and additionally the effect of introducing a known vulnerability v_{rsh} into that service. To existing techniques, such as an attack graph-based analysis, these may seem irrelevant to the security of host 5 since host 5 cannot be reached from host 0 anyway (due to firewall 3). However, by applying our metric, we will reach different conclusions.

The lower half of Fig. 5 shows two attack sequences leading to the root privilege on host 5 (note that we have omitted other, longer attack sequences for simplicity). The edges in dashed lines correspond to attacks that become possible after introducing the *rsh* service and the corresponding known vulnerability mentioned above.

First, without the *rsh* service on host 4, as indicated by the lower attack sequence, the attacker would need to first exploit a zero day vulnerability v_{http} on host 1, v_{ssh} on host 3, and subsequently he/she will have to get around firewall 3 and 4 through $v_{firewall3}$ and $v_{firewall4}$ (assumed to be different), before he/she can attack host 5 from host 3 through exploiting v_{ssh} again. Therefore, totally four different zero day vulnerabilities will be needed in this case.

Now if service *rsh* is left running on host 4, but without any known vulnerability, then the upper attack sequence (part of which is in dashed lines) will become possible, with a new zero day vulnerability v_{rsh}. Although this does not actually change *k* in this case (with v_{rsh} replacing $v_{firewall4}$), it is easy to see that by further assuming v_{rsh} to be a known vulnerability, *k* will be reduced by 1.

Next, consider introducing a known vulnerability in the *ftp* service on host 2. From the attack sequences shown in the lower half of Fig. 5, it is clear that such a known vulnerability does not give attackers any advantage in terms of reducing *k*, and therefore patching this vulnerability will not help to make the network more secure.

This case study illustrates that not every unnecessary service or known vulnerability will have the same effect on security. In practice, since removing a service or patching known vulnerabilities will usually incur a cost (e.g., administrative

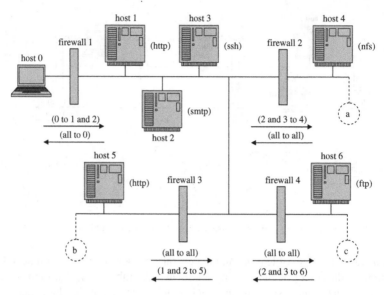

Fig. 6 Case study: asset backup

effort and cost for software patch or hardware upgrade), these activities should be prioritized based on their actual effect on security of the network.

5.3   Backup of Asset

In this case study, we will show that by placing an asset backup at different locations inside a network, the amount of security with respect to that asset may actually either increase, decrease, or remain the same.

In Fig. 6, assume we are most concerned by the root privilege on host 4. We also assume that a known vulnerability exists in the *http* service on both host 1 and 5, exploiting which provides root privilege on the host. Finally, assume we have chosen three candidate positions for placing a backup server for host 4, as indicated by the three dashed line circles.

First of all, without introducing any asset backup, we may find the three shortest attack sequences to be: $[\langle v_{http}, 0, 1\rangle, \langle v_{ssh}, 1, 3\rangle, \langle v_{nfs}, 3, 4\rangle]$, $[\langle v_{http}, 0, 1\rangle, \langle v_{smtp}, 1, 2\rangle, \langle v_{nfs}, 2, 4\rangle]$, and $[\langle v_{smtp}, 0, 2\rangle, \langle v_{nfs}, 2, 4\rangle]$. Note that v_{http} is a known vulnerability, and therefore, two different zero day vulnerabilities are needed to compromise host 4.

Next, consider setting up a backup server for host 4:

- First, consider placing the backup server, host 7, at location *a*. We can see that *k* will not change, because the same zero day vulnerability of the *nfs* service can compromise both host 4 and 7.
- Second, consider placing host 7 at location *b*, and changing firewall rules such that host 4 is directly accessible from host 7 for backup purposes. We can now find that the shortest attack sequence becomes $[\langle v_{http}, 0, 1\rangle, \langle v_{http}, 1, 5\rangle, \langle v_{nfs}, 5, 7\rangle, \langle v_{nfs}, 7, 4\rangle]$. Now, only one zero day vulnerability (recall v_{http} is a known vulnerability) is required, and *k* actually decreases by 1.
- Third, if we place host 7 at location *c*, we can see that the shortest attack sequence to gain root privileges on both host 4 and 7 now becomes longer: $[\langle v_{smtp}, attacker, 2\rangle, \langle v_{ftp}, 2, 6\rangle, \langle v_{nfs}, 6, 7\rangle, \langle v_{nfs}, 7, 4\rangle]$, which requires three different zero day vulnerabilities.

5.4 Firewall

In this case study, we apply the metric to evaluate the effectiveness of firewalls.

In Fig. 7, a personal firewall on host 3 allows inbound connection requests from host 1 and outbound requests to host 4 only. The firewall on host 4 allows inbound requests from host 3 and outbound requests to host 5. The firewall on host 6 allows inbound requests from 5 or 7. Moreover, we assume the personal firewall service on host C has a known vulnerability that may allow attackers to establish connections to the *ftp* service running on host 3. We are most concerned with the root privilege on host 6.

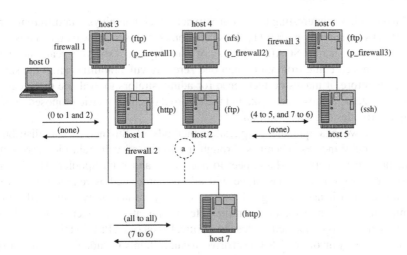

Fig. 7 Case study: firewall

We can show that the shortest attack sequences are $[\langle v_{ftp}, 0, 2\rangle, \langle v_{pfirewall1}, 2, 3\rangle,$ $\langle v_{ftp}, 2, 3\rangle, \langle v_{nfs}, 3, 4\rangle, \langle v_{ssh}, 4, 5\rangle, \langle v_{ftp}, 5, 6\rangle]$ and $[\langle v_{ftp}, 0, 2\rangle, \langle v_{firewall2}, 2, firewall2\rangle,$ $\langle v_{http}, 2, 7\rangle, \langle v_{ftp}, 7, 6\rangle]$. Since $v_{pfirewall1}$ is known, both sequences require two different zero day vulnerabilities.

Suppose now, as a temporary workaround, the administrator decides to move host 3 to location a behind firewall 2, and remove its personal firewall *pfirewall1* but keep the same network access control by adding extra rules to firewall 2 to only allow connection requests from 1 to 3 and from 3 to 4.

On first glance, the above solution may seem a reasonable approach. However, by applying the metric, we can show that doing this will actually render the network less secure. Specifically, after moving host 3 to new location a, it can be shown that the shortest attack sequence becomes $[\langle v_{http}, 0, 1\rangle, \langle v_{ftp}, 1, 3\rangle, \langle v_{http}, 3, 7\rangle, \langle v_{ftp}, 7, 6\rangle]$, which requires only 2 different zero day vulnerabilities, and k decreases by 1 (this is mainly due to the new connectivity from 3 to 7).

5.5   Stuxnet and SCADA Security

The discovery of the high profile worm Stuxnet has drawn much attention to the security of supervisory control and data acquisition (SCADA) systems. This section presents a case study of Stuxnet and SCADA security in order to demonstrate

- why a network needs to be evaluated against the threat of (multiple) zero day attacks.
- how a threat such as Stuxnet may potentially be mitigated by applying our metric.
- how industry best practices on SCADA security are captured, and may be evaluated, by our metric.

First of all, one interesting fact about Stuxnet is that it employs four different zero day attacks for spreading itself [1]. This fact alone suffices to show that, in a mission critical system such as SCADA, the risk of zero day attacks is very real, and such risk may indeed come from more than one zero day vulnerabilities all at the same time. Therefore, it makes perfect sense for administrators to evaluate the security of such systems against such risk, and the k-zero day safety metric proposed in this chapter provides one such solution.

Second, we examine the propagation methods of Stuxnet. It can distribute itself among Windows machines through a number of vulnerabilities involving USB flash drive, network share, peer-to-peer RPC, and Print Spooler [1]. Among those we can see that the last three will all be represented as remote services in our model, and hence is assigned with a zero day vulnerability. This will allow administrators to immediately identify potential threats if a machine with those services running is connected or close to a critical asset (e.g., PLC in this case). As to the vulnerability involving USB flash drive, it can certainly be modeled as a potential user mistake through an initial condition representing attackers' privilege, although

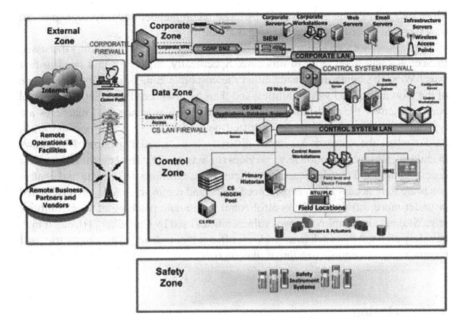

Fig. 8 Case study: SCADA security [7]

such modeling is only helpful if appropriate policies about physical security are in place (e.g., policies preventing USB drives to be used on critical machines). In summary, applying our metric may help administrators to identify and hence mitigate such potential threats of zero day attacks.

Next, we study the recommended practice on improving SCADA security by Homeland Security [7], as illustrated in Fig. 8, which entails:

– The enterprise network is divided into different architectural zones, as illustrated by four different colored background, with the most critical zone (the control zone) being furthermost from external infrastructures.
– Firewalls are placed between different zones and besides the DMZs to regulate traffic flows.
– Multiple DMZs are created for separate functionalities and access privileges.
– IDS sensors, as illustrated by the blue dots, are placed at strategic locations in the network.

Clearly, those security strategies closely match the network hardening options described in Sect. 4.1. Specifically, dividing the network into different zones, placing more critical zones further away from the network perimeter, and regulating network traffic using firewalls and DMZs all have the effect of increasing the length of shortest attack sequences, and thus may lead to better security. Introducing IDSs has the potential effect of forcing attackers to avoid certain hosts to evade detection, captured by negation in the asset formula (details can be found in [9]).

More importantly, the effectiveness of those recommended security strategies can now be more precisely evaluated using our metric.

In addition, we can easily see that all the network hardening options discussed in Sect. 4.1 will also apply in this case. Specifically, Stuxnet would need to first infect Windows computers inside either the corporate zone or data zone using one of the aforementioned vulnerabilities, and then it must spread itself into the control zone, and cover the final hop through removable drives (since field machines are typically never connected to an untrusted network) [1]. This will become much harder when the network has more diversity (e.g., smaller groups of Windows machines), stronger isolation (e.g., services running inside virtual machines), stricter access control and physical security policies (e.g., machines in the data and control zones are only accessible to experienced users, and removable media are prohibited or under more scrutiny in the control zone), up-to-date patching of vulnerabilities (e.g., Stuxnet also employs known vulnerabilities used by Conficker [1]), etc. It may be safely claimed that such a network, if sufficiently hardened using our metric, will be much less susceptible to a threat like Stuxnet.

6 Conclusion

In this chapter, we have described the k-zero day safety as a novel network security metric, discussed its application and demonstrated its power in practical scenarios. Several aspects of the proposed metric may need further improvements as detailed below. First, we have regarded all zero day vulnerabilities as equally likely due to their commonly perceived unmeasurability. However, in some cases certain assumptions can be safely made about the relative likelihood of different zero day vulnerabilities (e.g., some OSs are generally considered more secure than others). Assigning different weights or probabilities to different (types of) zero day vulnerabilities would be a natural extension to our model. Second, as discussed above, instantiating the metric model may involve uncertain input information (e.g., the possibility of insider attacks). An important future direction would be to develop a probabilistic approach to model such uncertain information. Third, the scope of our metric is limited by the three basic assumptions about zero day vulnerabilities (the existence of network connectivity, vulnerable services on destination host, and initial privilege on source host). The model will be more suitable for application to the evaluation of penetration attacks launched by human attackers or network propagation of worms or bots in mission critical networks. An important future work is to broaden the scope by accommodating other types of attacks (e.g., a time bomb which requires no network connection).

Acknowledgements Authors with Concordia University were partially supported by the Natural Sciences and Engineering Research Council of Canada under Discovery Grant N01035. Sushil Jajodia was partially supported by the by Army Research Office grants W911NF-13-1-0421 and

W911NF-15-1-0576, by the Office of Naval Research grant N00014-15-1-2007, National Institutes of Standard and Technology grant 60NANB16D287, and by the National Science Foundation grant IIP-1266147.

References

1. N. Falliere, L.O. Murchu, E. Chien, W32.stuxnet dossier. Symantec Security Response (2011)
2. S. Jajodia, S. Noel, B. O'Berry, Topological analysis of network attack vulnerability, in *Managing Cyber Threats: Issues, Approaches and Challenges*, ed. by V. Kumar, J. Srivastava, A. Lazarevic (Kluwer Academic Publisher, Dordrecht, 2003)
3. S. Jha, O. Sheyner, J.M. Wing, Two formal analysis of attack graph, in *Proceedings of the 15th Computer Security Foundation Workshop (CSFW'02)* (2002)
4. J. McHugh, Quality of protection: measuring the unmeasurable? in *Proceedings of the 2nd ACM QoP* (2006), pp. 1–2
5. X. Ou, W.F. Boyer, M.A. McQueen, A scalable approach to attack graph generation, in *Proceedings of the 13th ACM conference on Computer and communications security*, CCS'06 (ACM, New York, 2006), pp. 336–345
6. O. Sheyner, J. Haines, S. Jha, R. Lippmann, J.M. Wing, Automated generation and analysis of attack graphs, in *Proceedings of the IEEE S&P'02* (2002)
7. U.S. Department of Homeland Security, Recommended practice: improving industrial control systems cybersecurity with defense-in-depth strategies. https://www.us-cert.gov/control_systems/practices/Recommended_Practices.html (2009)
8. L. Wang, S. Noel, S. Jajodia, Minimum-cost network hardening using attack graphs. Comput. Commun. **29**(18), 3812–3824 (2006)
9. L. Wang, S. Jajodia, A. Singhal, S. Noel, k-zero day safety: measuring the security risk of networks against unknown attacks, in *Proceedings of the 15th ESORICS* (2010), pp. 573–587

Using Bayesian Networks to Fuse Intrusion Evidences and Detect Zero-Day Attack Paths

Xiaoyan Sun, Jun Dai, Peng Liu, Anoop Singhal, and John Yen

Abstract This chapter studies the zero-day attack path identification problem. Detecting zero-day attacks is a fundamental challenge faced by enterprise network security defense. A multi-step attack involving one or more zero-day exploits forms a zero-day attack path. This chapter describes a prototype system called ZePro, which takes a probabilistic approach for zero-day attack path identification. ZePro first constructs a network-wide system object instance graph by parsing system calls collected from all hosts in the network, and then builds a Bayesian network on top of the instance graph. The instance-graph-based Bayesian network is able to incorporate the collected intrusion evidence and infer the probabilities of object instances being infected. By connecting the instances with high probabilities, ZePro is able to generate the zero-day attack paths. This chapter evaluated the effectiveness of ZePro for zero-day attack path identification.

1 Motivation

In enterprise network security defense, detecting zero-day exploits is extremely difficult. By leveraging unknown vulnerabilities, zero-day attacks can evade traditional intrusion detection systems (IDSs) at ease. Signature-based IDSs rely on known features of detected attacks for effective intrusion detection. However, for zero-day attacks, such known features are usually not available. Anomaly IDSs [1–3] have the potential of detecting zero-day attacks in that anomaly detection distinguishes the abnormal behaviors from normal behaviors and does not require signatures. However, high false positive is the major weakness of anomaly detection

X. Sun • J. Dai
California State University, Sacramento, CA 95819, USA

P. Liu (✉) • J. Yen
The Pennsylvania State University, University Park, PA 16802, USA
e-mail: pliu@ist.psu.edu

A. Singhal
Computer Security Division, NIST, Gaithersburg, MD 20899, USA

© Springer International Publishing AG 2017
L. Wang et al., *Network Security Metrics*,
https://doi.org/10.1007/978-3-319-66505-4_5

that has to be addressed. In addition, the information asymmetry between attackers and defenders makes zero-day attacks even harder to detect.

Zero-Day Attack Path Considering that current enterprise networks are usually under the protection of security deployments such as IDSs and firewalls, it's very difficult for attackers to directly break into their final target. Instead, they may use some stepping stones. For example, they may first hack into a web server, then use the acquired privilege to further compromise a database server, and finally break into a workstation. These attack actions form a multi-step attack path. If one or more zero-day exploits are included in this path, the path is called a *zero-day attack path*.

Our strategy to attack the zero-day exploit problem is based on a key observation that in many cases identifying zero-day attack paths is substantially more feasible than identifying individual zero-day exploits. A zero-day attack path usually contains one or more zero-day exploits. When not every exploit in a zero-day attack path is zero-day, parts of the path can already be detected by commodity signature-based IDS. These parts are the non-zero-day segments in the zero-day attack path. That is, the defender can leverage one weakness of attackers: in many cases, they are unable to let an attack path be completely composed of zero-day exploits. Therefore, detecting and connecting the non-zero-day segments in a path can help reveal the zero-day segments in the same path.

Possible Solutions Attack graphs [4–7] and alert correlation [8, 9] are possible approaches of attack path generation. However, they both have limitations for revealing zero-day attack paths. By combining the vulnerabilities in an enterprise network, an attack graph is able to show potential multi-step attacks in a path. Nevertheless, attack graphs can only capture known vulnerabilities. As a result, when a multi-step attack path contains exploits exploiting unknown vulnerabilities, the attack path is usually not shown in the attack graph. What the analyst can see from the attack graph is only seemingly unrelated segments. Such segments are usually not sufficient to reveal the true intent of the attacker. Even worse, some non-zero day segments in latter attack steps may not even show up in the attack path due to the lack of satisfying preconditions that should be generated by former attack steps, such as required privileges. Alert correlation shares similar problems as attack graphs. It can identify the non-zero-day segments, but cannot combine these segments into a meaningful path that help reveal the zero-day exploits.

Our previous research designed and implemented a system called Patrol [10] to address these fundamental limitations. With Patrol, not-shown-in-attack-graph attack paths could be identified even if they are exploiting unknown vulnerabilities (i.e., zero-day exploits). This new system is essentially an innovative combination of two components: concatenated cross-machine *System Object Dependency Graphs (SODGs)* and *vulnerability shadows*. System objects refer to processes, files and sockets. We use concatenated SODGs because of the following observation: although attack paths exploiting unknown vulnerabilities can make themselves invisible in attach graphs, they usually cannot make themselves invisible in concatenated SODGs. As the bridge between user programs and kernel operating system, system calls are hard to avoid. Most attack goals are achieved by malware through system calls. When the infection propagates from one process (application or service) to another, the propagation causality is typically reflected in some data dependencies between system objects. These data dependencies are typically caused by certain system calls. When the infection propagates from one machine to another, socket system calls can capture such propagation causality. The concatenated cross-machine SODG would result in a single dependency graph for the whole enterprise network. When security sensors such as IDSs raise alerts, the involved system objects will be mapped to the SODG as trigger nodes. Patrol then performs backward and forward tracking from the trigger nodes to identify the suspicious intrusion propagation paths. To distinguish real zero-day attack paths from suspicious ones, Patrol checks suspicious paths against *shadow indicators*. Shadow indicators specify the common (anomaly) properties shared by a set of known vulnerabilities at the system call abstraction layer. The common properties can be used to identify future unknown exploitations if similar properties appear again. The set of known vulnerabilities that share a shadow indicator is called a *vulnerability shadow*.

Patrol is an effective approach of detecting zero-day attack paths. Nevertheless, this approach has a main limitation, namely the explosion in the number and size of zero-day attack path candidates. The forward and backward tracking from intrusion detection points can result in a large number of candidate paths, especially when lots of trigger nodes are available. In addition, a candidate path can be too big because it preserves every tracking-reachable object. Discerning real zero-day attack paths from suspicious ones relies on shadow indicators, which are not easy to acquire. Investigating and generating shadow indicators at system call abstraction layer for varieties of vulnerability shadows demands huge amount of efforts. As a consequence, in many cases this approach may generate a big "haystack" for the defender to find a "needle" in it.

Our Approach This book chapter summarizes a new probabilistic approach proposed in [11] for zero-day attack path identification. The approach is implemented in a system called ZePro [11]. By parsing system calls collected from hosts in the network, ZePro also generates a network-wide graph. However, this graph is not the SODG, but the *object instance graph*. Each instance represents an object at a specific timestamp. Based on the instance graph, ZePro builds a Bayesian network (BN) to leverage the intrusion evidence collected in the network. The intrusion evidence usually includes alerts generated by security sensors such as IDSs, Tripwire, and information from vulnerability scanners, system logs, etc. Human admins can also provide intrusion evidence if abnormal system or network behavior is noticed. With the intrusion evidence, instance-graph-based BN is able to infer the probabilities of instances being infected. By connecting those instances with high infection probabilities through dependency relations, ZePro is able to generate a path, which is regarded as the zero-day attack path. Compared with Patrol, ZePro only relies on the collected intrusion evidence and does not have any requirement on the availability of shadow indicators. The identified paths are of manageable size in that the BN can significantly narrow down the set of suspicious objects.

Our new insights are as follows. First, due to path explosion, deterministic dependency analysis is not adequate and will fall short. Innovative ways are required to help separate the dependency paths introduced by legitimate activities and dependency paths introduced by zero-day attacks. Second, through BNs, a key difference between the two types of dependency paths becomes visible. In a BN, a dependency path becomes a causality path associated with the probabilities of system objects being infected. Typically, the infection probabilities for system objects involved in a zero-day dependency path are substantially higher than the infection probabilities of objects involved in legitimate paths. Therefore, our approach does not require any pre-knowledge to distinguish the real zero-day attack paths from the legitimate ones.

The work of ZePro has the following advantages. First, the approach is systematic. The instance-graph-based BN is able to perform evidence fusion towards all types of knowledge available to network defenders, such as security alerts, system logs, and even human inputs. Second, the approach does not rely on the availability of common properties shared by vulnerabilities at OS-level to distinguish real zero-day attack paths from suspicious ones. Third, the approach is elastic. New knowledge can be incorporated to BN as it becomes available. The knowledge may change previous probability inference results. In addition, as more evidence is incorporated, the erroneous knowledge can be ruled out. Fourth, the tool of ZePro is automated. It saves human analysts' time and efforts by reducing the amount of manual work.

In a word, the contribution of ZePro is as follows. (1) To the best of our knowledge, ZePro is the first work that takes a probabilistic approach to identify the zero-day attack paths. (2) We made the first effort to build Bayesian network at system object level. (3) We designed and developed the system ZePro and evaluated its effectiveness for zero-day attack path identification.

Organization of This Chapter This chapter is an adaption of the work published in [11]. The following of this chapter will be structured as follows: Section 2 describes the rationales of using Bayesian networks for zero-day attack path identification, explains the problems of constructing Bayesian networks directly on top of the SODGs, and then introduces a new type of system level dependency graph, the object instance graph, to solve the problems existing in SODGs. Section 3 presents the infection propagation models used the instance-graph-based Bayesian networks, and discusses approaches for incorporating intrusion evidence. Sections 4 and 5 introduce the system design and implementation of ZePro. Section 6 evaluates the effectiveness of ZePro for zero-day attack path identification. Section 7 concludes the entire chapter.

2   Rationales and Models

The OS-level entities in UNIX-like systems can be categorized into three types of system objects, including processes, files and sockets. These system objects interact with each other through system calls such as *read, write*, and so on. For example,

Table 1 System call dependency rules

Dependency	System calls
process→file	write, pwrite64, rename, mkdir, fchmod, chmod, fchownat, etc.
file→process	stat64, read, pread64, execve, etc.
process→process	vfork, fork, kill, etc.
process→socket	write, pwrite64, send, sendmsg, etc.
socket→process	read, pread64, recv, recvmsg, etc.
socket→socket	sendmsg, recvmsg, etc.

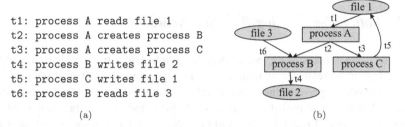

```
t1: process A reads file 1
t2: process A creates process B
t3: process A creates process C
t4: process B writes file 2
t5: process C writes file 1
t6: process B reads file 3
```

(a)   (b)

Fig. 1 An SODG generated by parsing an example set of simplified system call log [11]. The label on each edge shows the time associated with the corresponding system call. (**a**) Simplified system call log in time-order. (**b**) SODG

in a *read* system call, a process may read a file; in a subsequent *write* system call, the process may write to a socket. After an intrusion starts with one or more seed objects, interactions among system objects cause the intrusion to propagate through the system or even the network. Intrusion seeds are usually system objects that are created or by touched by attackers, such as modified files or viruses, compromised processes, or corrupted data, etc. Through object interactions happened in system calls, the innocent system objects can get infected by other malicious or infected objects. This process is called *infection propagation*. The infection propagation among system objects enables intrusions to propagate in the system, or to the network through socket communications.

Previous work [12, 13] has studied constructing operating system level dependency graphs. In Patrol, this type of dependency graph is called System Object Dependency Graphs (SODGs). The SODGs are generated by parsing system calls. Each system call is parsed into a source object, a sink object, and a dependency relation between them according to a set of dependency rules. For example, if a process A reads a file B in a *read* system call, the system call is parsed into A, B, and a dependency relation of $B \rightarrow A$. Each object becomes a node and each dependency relation becomes a directed edge in SODGs. Similar dependency rules for parsing other system calls is shown in Table 1. Figure 1b is an example SODG created by parsing the simplified system calls in Fig. 1a.

Fig. 2 An example Bayesian
network [11]

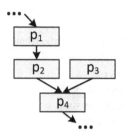

CPT at node p_2

	p_1=T	p_1=F
p_2=T	0.9	0.01
p_2=F	0.1	0.99

2.1 Rationales of Using Bayesian Networks

The Bayesian network is a Directed Acyclic Graph (DAG) that is able to model the cause-and-effect relations. A node in the BN represents a variable of interest, and a directed edge represents the causality relation between the cause nodes and effect nodes. A conditional probability table (CPT) for a node shows the strength of the causality relation. Figure 2 is an example BN. The CPT at node p_2 indicates the strength of the causality relation between p_1 and p_2. According to the CPT, if p_1 is true, the probability of p_2 being true is 0.9. It can be denoted with $P(p_2 = T|p_1 = T) = 0.9$. Similarly, the states of p_2 and p_3 can further determine the probability of p_4 according to the CPT at p_4. When evidence is collected, the BN can incorporate the evidence through updating the posterior probabilities of nodes. For example, if evidence $p_2 = T$ is observed, the probability $P(p_2 = T)$ will be set to 1, and the probability $P(p_1 = T|p_2 = T)$ will be updated correspondingly. In this way, the likelihood for p_1 being true is changed due to incorporating the evidence of $p_2 = T$.

The features and functionality of BN makes it applicable to the operating system level. The major reason is that operating system level also has causality relations: an infected system object can cause an innocent system object to be infected. Since the system level dependency graphs such as SODGs have already captured the OS-level dependency relations, BN can be constructed directly on top of the dependency graphs by interpreting dependency relations into causality relations.

Applying BN towards the system level dependency graphs enables zero-day attack path identification for the following reasons. First, BN is able to incorporate the collected intrusion evidence. The deployed security sensors are able to raise alerts towards suspicious activities. However, these security sensors usually suffer from high false rates. Moreover, the raised alerts are isolated from each other and it's hard to correlate them. With BN, these alerts can be leveraged as the attack evidence to identify the potential zero-day attack paths. In addition, as more alerts are incorporated by BN, the impact of false alerts will be gradually reduced. Second, the BN is able to provide quantitative analysis by computing the probabilities of objects being infected. These probabilities help identify the most suspicious objects along the zero-day attack paths. That is, the suspicious objects reveal themselves gradually as more attack evidence is incorporated. By connecting the objects with high infection probabilities, the zero-day attack path can be identified.

The identified path is of manageable size because the set of suspicious objects have been significantly narrowed down by only considering objects with high infections probabilities.

2.2 Problems of Constructing BN Based on SODG

As the SODG has already captured the OS-level dependencies, it is possible to construct BN on top of the SODG. The dependency relations in an SODG can be interpreted into infection causality relations in the BN. For example, the dependency *process A → file 1* in an SODG represents *file 1* depends on *process A*, which implies the infection causality that "*file 1* is likely to be infected if *process A* is already infected". Therefore, the BNs can possibly be constructed by taking structure of dependencies from SODGs.

Nevertheless, in spite of the SODG's potential, it cannot serve as the base of BN due to the following reasons.

First, the SODG has cycles among nodes. For example, in Fig. 1b, *file 1*, *process A* and *process C* form a cycle. If a BN directly takes the topology of the SODG, the constructed BN will get cycles as well. However, the BN does not allow any cycles because it is an *acyclic* graphical model.

Second, an SODG cannot reflect the correct information flow if the time labels associated with edges are removed. This is problematic when a BN is constructed on top of the SODG. BN is only able to inherit the topology of an SODG and cannot preserve the time labels. The topology itself without time information may lead to incorrect causality inference in the SODG-based BNs. For instance, if the time information is not considered, the topology in Fig. 1b shows that infection causality relations exist among *file 3*, *process B* and *file 2*. That is, if *file 3* is infected, *process B* and *file 2* have the likelihood of getting infected by *file 3*. However, the system log indicates that the system call "*t6: process B reads file 3*" occurs after the system call "*t4: process B writes file 2*". Therefore, *file 3* should not influence the status of *file 2*.

Third, a node in an SODG can end up with having too many parent nodes, which will render the CPT assignment difficult and even impractical in the SODG-based BN. For example, if *process B* in Fig. 1b continuously reads hundreds of files (which is normal in a practical operating system), it will get hundreds of file nodes as its parents. In the corresponding SODG-based BN, if each file node has two possible states that are "*infected*" and "*uninfected*", and the total number of parent file nodes are denoted as n, then the CPT table at *process B* has to assign 2^n numbers in order to specify the infection causality of the parent file nodes to *process B*. This is impractical when n is very large.

Considering above issues, our work proposes a new type of system level dependency graph, called the *object instance graph*, to serve as the base of Bayesian networks.

2.3 Object Instance Graph

Due to system call operations, a system object may change its status as it interacts with other objects. For example, an "innocent" file may become "infected" if it is written by an infected process. Therefore, we use the term "instance" to represent a "version" of an object at a specific time. Different instances of the same object could have different infection status. In an object instance graph, each node is an instance, rather than an object. The object instance graphs capture the dependency relations among instances, and can thus reflect the infection causality relations among them as well.

Definition 1 *Object Instance Graph [11].*
If the system call trace in a time window $T[t_{begin}, t_{end}]$ is denoted as Σ_T and the set of system objects (mainly processes, files or sockets) involved in Σ_T is denoted as O_T, then the object instance graph is a directed graph $G_T(V, E)$, where:

- V is the set of nodes, and initialized to empty set $\varnothing$;
- E is the set of directed edges, and initialized to empty set $\varnothing$;
- If a system call $syscall \in \Sigma_T$ is parsed into two system object instances src_i, $sink_j$, $i, j \geq 1$, and a dependency relation dep_c: $src_i \rightarrow sink_j$, where src_i is the ith instance of system object $src \in O_T$, and $sink_j$ is the jth instance of system object $sink \in O_T$, then $V = V \cup \{src_i, sink_j\}$, $E = E \cup \{dep_c\}$. The timestamps for $syscall$, dep_c, src_i, and $sink_j$ are respectively denoted as $tsyscall$, $tdep_c$, $tsrc_i$, and $tsink_j$. The $tdep_c$ inherits $tsyscall$ from $syscall$. The indexes i and j are determined before adding src_i and $sink_j$ into V by:

  - For $\forall\ src_m, sink_n \in V$, $m, n \geq 1$, if i_{max} and j_{max} are respectively the maximum indexes of instances for object src and $sink$, and;
  - If $\exists\ src_k \in V$, $k \geq 1$, then $i = i_{max}$, and $tsrc_i$ stays the same; Otherwise, $i = 1$, and $tsrc_i$ is updated to $tsyscall$;
  - If $\exists\ sink_z \in V$, $z \geq 1$, then $j = j_{max} + 1$; Otherwise, $j = 1$. In both cases $tsink_j$ is updated to $tsyscall$; If $j \geq 2$, then $E = E \cup \{dep_s: sink_{j-1} \rightarrow sink_j\}$.

- If $a \rightarrow b \in E$ and $b \rightarrow c \in E$, then c transitively depends on a.

Based on the dependency rules, a system call can be parsed into a dependency relation $src \rightarrow sink$ where src represents the source object and $sink$ represents the sink object. According to Definition 1, if no instance of src exists in the instance graph, a new instance will be created for it. If instances of src already exist, no new instances will be created. However, for $sink$ object, a new instance will always be created for it whenever a new $src \rightarrow sink$ appears. The reason is that the dependency relation $src \rightarrow sink$ will not change the status of src, but may change the status of $sink$. A new instance is needed only when the status of an object may be changed by the dependency relations.

With new instances being created, two types of dependency relations may be added: *contact dependency* and *state transition dependency*. First, a dependency dep_c is added between the most recent instances of src and $sink$ (src and $sink$ are

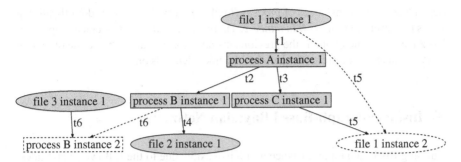

Fig. 3 An instance graph generated by parsing the same set of simplified system call log as in Fig. 1a [11]. The label on each edge shows the time associated with the corresponding system call operation. The *dotted rectangle* and *ellipse* are new instances of already existed objects. The *solid edges* and the *dotted edges* respectively denote the contact dependencies and the state transition dependencies

different system objects). The dep_c is called *contact dependency* because it is caused by contact between two system objects through a system call. Second, a dep_s is also added between the most recent instance and the new instance of the same object. An object's previous status can impact its current status. That is, the status of the most recent instance of an object will impact the status of its new instance. For example, a previously "infected" system object will keep the status of "infected". Therefore, if the most recent instance of an object has the state of "infected", the new instance will likely to have the same state of "infected". The dep_s is named as *state transition dependency* because it reflects the state transition between different instances of the same system object.

The instance graph addresses the issues of SODGs for constructing BNs. This is demonstrated using Fig. 3, which is the instance graph generated for the log in Fig. 1a.

First, instance graphs break cycles in SODGs. For example, in Fig. 1b, a cycle exists among *file 1, process A* and *process C*. In Fig. 3, the system call "t5: process C writes file 1" is parsed into *process C instance 1 → file 1 instance 2*, rather than *process C → file 1* as in Fig. 1b. In this way, the edge from process C will not connect back to *file 1*, but point to a new instance of *file 1*. The cycle is thus broken.

Second, instance graphs can reflect correct information flows because object instances imply the time sequence of causality relations. For example, in Fig. 3, the system call "t6: process B reads file 3" is parsed into *file 3 instance 1 → process B instance 2*, instead of *file 3 → process B* as in Fig. 1b. In this case, *file 3* can only infect *instance 2* of *process B* but not cannot impact any previous instances. As a result, *file 3* cannot not impact the status of *file 2* through *process B* any more.

Third, the mechanism of creating new *sink* instances for a relation *src → sink* prevents the nodes in instance graphs from getting too many parents. For example, *process B instance 2* in Fig. 3 has two parents: *process B instance 1* and *file 3 instance 1*. If *process B* appears again as the *sink* object in later *src → sink* dependencies, new instances of *process B* will be created instead of directly adding *src* as the parent to *process B instance 2*. Therefore, a node in an instance graph only has 2 parents at most: one is the previous instance for the same object; the other one is an instance for a different object that the node depends on.

3 Instance-Graph-Based Bayesian Networks

Building BN based on an instance graph is feasible due to the following rationales. First, a BN is able to capture cause-and-effect relations, and thus can be used to model the infection propagation among instances: the cause is an already infected instance, while the effect is its infection to another innocent instance. We name this cause-and-effect relation as *infection causality*. Second, an instance graph can reflect the infection propagation process by capturing the dependencies among instances of different system objects. Third, a BN can be constructed on top of the instance graph as they couple well with each other: the dependencies among instances of different system objects can be directly interpreted into infection causalities in the BN. The BN's graphical nature makes it fit well with an instance graph.

Constructing an instance-graph-based Bayesian network and inferring the probabilities of interested variables contain two steps: (1) Specifying the CPTs of the nodes through infection propagation models; (2) Incorporating the collected attack evidence for probability inference.

3.1 The Infection Propagation Models

The infection propagation models describe the infection causalities among object instances, including *contact infection causalities* and *state transition infection causalities*. Each instance has two possible states, *"infected"* and *"uninfected"*. The contact infection causalities and state transition infection causalities are corresponding to the contact dependencies and state transition dependencies in instance graphs respectively.

Contact Infection Causality Model This model describes the infection causalities between instances of two different objects involved in a system call operation. Figure 4 is part of a BN constructed given the dependency $src \rightarrow sink$. The CPT for $sink_{j+1}$ indicates the infection propagation models. If $sink_j$ is uninfected, the likelihood of $sink_{j+1}$ being infected is determined by the infection status of src_i, a *contact infection rate* τ and an *intrinsic infection rate* ρ, $0 \leq \tau, \rho \leq 1$.

The contact infection rate τ reflects the likelihood of $sink_{j+1}$ getting infected given src_i is infected. If src_i is infected and $sink_j$ is innocent, the likelihood for $sink_{j+1}$ getting infected is τ. The value of τ impacts the range of infection

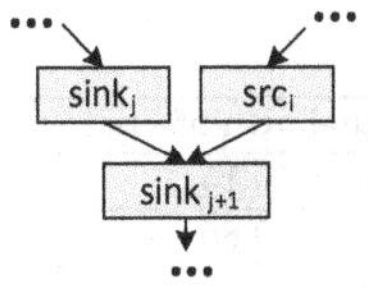

		CPT at node $sink_{j+1}$		
		$sink_j$=Infected		$sink_j$=Uninfected	
		src_i=Infected	src_i=Uninfected	src_i=Infected	src_i=Uninfected
$sink_{j+1}$=Infected		1	1	τ	ρ
$sink_{j+1}$=Uninfected		0	0	$1-\tau$	$1-\rho$

Fig. 4 The infection propagation models [11]

propagation. For example, $\tau = 1$ means all instances that have interacted with infected objects will get infected, while $\tau = 0$ means the infection will not be propagated to other instances at all. The system security experts can tune the value of τ within the range of 0–1.

The intrinsic infection rate ρ reflects the likelihood of $sink_{j+1}$ getting infected given src_i is uninfected. In this case, the infection of $sink_{j+1}$ is not caused by the interaction with src_i. Therefore, the intrinsic infection rate ρ is usually determined by the prior probability of the object being infected. In our experiments, we set all such prior probabilities to be small constant numbers by making assumptions that system objects are most likely innocent when no attack evidence is observed.

Since a large number of system call traces with ground truths are often unavailable, currently it is very unlikely to learn the parameters of τ and ρ using statistical techniques. Hence, now these parameters have to be assigned by security experts. Security experts can assign parameters in batch mode or provide different parameters for specific nodes based on their knowledge. We will evaluate the impact of τ and ρ in Sect. 6. Bayesian network training and parameter learning is beyond the scope of this paper and will be investigated in future work.

State Transition Infection Causality Model This model describes the infection causalities between instances of the same objects. Given the assumption that no intrusion recovery operations are performed, an object cannot get back to the state of *"uninfected"* from the state of *"infected"*. Therefore, an implicit rule exists in the infection causalities between an objects' different instances: if an instance of an object gets infected, all future instances of the object will keep the "infected" state. The rule can be enforced in the CPTs. For example, in Fig. 4, if $sink_j$ is infected, the likelihood of $sink_{j+1}$ being infected remains to be 1, regardless of src_i being infected or not. When $sink_j$ is uninfected, the likelihood of $sink_{j+1}$ being infected will be determined by the states of src_i based on the contact infection causality model.

3.2 Evidence Incorporation

Numerous ways have been developed to capture intrusion symptoms, which can be caused by attacks exploiting both known vulnerabilities and zero-day vulnerabilities. A tool Wireshark [14] can notice a back telnet connection that is instructed

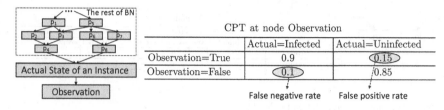

Fig. 5 Local observation model [17]

to open; an IDS such as Snort [15] may recognize a malicious packet; a packet analyzer tcpdump [16] can capture suspicious network traffic, etc. In addition, human security admins can also manually check the system or network logs to discover other abnormal activities that cannot be captured by security sensors. As more correct evidence is fed into BN, the identified zero-day attack paths get closer to real facts.

Evidence can be incorporated in two methods. First, the evidence can be added by setting the infection status of an instance. For example, if the security admins noticed some abnormal behaviors of a system object and verified that the object is infected at a specific time, they can directly set the status of the corresponding instance into "infected". Second, the local observation model (LOM) [17] can be used if the observed evidence contains uncertainty. Both security admins or security sensors may notice suspicious system behaviors or activities, but such observations may not be 100% correct in reflecting the truth. In this case, the LOM is useful for modeling the uncertainty of observations. In the LOM, an observation node is added as the child node to an object instance, as shown in Fig. 5. That is, the actual status of the instance will possibly impact the observation being made. When an observation is provided by security sensors, the values in CPT reflect the false rates of security sensors. For instance, the false positive rate is reflected by $P(Observation = True \mid Actual = Uninfected)$ and the false negative rate is reflected by $P(Observation = False \mid Actual = Infected)$.

4 System Overview

The overall system overview is illustrated in Fig. 6, consisting of the following modules [11].

System Call Auditing and Filtering We perform system call auditing in a network-wide and system-wide way. In addition, we keep OS-aware information like process IDs and file descriptor numbers, so that the OS objects can be later identified accurately. We also perform system call pruning to get rid of redundant and largely possibly innocent objects, including dynamic linked library files and some dummy objects like *stdin/stdout* and */dev/null* [10].

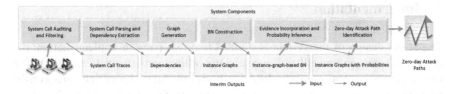

Fig. 6 System design [11]

System Call Parsing and Dependency Extraction We perform system call parsing by collecting and analyzing system call trace data from individual systems. The parsing results in system object dependency relations extracted from system calls. This module is central and off-line, in favor of not hurting the individual original system performance.

Graph Generation We generate object instance graphs by applying the logic in Definition 1 towards the dependencies extracted above. The instance graphs can be either host-wide or network-wide, where the instances of the communicating sockets can be used as glues to concatenate the separate host-wide instance graphs into a network-wide one.

BN Construction The topology of the built instance graph is used to construct BN, where the BN nodes are graph instances and BN edges are graph dependencies. A *.net* file is utilized to carry the node and associated CPT table information, which inherently defines the instance-graph-based BN.

Evidence Incorporation and Probability Inference The integration of evidence information into BN is done in two possible ways: one is to directly initiate the infection state of an object instance, the other is to give an LOM (local observation model) as parent node for the instance. Probability inference will cause the probability propagate to all nodes in the instance graph via BN.

Zero-Day Attack Path Identification The built instance graphs are normally with too many nodes and edges which render a mess to the audience. The merit of our system is to identify the attack paths that are flooded inside the instance graphs, for which the system targets at finding the nodes and edges with high probabilities in BN. These high probability objects indicate the propagation of infection across the networked systems, and could be highlighted with one DFS (depth-first search) algorithm that traverses the structure of the instance graphs to preserve a node either it owns a high probability by itself, or it has high-probability predecessors or successors. We use a probability *threshold* to allow the fine-tuning of the confidence level in identification results.

5 Implementation

The above design of the system is divided into two parts in implementation: the online part (for system call auditing) and the offline parts (for data analysis). The online part is implemented as a loadable kernel module. The offline parts consist of gawk code and Java code for different purposes. Specifically, the gawk code is for the generation of the *.net* file for the instance-graph-based BN, and the *dot*-compatible file for Graphviz-based data visualization [18]. The Java code is to compute probability inference, based on the BN API provided by SamIam [19].

The instance graph is featured by introducing difference instances for the same system object, but this feature also causes it to be too complex for a comprehensible view. Hence, we invent the following ways (other than the optional system call filtering) for graph pruning to gain simplicity and elegance, without hurting the nature of capturing infection propagation [11].

One common reason of the graph complexity is repeated dependencies due to multiple operations between the same pair of system objects, even if the operations are enabled by different system calls. A good example is the multi-occurrence of *write* operation between the same *process-file* pair. Each time the *write* system call is invoked, a new instance of the *file* will be created with a new dependency relation added to the most recent instance of *process*. In this case, the new *file* instance and dependency are actually redundant, if that *process* has not been affected by any other system objects. Based on such objective observations, we ignore all the repeated *src* → *sink* dependency relations if and only if it's detected that *src* not updated after the last time it is involved in the same *src* → *sink* dependency.

The second way to reduce complexity is to trim the *root* instance node that has a positive out-degree while has zero in-degree, where *out-degree* is the number of edges from a node and *in-degree* is the number of edges leading to a node. The *file 3* node in Fig. 3 is a good illustration, as it never appears as a *sink* object in any *src* → *sink* dependency during the time span. We eliminate it from analysis with the belief that it is not affected by any other objects, nor manipulated by attackers. Such node elimination will not hurt the identification of zero-day attack paths, as zero-in-degree nodes are not sources of intrusion propagations unless they are directly tagged as malicious due to any confirmed intrusion alerts. Normally the system configuration or header files can get pruned using this method.

The third scenario where we can further diminish complexity is the occurrence of repeated mutual dependencies between the same pair of objects. In this case, the two objects will respectively get multiple instances as they keep interacting with each other. The typical examples include the communication between a *process* talking with a *socket* or *file* object. For instances, our experiment reveals the fact that the process (*pid:6706, pcmd:sshd*) and the socket (*ip:192.168.101.5, port: 22*) interact with each other, rendering 107 different instances. Actually, such instances are mostly redundant when the operations are contiguously happening, as there's no other object to cause the current infection status change in the middle. Our practice along this way is to preserve only the very beginning and ending dependency relations between the same pair.

6 Evaluation

6.1 Attack Scenario

The same attack scenario from Patrol [10] was implemented in [11] for comparison, to verify the pros of system ZePro. Figure 7 illustrates the three-step attack: (1) vulnerability CVE-2008-0166 [20] is exploited to launch a brute-force key guessing attack towards the SSH Server for root access; (2) a Trojan-horse file is uploaded from the SSH Server to the NFS Server's under the directory of */exports*, which is mis-configured to allow cross-user file sharing under this directory. Hence, this Trojan is downloaded by a Workstation from the inside network; (3) the Trojan file is mounted by the Workstation and its arbitrary malicious code gets executed. The Trojan file could carry exploits to different vulnerabilities on the Workstation. In Experiment 1, the malicious file contains a Trojan-horse that exploits CVE-2009-2692 [21] existing in the Linux kernel of workstation 3. CVE-2009-2692 is a vulnerability that allows local users to gain privileges by triggering a NULL pointer dereference. In Experiment 2, the malicious file contains another Trojan-horse leveraging CVE-2011-4089 [22] on workstation 4. This vulnerability allows attackers to execute arbitrary code by winning a race condition. Our goal is to test whether ZePro can reveal both of the attack paths enabled by different vulnerabilities. Here we only present the experiment results of Experiment 1 for illustration under space constraints.

Our philosophy to evaluate zero-day vulnerabilities or exploits is *emulation*, specifically by treating some known vulnerabilities as zero-day ones. For example, in the above attack scenario, we assume the current time is Dec 31, 2008, then CVE-2009-2692 can be regarded as a zero-day vulnerability, as long as the detection technique excludes the usage of any signature or pattern that was found after Dec 31, 2008. From this sense, the reconfiguration mistake on NFS Server can be regarded as another zero-day vulnerability, since none of the security scanners like Nessus [23] could detect it. Such emulation-based strategy also enables another advantage for our evaluation: all the information for such *"known* zero-day" vulnerabilities will be *available* for our verification regarding correctness and accuracy.

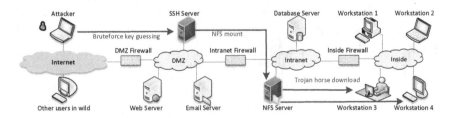

Fig. 7 Attack scenario: three-step attack [10, 11]

We deployed various sensors in our test-bed, including firewalls, Wireshark, Ntop, Nessus, Snort, and Tripwire. These sensors will capture different intrusion evidence to feed the BN for probability inference.

6.2 Experiment Results

The above attack scenario under security monitoring delivered 143,120 system calls generated by three hosts, based on which an instance-graph-based BN was built with 1853 nodes and 2249 edges. Table 2 lists the collected intrusion evidence.

Correctness Figure 8 shows the instance-graph-based zero-day attack path identified by ZePro, in which the rectangles are processes, the ellipses are files and the diamonds are sockets. The intrinsic parameters for our experiment are: 0.0001 as infection rate ρ, 80% as the probability threshold, and 0.9 as the contact infection rates τ. The dark grey color highlights the intrusion evidence fed into the algorithm, and the light grey color highlights the nodes that we verified as truly malicious. All such details testified that Fig. 8 correctly and accurately revealed the actual intrusion process described in our attack scenario.

Table 2 The collected evidence [11]

ID	Host	Evidence
E1	SSH Server	Snort messages "potential SSH brute force attack"
E2	Workstation 3	Tripwire reports "/virus is added"
E3	Workstation 3	Tripwire reports "/etc/passwd is modified"
E4	Workstation 3	Tripwire reports "/etc/shadow is modified"

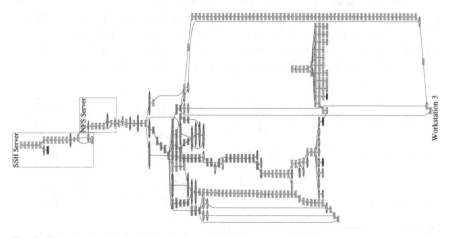

Fig. 8 The zero-day attack path in the form of an instance graph [11]

It's important to note that Fig. 8 successfully captured the *zero-day* intrusion symptoms, which were totally missed by the traditional intrusion detect techniques. For example, no alerts were listed in Table 2, however our system recognized the file *workstation_attack.tar.gz* contributing to the whole cross-machine intrusion propagation by being uploaded from SSH Server to NFS Server under */exports* directory, and then being mounted to */mnt* on workstation 3. Another example is the object *PAGE0: memory(0-4096)* on workstation 3, which was not listed in Table 2 as well, however it is the root cause why the attacker ultimately gained root access through NULL pointer de-reference. Without a zero-day attack path like Fig. 8 that is revealed by our system, the security administrator hardly could be exposed to such indicators of zero-day vulnerabilities and exploits. This makes our methodology unique and outstanding.

An additional merit of our approach is that the instance-graph-based BN can clearly show the state transitions of an object using instances. By matching the instances and dependencies back to the system call traces, it can even find out the exact system call that causes the state-changing of the object. For example, the node *x2086.4.:(6763:6719:tar)* in Fig. 8 represents the fourth instance of process *(pid:6763, pcmd:tar)*. Previous instances of the process are considered as innocent because of their low infection probabilities. The process becomes highly suspicious only after a dependency occurs between node *x2082.2:(/home/user/test-bed/workstation_attack.tar.gz:1384576)* and node *x2086.4*. Matching the dependency back to the system call traces reveals that the state change of the process is caused by "*syscall:read, start:827189, end:827230, pid:6763, ppid:6719, pcmd:tar, ftype:REG, pathname:/home/user/test-bed/workstation_attack.tar.gz, inode:1384576*", a system call indicating that the process reads a suspicious file.

Size of Instance Graph and Zero-day Attack Paths Table 3 illustrates our evaluation on the size of instance graphs, which also reflects the effectiveness of pruning techniques to gain reduction of instance number. According to the table, the number

Table 3 The impact of pruning the instance graphs [11]

	SSH server		NFS server		Workstation 3	
	Before	After	Before	After	Before	After
# of syscalls in raw data trace	82,133		14,944		46,043	
Size of raw data trace (MB)	13.8		2.3		7.9	
# of extracted object dependencies	10,310		11,535		17,516	
# of objects	349		20		544	
# of instances in instance graph	10,447	745	11,544	39	17,849	1069
# of dependencies in instance graph	20,186	968	19,863	37	34,549	1244
# of contact dependencies	9888	372	8329	8	17,033	508
# of state transition dependencies	10,298	596	11,534	29	17,516	736
Average time for graph generation(s)	14	11	6	5	13	11
.net file size (KB)	2000	123	2200	8	3600	180

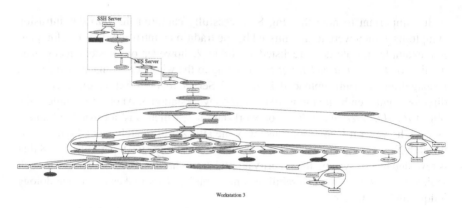

Fig. 9 The object-level zero-day attack path corresponding to Fig. 8 [11]

Table 4 The influence of evidence [11]

	SSH server			NFS server		Workstation 3			
	x4.1	x10.1	x253.3	x1007.1	x1017.1	x2006.2	x2083.1	x2108.1	x2311.32
Evidence	(%)	(%)	(%)	(%)	(%)	(%)	(%)	(%)	(%)
No Evi.	0.56	0.51	0.57	0.51	0.54	0.54	0.51	0.51	1.21
E1	63.76	57.38	79.13	57.38	46.54	41.92	37.75	24.89	26.93
E2	63.76	57.38	79.13	57.38	46.94	42.58	38.34	27.04	30.09
E3	86.82	78.14	80.76	84.50	75.63	81.26	79.56	75.56	81.55
E4	86.84	78.16	80.77	84.53	75.65	81.3	79.59	75.60	81.66

of instances for three hosts in graph is dropped from 39,840 to 1853 (averagely 2.03 instances per object). For better simplicity, elegance and comprehension at object level, ZePro also provides a reader-friendly view to aggregate different instances for the same object, which is inherently the System Object Dependency Graph (SODG) defined in [10]. Figure 9 shows the corresponding the SODG form for Figure 8.

Figure 9 also provides a solid demonstration that ZePro excels Patrol [10] in that ZePro generate more accurate but simpler results than Patrol, where it does not require any pre-knowledge (namely vulnerability indicators in [10]) that is necessary feeding for Patrol. Specifically, for the same attack scenario, ZeProl renders a 175-object SODG, while ZeProl only outputs a 77-object SODG without losing any key objects involved in the intrusion cascading. Comparing the size of 77 objects to the one 175 objects, the reduction is substantive and the result is much more comprehensible. Mostly importantly, considering the pre-knowledge (such as networking or system heuristics) may be usually unavailable, Patrol will easily fail while ZePro will remain effective.

Influence of Evidence Table 4 summarizes our evaluation on how the intrusion evidence as input impact the probability inference. We pick some representative nodes from Fig. 8, and feed the intrusion evidence into BN by the order shown in Table 4. The evaluation results reveal that when more evidence is integrated into

Table 5 The influence of false alerts [11]

Evidence		x4.1 (%)	x10.1 (%)	x253.3 (%)	x1007.1 (%)	x1017.1 (%)	x2006.2 (%)	x2083.1 (%)	x2108.1 (%)	x2311.32 (%)
Only E1	E4=True	98.46	88.62	81.59	98.20	88.30	97.78	97.67	90.23	94.44
	E4=False	56.33	50.70	78.60	48.65	37.60	29.96	24.92	10.89	12.48
All evidence	E4=True	86.84	78.16	80.77	84.53	75.65	81.3	79.59	75.60	81.66
	E4=False	86.74	78.06	80.76	84.41	75.54	81.13	79.42	75.39	81.38

the analysis, the identified zero-day attack path become more accurate reflecting the intrusion ground truth. Specifically, when *E1* is fed into the system, the probabilities (higher than 60%) only propagate to SSH Server. When *E2* appears, the probabilities for other hosts increase obviously, but still do not stand out. When *E3* and *E4* emerge, the representative nodes mostly tend to have much larger probabilities which indicate that they are suspicious. Put together, as more evidence speaks to reveal the attack contexts, the instances with high probabilities are left while those with low probabilities are removed.

Influence of False Alerts Through the evaluation on evidence impacting the detection results, one concern is whether the false alerts will falsify the results. For this, we assume that *E4* is a false positive alarm and Table 5 summarizes its impact to node probabilities. According to the table, if this false alert is the only evidence fed into BN, it will manipulate the results in a negative way; however, as more true evidences arrive, the influence of *E4* diminishes. For example, with all the other evidences available, the probability of node *x2006.2* almost does not change (81.13% vs. 81.3%) when *E4* turns true to false. Hence, the detection results of ZePro tend to be robust.

Influence of Parameters τ and ρ Sensitivity analysis was also performed to evaluate the influence of the parameters: ρ as the intrinsic infection rate, and τ as the contact infection rate. Our experiments show that ρ is not very influential to the results, as it is usually set to a very small number. However, a major drop of τ (e.g. from 0.9 to 0.5) will generate a huge impact to the node probabilities, compared to a minor decrease (from 0.9 to 0.8). It makes sense as τ is the value that defines the likelihood of src_i infecting $sink_j$ given a $src_i \to sink_j$ dependency relation. But, such disturbance caused by τ can be overcome by adjusting the probability threshold accordingly. The rationale is that when τ is small (for example, 50%), a low probability (around 40–60%) is already large enough to indicate a node is suspicious. Overall, by adjusting τ and probability threshold together, the identification of zero-day attack path will still tend to be robust with the parameter changes.

Complexity and Scalability To evaluate the complexity and the corresponding time overheads, we conducted off-line analysis on a host with 2.4 GHz Intel Core 2 Duo processor and 4G RAM [11]. Table 3 shows the results for a 1854-node BN with *recursive conditioning* [26] as the analysis algorithm. Specifically, the total time for BN construction is around 27 s, the average time cost for BN compilation and probability inference is 1.57 s, the average time cost for zero-day attack path identification is 59 s, the average data analysis speed is 280 KB/s, and the average memory used for compiling the BN is 4.32 Mb. The overall penalty on individual systems for runtime system call auditing is around 15–20% slow-down based on the evaluation with UnixBench and kernel compilation as benchmarks.

ZePro can be scalable based on the following two efforts: (1) adjusting the time windows size. For example, system calls can be fetched every 30 or 40 min, and sent for central and offline analysis. Usually, the larger the time window size is, the more time overhead the data analysis takes. The optimal time window size could not be fixed in a determined way, but can be approached through tests given the normal business workloads on enterprise network servers usually yield stable system behavior. For example, we recommend 15 min as the time windows size for our testbed; (2) employ parallel computing. For instance, with 512 processors in a HPC cluster to process data from a 10,000-host enterprise network, the time cost is estimated to be 2.93 min for instance graph generation and 6.3 min for zero-day attack path identification. Interested readers can refer to [24, 25] for the scalability of Bayesian networks.

7 Conclusion

This chapter is an adaption of the work in [11]. To identify the zero-day attack paths, this chapter uses a probabilistic approach and implemented a system called ZePro. Simply put, ZePro first constructs a Bayesian network on top of a network-wide system object instance graph, and then computes the probabilities of instances being infected by leveraging the intrusion evidence collected from security sensors. The experiment results show that ZePro can effectively identify zero-day attack paths.

Acknowledgements This work was supported by ARO W911NF-15-1-0576, ARO W911NF-13-1-0421 (MURI), CNS-1422594, NIETP CAE Cybersecurity Grant, and NIST 60NANB16D241.

References

1. V. Chandola, A. Banerjee, V. Kumar, in *Anomaly Detection: A Survey.* ACM Computing Surveys (CSUR) (2009)
2. C. Kruegel, D. Mutz, F. Valeur, G. Vigna, in *On the Detection of Anomalous System Call Arguments.* ESORICS (2003)
3. S. Bhatkar, A. Chaturvedi, R. Sekar, in *Dataflow Anomaly Detection.* IEEE S&P (2006)
4. S. Jajodia, S. Noel, B. O'Berry, in *Topological Analysis of Network Attack Vulnerability.* Managing Cyber Threats (2005)

5. P. Ammann, D. Wijesekera, S. Kaushik, in *Scalable, Graph-Based Network Vulnerability Analysis*. ACM CCS (2002)
6. X. Ou, W.F. Boyer, M.A. McQueen, in *A Scalable Approach to Attack Graph Generation*. ACM CCS (2006)
7. X. Ou, S. Govindavajhala, A.W. Appel, in *MulVAL: A Logic-Based Network Security Analyzer*. USENIX security (2005)
8. S.T. King, Z.M. Mao, D.G. Lucchetti, P.M. Chen, in *Enriching intrusion alerts through multi-host causality*. NDSS (2005)
9. Y. Zhai, P. Ning, J. Xu, in *Integrating IDS Alert Correlation and OS-Level Dependency Tracking*. IEEE Intelligence and Security Informatics (2006)
10. J. Dai, X. Sun, P. Liu, in *Patrol: Revealing Zero-Day Attack Paths Through Network-Wide System Object Dependencies*. ESORICS (2013)
11. X. Sun, J. Dai, P. Liu, A. Singhal, J. Yen, in *Towards Probabilistic Identification of Zero-day Attack Paths*, IEEE Conference on Communications and Network Security (CNS 2016), Philadelphia, PA USA (2016)
12. S.T. King, P.M. Chen, in *Backtracking Intrusions*. ACM SIGOPS (2003)
13. X. Xiong, X. Jia, P. Liu, in *Shelf: Preserving Business Continuity and Availability in an Intrusion Recovery System*. ACSAC (2009)
14. Wireshark. https://www.wireshark.org/.
15. Snort. https://www.snort.org/.
16. Tcpdump. http://www.tcpdump.org/.
17. P. Xie, J. H. Li, X. Ou, P. Liu, R. Levy, in *Using Bayesian Networks for Cyber Security Analysis*. DSN (2010)
18. GraphViz. http://www.graphviz.org/.
19. SamIam. http://reasoning.cs.ucla.edu/samiam/.
20. https://cve.mitre.org/cgi-bin/cvename.cgi?name=CVE-2008-0166
21. https://cve.mitre.org/cgi-bin/cvename.cgi?name=CVE-2009-2692
22. https://cve.mitre.org/cgi-bin/cvename.cgi?name=CVE-2011-4089
23. Nessus, http://www.tenable.com/products/nessus-vulnerability-scanner
24. O.J. Mengshoel, Understanding the scalability of Bayesian network inference using clique tree growth curves. Artif. Intell. **174**(12), 984–1006 (2010)
25. V. Krishna Namasivayam, V.K. Prasanna, in *Scalable parallel implementation of exact inference in Bayesian networks*. ICPADS (2006)
26. A. Darwiche, Recursive conditioning Artif. Intell. **126**(1), 5–41 (2001)

Evaluating the Network Diversity of Networks Against Zero-Day Attacks

Mengyuan Zhang, Lingyu Wang, Sushil Jajodia, and Anoop Singhal

Abstract Diversity has long been regarded as a security mechanism and it has found new applications in security, e.g., in cloud, Moving Target Defense (MTD), and network routing. However, most existing efforts rely on intuitive and imprecise notions of diversity, and the few existing models of diversity are mostly designed for a single system running diverse software replicas or variants. At a higher abstraction level, as a global property of the entire network, diversity and its effect on security have received limited attention. In this chapter, we present a formal model of network diversity as a security metric. Specifically, we first devise a biodiversity-inspired metric based on the effective number of distinct resources. We then propose two complementary diversity metrics, based on the least and the average attacking efforts, respectively. Finally, we evaluate the proposed metrics through simulation.

1 Introduction

Diversity has long been regarded as a security solution because it may improve the resilience of a software system against both known and unknown vulnerabilities [28]. Security attacks exploiting unknown vulnerabilities may be detected and tolerated as Byzantine faults by comparing either the outputs [10] or behaviors [18] of multiple software replicas or variants [9]. Although the earlier diversity-by-design approaches usually suffer from prohibitive development and deployment cost, recent works show more promising results on employing either opportunistic

M. Zhang • L. Wang (✉)
Concordia Institute for Information Systems Engineering, Concordia University, Montreal, QC, Canada H3G 1M8
e-mail: mengy_zh@ciise.concordia.ca; wang@ciise.concordia.ca

S. Jajodia
Center for Secure Information Systems, George Mason University, Fairfax, VA 22030-4444, USA
e-mail: jajodia@gmu.edu

A. Singhal
Computer Security Division, NIST, Gaithersburg, MD 20899, USA
e-mail: anoop.singhal@nist.gov

© Springer International Publishing AG 2017
L. Wang et al., *Network Security Metrics*,
https://doi.org/10.1007/978-3-319-66505-4_6

diversity [19] or automatically generated diversity [5, 6, 25]. More recently, diversity has found new applications in cloud computing security [36], Moving Target Defense (MTD) [22], resisting sensor worms [40], and network routing [8].

Most of those existing efforts rely on either intuitive notions of diversity or models mostly designed for a single system running diverse software replicas or variants. At a higher abstraction level, as a global property of an entire network, the concept of *network diversity* and its effect on security has received limited attention. In this chapter, we describe a formal model of network diversity as a security metric for the purpose of evaluating the resilience of networks with respect to zero day attacks.

More specifically, we propose a network diversity metric by adapting well known mathematical models of biodiversity in ecology. The metric basically counts the number of distinct resources inside a network, while considering the uneven distribution of resources and varying degree of similarity between resources. Second, we design a network diversity metric based on the least attacking effort required for compromising certain important resources, while taking into account the causal relationships between resources. Third, we devise a probabilistic network diversity metric to reflect the average attacking effort required for compromising critical assets. This metric serves as a complementary measure to the above second metric in depicting the effect of diversity on security.

2   Use Cases

We first describe several use cases in order to motivate our study and illustrate various requirements and challenges in modeling network diversity. Some of those use cases will also be revisited in later sections.

2.1   Use Case 1: Stuxnet and SCADA Security

Stuxnet is one of the first malware that employ multiple (four) different zero day attacks [15]. This clearly indicates, in a mission critical system, such as supervisory control and data acquisition (SCADA) in this case, the risk of zero day attacks and multiple unknown vulnerabilities is very real, and consequently network administrators will need a systematic way for evaluating such a risk. However, this is clearly a challenging task due to the lack of prior knowledge about vulnerabilities or attacking methods.

A closer look at Stuxnet's attack strategies will reveal how network diversity may help here. Stuxnet targets the programmable logic controllers (PLCs) on control systems of gas pipelines or power plants [15], which are mostly programmed using Windows machines not connected to the network. Therefore, Stuxnet adopts a multi-stage approach, by first infecting Windows machines owned by third parties (e.g.,

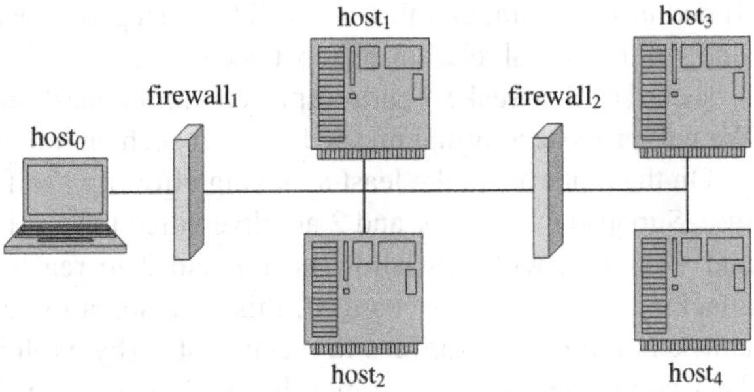

Fig. 1 The running example

contractors), next spreading to internal Windows machines through the LAN, and finally covering the last hop through removable flash drives [15]. Clearly, the degree of software diversity along potential attack paths leading from the network perimeter to the PLCs can be regarded as a critical metric of the network's resilience against a threat like Stuxnet. Our objective in this chapter is to provide a rigorous study of such network diversity metrics.

2.2 Use Case 2: Worm Propagation

To make our discussion more concrete, we will refer to the running example shown in Fig. 1 from now on. In this use case, our main concern is the potential propagation of worms or bots inside the network. A common belief here is that we can simply count the number (percentage) of distinct resources in the network as diversity. Although such a definition is natural and intuitive, it clearly has limitations.

For example, suppose host 1, 2, and 3 are Web servers running IIS, all of which access files stored on host 4. Clearly, the above count-based metric will indicate a lack of diversity and suggest replacing IIS with other software to prevent a worm from infecting all three at once. However, it is easy to see that, even if a worm can only infect one Web server after such a diversification effort (e.g,. it can infect IIS but not Apache), it can still propagate to all four hosts through the network share on host 4 (e.g., it may infect certain executable files stored on host 4 which are subsequently accessed by all Web servers). The reason that this naive approach fails in this case is that it ignores the existence of causal relationships between resources (due to the network share). Therefore, after we discuss the count-based metric in Sect. 3, we will address this limitation with a *goal oriented* approach in Sect. 4.

2.3 Use Case 3: Targeted Attack

Suppose now we are more concerned with a targeted attack on the storage server, host 4. Following above discussions, an intuitive solution is to diversify resources along any *path* leading to the critical asset (host 4), e.g., between hosts 1 (or 2,

3) and host 4. Although this is a valid observation, realizing it requires a rigorous study of the causal relationships between different resources, because host 4 is only as secure as the weakest path (representing the least attacking effort) leading to it. We will propose a formal metric based on such an intuition in Sect. 4.

On the other hand, the least attacking effort by itself only provides a partial picture. Suppose now host 1 and 2 are diversified to run IIS and Apache, respectively, and firewall 2 will only allow host 1 and 2 to reach host 4. Although the least attacking effort has not changed, this diversification effort has actually provided attackers more opportunities to reach host 4 (by exploiting either IIS or Apache). That is, misplaced diversity may in fact hurt security. This will be captured by a probabilistic metric in Sect. 5.

2.4   Use Case 4: MTD

Moving Target Defense (MTD) can be considered as a different approach to applying diversity to security, since it diversifies resources along the time dimension [22]. However, most existing work on MTD relies on intuitive notion of diversity which may lead to misleading results. This next case demonstrates the usefulness of our proposed metrics particularly for MTD. In this case, suppose host 1 and 2 are Web servers, host 3 an application server, and host 4 a database server. A MTD will attempt to achieve better security by varying in time the software components at different tiers. A common misconception here is that the combination of different components at different tiers will increase diversity, and the degree of diversity is equal to the product of diversity at those tiers. However, this is usually not the case. For example, a single flaw in the application server (host 3) may result in a SQL injection that compromises the database server (host 4) and consequently leaks the root user's password. Also, similar to the previous case, more diversity over time may actually provide attackers more opportunities to find flaws. The lesson here is again that, an intuitive observation may be misleading, and formally modeling network diversity is necessary.

3   Biodiversity-Inspired Network Diversity Metric

Although the notion of network diversity has attracted limited attention, its counterpart in ecology, *biodiversity*, and its positive impact on the ecosystem's stability has been investigated for many decades [13]. While many lessons may potentially be borrowed from the rich literature of biodiversity, in this chapter we will focus on adapting existing mathematical models of biodiversity for modeling network diversity.

Specifically, the number of different species in an ecosystem is known as *species richness* [34]. Similarly, given a set of distinct resource types (we will consider similarity between resources later) R in a network, we call the cardinality $|R|$ the *richness* of resources in the network. An obvious limitation of this richness metric is that it ignores the relative abundance of each resource type. For example, the two sets $\{r_1, r_1, r_2, r_2\}$ and $\{r_1, r_2, r_2, r_2\}$ have the same richness of 2 but clearly different levels of diversity.

To address this limitation, the Shannon-Wiener index, which is essentially the Shannon entropy using natural logarithm, is used as a *diversity index* to group all systems with the same level of diversity, and the exponential of the diversity index is regarded as the *effective number* metric [20]. The effective number basically allows us to always measure diversity in terms of the number of equally-common species, even if in reality those species may not be equally common. In the following, we borrow this concept to define the effective resource richness and our first diversity metric.

Definition 1 (Effective Richness and d_1-Diversity) In a network G with the set of hosts $H = \{h_1, h_2, \ldots, h_n\}$, set of resource types $R = \{r_1, r_2, \ldots, r_m\}$, and the resource mapping $res(.) : H \rightarrow 2^R$ (here 2^R denotes the power set of R), let $t = \sum_{i=1}^{n} |res(h_i)|$ (total number of resource instances), and let

$$p_j = \frac{|\{h_i : r_j \in res(h_i)\}|}{t} (1 \le i \le n, 1 \le j \le m)$$

(relative frequency of each resource). We define the network's diversity as $d_1 = \frac{r(G)}{t}$, where $r(G)$ is the network's effective richness of resources, defined as

$$r(G) = \frac{1}{\prod_1^n p_i^{p_i}}$$

One limitation of the effective number-based metric is that similarity between different resource types is not taken into account and all resource types are assumed to be entirely different, which is not realistic (e.g., the same application can be configured to fulfill totally different roles, such as NGinx as a reverse proxy or a web server, respectively, in which case these should be regarded as different resources with high similarity). Therefore, we borrow the similarity-sensitive biodiversity metric recently introduced in [27] to re-define resource richness. With this new definition, the above diversity metric d_1 can now handle similarity between resources.

Definition 2 (Similarity-Sensitive Richness) In Definition 1, suppose a similarity function is given as $z(.) : [1, m] \times [1, m] \rightarrow [0, 1]$ (a larger value denoting higher similarity and $z(i, i) = 1$ for all $1 \le i \le m$), let $zp_i = \sum_{j=1}^{m} z(i, j)p_j$. We define the network's effective richness of resources, considering the similarity function, as

$$r(G) = \frac{1}{\prod_1^n zp_i^{p_i}}$$

The effective richness-based network diversity metric d_1 is only suitable for cases where all resources may be treated equally, and causal relationships between resources either do not exist or may be safely ignored. On the other hand, this metric may also be used as a building block inside other network diversity metrics, in the sense that we may simply say "the number of distinct resources" without worrying about uneven distribution of resource types or similarity between resources, thanks to the effective richness concepts given in Definitions 1 and 2.

The effect of biodiversity on the stability of an ecosystem has been shown to critically depend on the interaction of different specifies inside a food Web [29]. Although such interaction typically takes the form of a "feed-on" relationship between different specifies, which does not directly apply to computer networks, this observation has inspired us to model diversity based on the structural relationship between resources, which will be detailed in the coming sections.

4   Least Attacking Effort-Based Network Diversity Metric

This section models network diversity based on the least attacking effort. In order to do so while considering causal relationships between different resources, we first need a model of such relationships and possible zero day attacks. Our model is similar to the *attack graph* model [3, 38], although our model focuses on remotely accessible resources (e.g., services or applications that are reachable from other hosts in the network), which will be regarded as placeholders for potential zero day vulnerabilities instead of known vulnerabilities as in attack graphs.

To build intuitions, we revisit Fig. 1 by making the following assumptions. Accesses from outside firewall 1 are allowed to host 1 but blocked to host 2; accesses from host 1 or 2 are allowed to host 3 but blocked to host 4 by firewall 2; hosts 1 and 2 provide *http* service; host 3 provides *ssh* service; Host 4 provides both *http* and *rsh* services.

Figure 2 depicts a corresponding *resource graph*, which is syntactically equivalent to an attack graph, but models zero day attacks rather than known vulnerabilities. Each pair in plaintext is a self-explanatory security-related condition (e.g., connectivity $\langle source, destination \rangle$ or privilege $\langle privilege, host \rangle$), and each triple inside a box is a potential exploit of resource $\langle resource, source\ host, destination\ host \rangle$; the edges point from the pre-conditions to a zero day exploit (e.g., from $\langle 0, 1 \rangle$ and $\langle user, 0 \rangle$ to $\langle http, 0, 1 \rangle$), and from that exploit to its post-conditions (e.g., from $\langle http, 0, 1 \rangle$ to $\langle user, 1 \rangle$). Exploits or conditions involving firewall 2 are omitted for simplicity.

We simply regard resources of different types as entirely different (their similarity can be handled using the effective resource richness given in Definition 2). Also, we take the conservative approach of considering all resources (services and firewalls) to be potentially vulnerable to zero day attacks. Definition 3 formally introduces the concept of resource graph.

Fig. 2 An example resource
graph

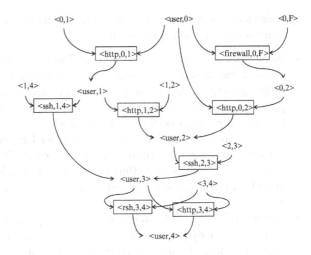

Table 1 Attack paths

Attack path	# of steps	# of resources
1. $\langle http, 0, 1 \rangle \rightarrow \langle ssh, 1, 4 \rangle \rightarrow \langle rsh, 4, 5 \rangle$	3	3
2. $\langle http, 0, 1 \rangle \rightarrow \langle ssh, 1, 4 \rangle \rightarrow \langle http, 4, 5 \rangle$	3	2
3. $\langle http, 0, 1 \rangle \rightarrow \langle http, 1, 2 \rangle \rightarrow \langle ssh, 2, 4 \rangle \rightarrow \langle rsh, 4, 5 \rangle$	4	3
4. $\langle http, 0, 1 \rangle \rightarrow \langle http, 1, 2 \rangle \rightarrow \langle ssh, 2, 4 \rangle \rightarrow \langle http, 4, 5 \rangle$	4	2
5. $\langle firewall, 0, F \rangle \rightarrow \langle http, 0, 2 \rangle \rightarrow \langle ssh, 2, 4 \rangle \rightarrow \langle rsh, 4, 5 \rangle$	4	4
6. $\langle firewall, 0, F \rangle \rightarrow \langle http, 0, 2 \rangle \rightarrow \langle ssh, 2, 4 \rangle \rightarrow \langle http, 4, 5 \rangle$	4	3

Definition 3 (Resource Graph) Given a network with the set of hosts H, set of
resources R with the resource mapping $res(.) : H \rightarrow 2^R$, set of zero day exploits
$E = \{\langle r, h_s, h_d \rangle \mid h_s \in H, h_d \in H, r \in res(h_d)\}$ and their pre- and post-conditions
C, a resource graph is a directed graph $G(E \cup C, R_r \cup R_i)$ where $R_r \subseteq C \times E$ and
$R_i \subseteq E \times C$ are the pre- and post-condition relations, respectively.

Next consider how attackers may potentially attack a critical network asset,
modeled as a goal condition, with the least effort. In Fig. 2, by following the simple
rule that an exploit may be executed if all the pre-conditions are satisfied, and
executing that exploit will cause all the post-conditions to be satisfied, we may
observe six *attack paths*, as shown in Table 1 (the second and third columns can
be ignored for now and will be explained shortly). Definition 4 formally introduces
the concept of attack path.

Definition 4 (Attack Path) Given a resource graph $G(E \cup C, R_r \cup R_i)$, we call $C_I =$
$\{c : c \in C, (\nexists e \in E)(\langle e, c \rangle \in R_i)\}$ the set of initial conditions. Any sequence of zero
day exploits $e_1, e_2, \ldots, e_n$ is called an attack path in G, if $(\forall i \in [1, n])(\langle c, e_i \rangle \in$
$R_r \rightarrow (c \in C_i \vee (\exists j \in [1, i-1])(\langle e_j, c \rangle \in R_i)))$, and for any $c \in C$, we use $seq(c)$
for the set of attack paths $\{e_1, e_2, \ldots, e_n : \langle e_n, c \rangle \in R_i\}$.

We are now ready to consider how diversity could be defined based on the least
attacking effort (the shortest path). There are actually several possible ways for

choosing such shortest paths and for defining the metric, as we will illustrate through our running example in the following.

- First, as shown in the second column of Table 1, path 1 and 2 are the shortest in terms of the *steps* (i.e., the number of zero day exploits). Clearly, those do not reflect the least attacking effort, since path 4 may actually take less effort than path 1, as attackers may reuse their exploit code, tools, and skills while exploiting the same *http* service on three different hosts.
- Next, as shown in the third column, path 2 and 4 are the shortest in terms of the number of distinct resources (or effective richness). This seems more reasonable since it captures the saved effort in reusing exploits. However, although path 2 and 4 have the same number of distinct resources (2), they clearly reflect different diversity.
- Another seemingly valid solution is to base on the minimum ratio $\frac{\# of\ resources}{\# of\ steps}$ (which is given by path 4 in this example), since such a ratio reflects the potential improvements in terms of diversity (e.g., the ratio $\frac{2}{4}$ of path 4 indicates 50% potential improvement in diversity). However, we can easily imagine a very long attack path minimizing such a ratio but does not reflect the least attacking effort (e.g., an attack path with 9 steps and 3 distinct resources will yield a ratio of $\frac{1}{3}$, less than $\frac{2}{4}$, but clearly requires more effort than path 4).
- Finally, yet another option is to choose the shortest path that minimizes both the number of distinct resources (path 2 and 4) and the above ratio $\frac{\# of\ resources}{\# of\ steps}$ (path 4). However, a closer look will reveal that, although path 4 does represent the least attacking effort, it does not represent the maximum amount of potential improvement in diversity, because once we start to diversify path 4, the shortest path may change to be path 1 or 2.

Based on these discussions, we define network diversity by combining the first two options above. Specifically, the network diversity is defined as the ratio between the minimum number of distinct resources on a path and the minimum number of steps on a path (note these can be different paths). Going back to our running example above, we find path 2 and 4 to have the minimum number of distinct resources (two), and also path 1 and 2 to have the minimum number of steps (three), so the network diversity in this example is equal to $\frac{2}{3}$ (note that it is a simple fact that this ratio will never exceed 1). Intuitively, the numerator 2 denotes the network's current level of robustness against zero day exploits (no more than 2 different attacks), whereas the denominator 3 denotes the network's maximum potential of robustness (tolerating no more than 3 different attacks) by increasing the amount of diversity (from $\frac{2}{3}$ to 1). More formally, we introduce our second network diversity metric in Definition 5 (note that, for simplicity, we only consider a single goal condition for representing the given critical asset, which is not a limitation since multiple goal conditions can be easily handled through adding a few dummy conditions [1]).

Definition 5 (d_2-Diversity) Given a resource graph $G(E \cup C, R_r \cup R_i)$ and a goal condition $c_g \in C$, for each $c \in C$ and $q \in seq(c)$, denote $R(q)$ for

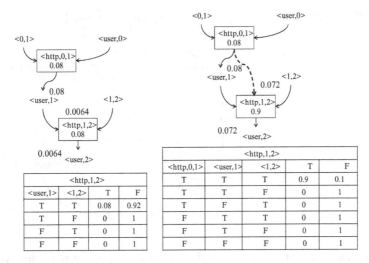

Fig. 3 Modeling network diversity using Bayesian networks

$\{r : r \in R, r \text{ appearsin } q\}$, the network diversity is defined as (where $min(.)$ returns the minimum value in a set)

$$d_2 = \frac{min_{q \in seq(c_g)} \mid R(q) \mid}{min_{q' \in seq(c_g)} \mid q' \mid}$$

5 Probabilistic Network Diversity

In this section, we develop a probabilistic metric to capture the effect of diversity based on average attacking effort by combining all attack paths.

5.1 Overview

This section first reviews the probabilistic model of network diversity introduced in [39] and then points out its limitations. This model defines network diversity as the ratio between two probabilities, namely, the probability that given critical assets may be compromised, and the same probability but with an additional assumption that all resource instances are distinct (which means attackers cannot reuse any exploit). Both probabilities represent the *attack likelihood* with respect to goal conditions, which can be modeled using a Bayesian network constructed based on the resource graph [16].

For example, Fig. 3 demonstrates this model based on our running example (only part of the example is shown for simplicity). The left-hand side represents the case

Fig. 4 The redesigned model

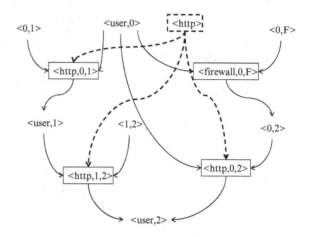

in which the effect of reusing an exploit is not considered, that is, the two *http* service instances are assumed to be distinct. The right-hand side considers that effect and models it as the conditional probability that the lower *http* service may be exploited given that the upper one is already exploited (represented using a dotted line). The two conditional probability tables (CPTs) illustrate the effect of reusing the *http* exploit (e.g., probability 0.9 in the right CPT), and not reusing it (e.g., probability 0.08 in the left CPT), respectively. The network diversity in this case will be calculated as the ratio $d_3 = \frac{0.0064}{0.072}$.

We realized that the above model has certain limitations when a few invalid results (larger than 1) were returned during our simulations. More specifically, in the above model, modeling the effect of reusing exploits as a conditional probability (that a resource may be exploited given that some other instances of the same type are already exploited) essentially assumes a total order over different instances of the same resource type in any resource graph, which comprises a major limitation. For example, in Fig. 4 (the dashed line and box, and the CPT table may be ignored for the time being), although the reused *http* exploit $\langle http, 1, 2 \rangle$ (after exploiting $\langle http, 0, 1 \rangle$) may be handled using the above model by adding a dotted line pointing to it from its ancestor $\langle http, 0, 1 \rangle$, the same method will not work for the other potentially reused *http* exploit $\langle http, 0, 2 \rangle$, since there does not exist a definite order between $\langle http, 0, 1 \rangle$ and $\langle http, 0, 2 \rangle$, which means an attacker may reach $\langle http, 0, 2 \rangle$ before, or after, reaching $\langle http, 0, 1 \rangle$. Therefore, we cannot easily assume one of them to be exploited first. Considering that the resource graph model is defined based on a Bayesian network, which by definition requires acyclic graphs, we cannot add bi-directional dotted lines between exploits, either.

Another related limitation is that, once exploits are considered to be partially ordered, the attack likelihood will not necessarily be the lowest when all the resources are assumed to be distinct. For example, in Fig. 4, an attacker may reach condition $\langle user, 2 \rangle$ through two paths, $\langle http, 0, 1 \rangle \rightarrow \langle http, 1, 2 \rangle$ and $\langle firewall, 0, F \rangle \rightarrow \langle http, 0, 2 \rangle$. Intuitively, the attack likelihood will actually be higher if the *http* exploits in the two paths are assumed to be distinct, since now an attacker would have more choices in reaching the goal condition $\langle user, 2 \rangle$. Those limitations will be addressed in following sections through a redesigned model.

5.2 Redesigning d_3 Metric

To address the aforementioned limitations of the original d_3 metric [39], we redesign the model of reusing exploits of the same resource type. Intuitively, what allows an attacker to more likely succeed in exploiting a previously exploited type of resources is the knowledge, skills, or exploit code he/she has obtained. Therefore, instead of directly modeling the casual relationship between reused exploits, we explicitly model such advantages of the attacker as separate events, and model their effect of increasing the likelihood of success in subsequent exploits as conditional probabilities.

More specifically, a new parent node common to exploits of the same resource type will be added to the resource graph, as demonstrated in Fig. 4 using dashed lines and box. This common parent node represents the event that an attacker has the capability to exploit that type of resources. However, unlike nodes representing initial conditions, which will be treated as evidence for calculating the posterior probability of the goal condition, the event that an attacker can exploit a type of resources will not be considered observable. Adding a common parent node to exploits of the same resource type will introduce probabilistic dependence between the children nodes such that satisfying one child node will increase the likelihood of others, which models the effect of reusing exploits.

For example, in Fig. 4, the dashed line box indicates a new node $\langle http \rangle$ representing the event that an attacker has the capability to exploit *http* resources. The dashed lines represent conditional probabilities that an attacker can exploit each *http* instance, and the CPT table shows an example of such conditional probability for $\langle http, 1, 2 \rangle$. The marginal probability 0.08 assigned to $\langle http \rangle$ represents the likelihood that an attacker has the capability of exploiting *http* resources, and the conditional probability 0.9 assigned to $\langle http, 1, 2 \rangle$ represents the likelihood for the same attacker to exploit that particular instance. The existence of such a common parent will introduce dependence between those *http* exploits, such that satisfying one will increase others' likelihood.

Formally, Definition 6 characterizes network diversity using this approach. In the definition, the second set of conditional probabilities represent the probability that an attacker is capable of exploiting each type of resources. The third and fourth sets together represent the semantics of a resource graph. Finally, the fifth set represents the conditional probability that an exploit may be executed when its pre-conditions are satisfied (including the condition that represents the corresponding resource type).

Definition 6 (d_3 **Diversity**) Given a resource graph $G(E \cup C, R_r \cup R_i)$, let $R' \subseteq R$ be the set of resource types each of which is shared by at least two exploits in E, and let $R_s = \{(r, \langle r, h_s, h_d \rangle) : r \in R', \langle r, h_s, h_d \rangle \in E\}$ (that is, edges from resource types to resource instances). Construct a Bayesian network $B = (G'(E \cup C \cup R', R_r \cup R_i \cup R_s), \theta)$, where G' is obtained by injecting R' and R_s into the resource graph G, and regarding each node as a discrete random variable with two states T and F, and θ is the set of parameters of the Bayesian network given as follows.

1. $P(c = T) = 1$ for all the initial conditions $c \in C_I$.
2. $P(r = T)$ are given for all the shared resource types $r \in R'$.
3. $P(e \mid \exists c_{(c,e) \in R_r} = F) = 0$ (that is, an exploit cannot be executed until all of its pre-conditions are satisfied).
4. $P(c \mid \exists e_{(e,c) \in R_i} = T) = 1$ (that is, a post-condition can be satisfied by any exploit alone).
5. $P(e \mid \forall c_{(c,e) \in R_r \cup R_s} = T)$ are given for all $e \in E$ (that is, the probability of successfully executing an exploit when its pre-conditions have all been satisfied).

Given any $c_g \in C$, the network diversity d_3 is defined as $d_3 = \frac{p'}{p}$ where $p = P(c_g \mid \forall c_{c \in CI} = T)$ (that is, the conditional probability of c_g being satisfied given that all the initial conditions are true), and p' denotes the minimum possible value of p when some edges are deleted from R_s (that is, the lowest attack likelihood by assuming certain resource types are no longer shared by exploits).

Figure 5 shows two simple examples in which the first depicts a conjunction relationship between the two exploits (in the sense that both upper exploits must be executed before the lower exploit can be reached), whereas the second a disjunction relationship (any of the two upper exploits can alone lead to the lower exploit). In both cases, assuming $c_g = \langle c_3, 1 \rangle$, the probability $p = P(c_g \mid \forall c_{c \in CI} = T)$ is shown in the figure. We now consider how to calculate the normalizing constant p'. For the left-hand side case, the probability $p = P(c_g \mid \forall c_{c \in CI} = T)$ would be minimized if we delete both edges from the top node (v_1) to its two children (that is, those

Fig. 5 Two examples of applying d_3

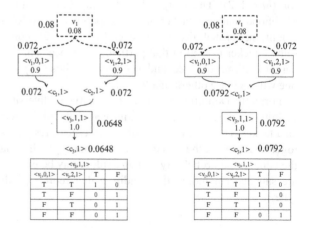

two exploits no longer share the same resource type). It can be calculated that $p' = 0.0064$, and hence the diversity $d_3 = \frac{0.0064}{0.0648}$ in this case. The right-hand case is more interesting, since it turns out that p is already minimized because deleting edges from the top node (v_1) will only result in a higher value of p (since an attacker would have two different ways for reaching the lower exploit), which can be calculated as 0.1536. Therefore, diversity in this case is $d_3 = \frac{0.0792}{0.0792}$, that is, improving diversity will not enhance (in fact it hurts) security in this case. This example also confirms our earlier observation that assuming all resources to be distinct does not necessarily lead to the lowest attack likelihood.

6 Applying the Network Diversity Metrics

The network diversity metrics we have proposed are based on abstract models of networks and attacks. How to instantiate such models for a given network is equally important. This section discusses various practical issues in applying the metrics and provides a case study on instantiating the models.

6.1 Guidelines for Instantiating the Network Diversity Models

To apply the proposed network diversity metrics, necessary input information needs to be collected. We describe how such inputs may be collected from a given network and discusses the practicality and scalability.

6.1.1 The d_1 Diversity Metric

To instantiate d_1, we need to collect information about

- hosts (e.g., computers, routers, switches, firewalls),
- resources (e.g., remotely accessible services), and
- similarity between resources.

Information about hosts and resources is typically already available to administrators in the form of a network map. A network scanning will assist in collecting or verifying information about active services. A close examination of host configurations (e.g., the status of services and firewall rules) may also be necessary since a network scanning may not reveal services that are currently disabled or hidden by security mechanisms (e.g., firewalls) but may be re-enabled once the security mechanisms are compromised.

Collecting and updating such information for a large network certainly demands substantial time and efforts. Automated network scanning or host-based tools exist to help simplify such tasks. Moreover, focusing on remotely accessible resources allows our model to stay relatively manageable and scalable, since most hosts typically only have a few open ports but tens or even hundreds of local applications. A challenge is to determine the similarity of different but related resources, which will be discussed in further details in Sect. 8.

6.1.2 The d_2-Diversity Metric

To instantiate the least attacking effort-based d_2 network diversity metric, we need to collect the following, in addition to what is already required by d_1,

- connectivity between hosts,
- security conditions either required for, or implied by, the resources (e.g., privileges, trust relationships, etc.), and
- critical assets.

The connectivity information is typically already available as part of the network map. A network scanner may help to verify such information. A close examination of host configurations (e.g., firewall rules) and application settings (e.g., authentication policies) is usually sufficient to identify the requirements for accessing a resource (pre-conditions), and an assessment of privilege levels of applications and the strength of isolation around such applications will reveal the consequences of compromising a resource (post-conditions). Critical assets can be identified based on an organization's needs and priority.

The amount of additional information required for applying d_2 is comparable to that required for d_1, since a resource typically has a small number of pre- and post-conditions. Once such information is collected, we can construct a resource graph using existing tools for constructing traditional attack graphs due to their syntactic equivalence, and the latter is known to be practical for realistic applications [21, 33].

6.1.3 The d_3-Diversity Metric

To instantiate the probabilistic network diversity metric d_3, we need to collect the following, in addition to what is already required for d_2,

- marginal probabilities of shared resource types, and
- conditional probabilities that resources can be compromised when all the pre-conditions are satisfied.

Both groups of probabilities represent the likelihood that attackers have the capability of compromising certain resources. A different likelihood may be assigned to each resource type, if this can be estimated based on experiences or reputations (e.g., the history of past vulnerabilities found in the same or similar resource). When such an estimation is not possible or desirable (note that any assumption about attackers' capabilities may weaken security if the assumption turns to be invalid), we can assign the same nominal value as follows. Since a zero day vulnerability is commonly interpreted as a vulnerability not publicly known or announced, it can be characterized using the CVSS base metrics [31], as a vulnerability with a remediation level *unavailable*, a report confidence *unconfirmed*, and a maximum overall base score (and hence produce a conservative metric value). We therefore obtain a nominal value of 0.8, converting to a probability of 0.08. For reference purpose, the lowest existing CVSS score [32] is currently 1.7, so 0.08 is reasonably low for a zero day vulnerability. Once the probabilities are determined, applying d_3 amounts to constructing Bayesian networks and making probabilistic inferences based on the networks, which can be achieved using many existing tools (e.g., we use OpenBayes [17]). Although it is a well known fact that inference using Bayesian networks is generally intractable, our simulation results have shown that the particular inference required for applying the d_3 metric can actually be achieved under reasonable computational cost [39].

6.2   Case Study

We present a case study to demonstrate how our models may be instantiated by following the guidelines provided in previous section. The case study is based on a network configuration from the Penetration Testing Virtual Labs [35]. Despite its relatively small scale, the network configuration mimics a typical enterprise network, e.g., with DMZ, Web server behind firewall accessible from public Internet, and a private management network protected by the same firewall but with deep packet inspection and equipped with a domain controller and CITRIX server, as shown in Fig. 6. The following describes in details how we collect necessary input information for instantiating each metric, and the collected information is listed in Table 2.

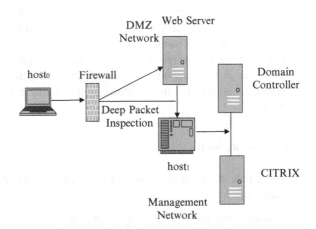

Fig. 6 An example network [35]

Table 2 Collected information

Hosts	Connectivity	Ports	Resources	Security conditions
Firewall	Web server, $host_1$	–	Egress traffic filtered, Deep content inspection rules	–
Web server	Firewall, $host_1$	80,43	Http services, SQLite1.2.4, Ubuntu 11.04	User, root
$Host_1$	Firewall, Web server, Domain controller, Citrix	80,3389	File Sharing, RDP Service, Windows 7,	Domain user, local administrator
Citrix	Domain controller, $host_1$	80,3389	Http services, Citrix Xen App, RDP service	User, local administrator
Domain controller	Citrix, $host_1$	3389	RDP service	User, domain administrator

6.2.1 The d_1 Metric

The information we collect for instantiating d_1 includes:

- Hosts: The network topological map clearly indicates these are the hosts: Firewall, Web Server, $host_1$, Citrix, and Domain Controller.
- Resources: The network configuration description indicates the firewall used in this network is Symantec Endpoint Protection, which deploys two different rules, for the DMZ network with egress traffic filtered and for the Management network with deep content inspection. We use nmap to scan the internal network in order to collect information about opening ports, applications running on the hosts and operating systems' information on the hosts, etc. For example, we determined that the public web server has opening ports 80 and 43, with SQLite and Appache running on top of Ubuntu 11.04.
- Similarity between resources: We take a simplistic approach of regarding resources in this network as either identical or different so the similarity score is either 1 or 0 (this can be refined by leveraging existing tools, as discussed in Sect. 8).

6.2.2 The d_2 Metric

To instantiate d_2, we need to collect the following, in addition to what is already collected for d_1:

- Connectivity: the network topological map clearly provides the connectivity between hosts.

- Security conditions: we study the applications and their existing vulnerabilities in order to collect corresponding security-related pre- and post-conditions. For example, SQLiteManager version 1.2.4 runs under user privilege on Web server, which indicates a post-condition of user privilege on the host, whereas Ubuntu 11.04 has root privilege as its post-condition due to potential privilege escalation vulnerabilities (there in fact exist such vulnerabilities [11]).
- Critical assets: in this network we consider the Domain Controller as critical asset due to its special role (actual system administrators will be in a better position to designate their critical assets).

6.2.3   The d_3 Metric

To instantiate d_3, we need to collect the following, in addition to what is already collected for d_2,

- Marginal probabilities of shared resource types and conditional probabilities that resources can be compromised when all the pre-conditions are satisfied: we assign 0.08 as a nominal value for both probabilities which may certainly be refined if additional information is available to administrators (see Sect. 6.1.3 for details).

7   Simulation

In this section, we study the three proposed metrics by applying them to different use cases through simulations. All simulation results are collected using a computer equipped with a 3.0 GHz CPU and 8 GB RAM in the Python environment under Ubuntu 12.04 LTS. The Bayesian network-based metric is implemented using OpenBayes [17]. To generate a large number of resource graphs for simulations, we first construct a small number of seed graphs based on real networks, and then generate larger graphs from those seed graphs by injecting new hosts and assigning resources in a random but realistic fashion (e.g., we vary the number of pre-conditions of each exploit within a small range since real world exploits usually have a small number of pre-conditions).

We apply the three network diversity metrics to different use cases, as presented in Sect. 2. Our objective is to evaluate the three metrics through numerical results and to examine those results together with statistically expected results represented by different attack scenarios.

The first two simulations compare the results of all three metrics to examine their different trends as graph sizes increase and as diversity increases. First of all, to convert the Bayesian network-based metric d_3 to a comparable scale of the other two, we use $\frac{\log_{0.08}(p')}{\log_{0.08}(p)}$ (i.e., the ratio based on equivalent numbers of zero day exploits) instead of d_3. In the left-hand side of Fig. 7, the scatter points marked with X in the red color are the individual values of d_2. The blue points marked with Y

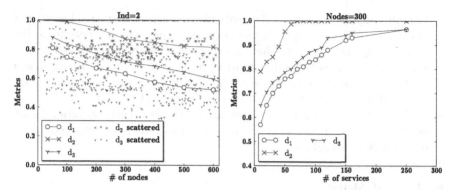

Fig. 7 Comparison of metrics (*left*) and the effect of increasing diversity (*right*) (Color figure online)

are the values of d_3 (converted as above). Also shown are their average values, and the average value of the effective richness-based metric d_1. The right figure shows the average value of the three metrics in increasing number of distinct resources for resource graphs of a fixed size.

Results and Implications: Both simulations show that, while all three metrics follow a similar trend (in the left figure, diversity will decrease in larger graphs since there will be more duplicated resources) and capture the same effect of increasing diversity (in the right figure), the Bayesian network-based metric d_3 somehow reflects an intermediate result between the two other extremes (d_1 can be considered as the average over all resources, whereas d_2 only depends on the shortest path). Those results show that applying all three metrics may yield consistent results and motivates us to compare them through further simulations.

Next we examine the metric results under different use cases, as described in Sect. 2. The first use case considers worms characterized as follows. First, each worm can only exploit a small number of vulnerabilities. In our implementation, we randomly choose one to three resource types as the capability of each worm. Second, the goal of a worm is infecting as many hosts as possible, does not need specific targets. Although some worms or bots may indeed in reality have a target, it is usually still necessary for them to first compromise a large number of machines before the target can be reached (e.g., Stuxnet [15]). In Fig. 8, the X-axis is the ratio of the number of resource types to the number of resource instances, which roughly represents the level of diversity in terms of richness (it can be observed that d_1 is close to a straight line). Y-axis shows the results of the three metrics as well as the ratio of hosts that are not infected by the simulated worms. The four lines represent the three metrics (marked with d_1, d_2, and d_3) and the ratio of hosts uninfected by simulated worms (marked with S_1). The left and right figures correspond to different percentage of first-level exploits (the exploits that only have initial conditions as their pre-conditions) among all exploits, which roughly depicts how well the network is safeguarded (e.g., 50% means a more vulnerable network than 10% since initially attackers can reach half, or five times more, exploits). For each configuration, we repeat 500 times to obtain the average result of simulated worms.

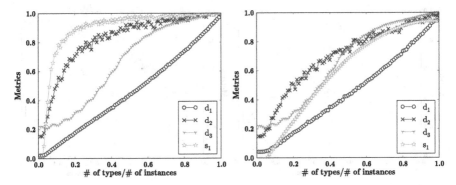

Fig. 8 Worm propagation (*left* 10% initially satisfied exploits, *right* 50% initially satisfied exploits)

Results and Implications: In this simulation, we can make the following observations. First of all, all three metrics still exhibit similar trends and relationships as discussed above. The left figure shows that, when the network is better safeguarded (with only 10% of exploits initially reachable), the effect of increasing diversity on simulated worms shows a closer relationship with the d_2 metric than the other two, both of which indicate that increasing diversity can significantly increase the percentage of hosts uninfected by worms. In comparison, the right figure shows a less promising result where both three metrics and the percentage of uninfected hosts all tend to follow a similar trend. Intuitively, in well guarded networks, many hosts cannot be reached until the worms have infected other adjacent hosts, so increasing diversity can more effectively mitigate worm propagation. In less guarded networks where half of the exploits may be reached initially, the effect of diversity on worms is almost proportional to the richness of resources (d_1), and all three metrics tend to yield similar results.

The second use case is targeted attacks (Sect. 2). We simulate attackers with different capabilities (sets of resources they can compromise) and the level of such capabilities (that is, the number of resources they can compromise) follows the Gamma distribution [30]. Similarly, we also repeat each experiment 500 times and we examine two different cases corresponding to different percentages of first-level exploits. In Fig. 9, S_2 is the result of simulated attacker, which means the percentages of attackers who cannot reach the randomly selected goal condition.

Results and Implications: From the results we can observe similar results as with the simulated worms. Specifically, increasing diversity can more effectively mitigate the damage caused by simulated attackers for well guarded networks (the left figure) than for less guarded networks (the right figure). Also, in the left figure, the simulated attackers' results are closer to that of d_2 than the other two metrics, whereas it is closer to both d_2 and d_3 in the right figure. In addition, by comparing the results in Fig. 9 (targeted attack) to that in Fig. 8 (worm), we can see that the same level of diversity can more effectively mitigate worm than it can do to simulated

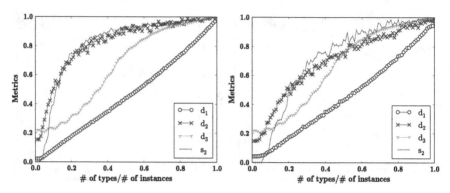

Fig. 9 Targeted attack (*left* 10% initially satisfied vulnerabilities, *right* 50% initially satisfied vulnerabilities)

attackers. This can be explained by the fact that a worm is assumed to have much less capability (set of resources it can compromise) than a simulated attacker.

8 Discussion

The similarity between resources is an important input to our metric models. In Sect. 6.2, we have taken a simplistic approach of regarding resources as either identical or completely different (the similarity score is either 1 or 0). Although such an approach may be acceptable in many cases, it certainly needs to be refined considering the fact that slight differences usually exist among different versions of the same software, whereas different software may share common code or libraries. Measuring such differences or similarity between resources will lead to more accurate results for the diversity metrics. This section discusses potential solutions.

Most of today's complex software are developed under established software engineering principles which encourage modularity, software reuse, the use of program generators, iterative development, and open-source packages. As a result, many software may share common code blocks or employ common libraries, both of which may result in significant similarity between those software. For example, Chrome and Opera have both been using Blink as their rendering engine since 2013 so both include common code blocks. A well known example of sharing common library functions in different software is the recent Heartbleed bug in which many popular Web servers, including Apache HTTP Server, IBM HTTP Server, and Nginx, all employ the common openssl library to establish SSL connections. To measure such similarity between different software, we believe existing efforts, such as clone detection at both source code and binary levels, should be leveraged and extended to develop practical solutions. Although this is not the main focus of this chapter, we provide a brief overview of existing approaches which we believe are promising in this regard.

At source code level, there exists a rich literature on clone detection, which attempts to match code fragments through both syntax and semantic features. For example, text-based approach extracts signatures of the lines and then match software based on substrings [24]. Such a technique provides basic matching results although it has many limitations, e.g., it cannot handle identifier renaming, since it does not transform source code into intermediate formats. Token-based approach parses the source code into a list of tokens [4] so that it can handle renaming, although it has its own limitations, e.g., it cannot deal with replacement of control flows. In a tree-based approach [14], an abstract syntax tree is generated from the source code for matching. Such technique provides more semantic features but it ignores data flows and therefore cannot deal with reordering statements. Apart from those matching-based approaches, a similarity distance-based approach [7] calculates a distance between two code segments and then compare to a given threshold. There exist many other approaches in this literature, all of which may be leveraged to identify and quantify similarity between open source software.

As to closed source software, identifying shared code or library functions is more challenging. Nonetheless, there are many existing efforts on assembly-level clone detection and library identification. The text-based approach regards the executable part of a binary as a sequence of bytes or lines of assembly and compares them to find identical sequences [23]. The token-based approach relies on feature vectors consisted of opcodes and operands and employs metrics to provide function-level clone detection [37]. The structural-based approach maps the code back to execution schema and compares their structural features [12]. Our recent work combines several existing concepts from classic program analysis, including control flow graph, register flow graph, and function call graph, to capture semantic similarity between two binaries [2]. Finally, the binary search engine provide an easy way for locating shared libraries inside a software binary [26]. Although more challenging than it is for open source software, We believe developing practical tools by leveraging such existing efforts to identify and estimate similarity for closed source software is still possible.

Finally, variations of software may also be caused by configuration differences (e.g., different settings of Sophos antivirus software), additional security hardening measures (e.g., SELinux and Grsecurity), add-ons and plugins, etc., which may sometimes offer even more substantial impact than different versions of a software. Taking into account such factors in measuring software similarity can be a real challenge and the only tangible solution may still be relying on administrators' manual inspection and estimation.

9   Conclusion

In this chapter, we have formally modeled network diversity as a security metric for evaluating networks' robustness against zero day attacks. We first devised an effective richness-based metric based on the counterpart in ecology. We then proposed a least attacking effort-based metric to address causal relationships between resources and a probabilistic metric to reflect the average attacking effort. We provided guidelines for instantiating the proposed metrics and discussed how software diversity may be estimated. Finally, we evaluated our algorithms and metrics through simulations. Our study has shown that an intuitive notion of diversity could easily cause misleading results, and the proposed formal models provided better understanding of the effect of diversity on network security.

Acknowledgements Authors with Concordia University were partially supported by the Natural Sciences and Engineering Research Council of Canada under Discovery Grant N01035. Sushil Jajodia was partially supported by the by Army Research Office grants W911NF-13-1-0421 and W911NF-15-1-0576, by the Office of Naval Research grant N00014-15-1-2007, National Institutes of Standard and Technology grant 60NANB16D287, and by the National Science Foundation grant IIP-1266147.

References

1. M. Albanese, S. Jajodia, S. Noel, A time-efficient approach to cost-effective network hardening using attack graphs, in *Proceedings of DSN'12* (2012), pp. 1–12
2. S. Alrabaee, P. Shirani, L. Wang, M. Debbabi, Sigma: a semantic integrated graph matching approach for identifying reused functions in binary code. Digit. Investig. **12**(Supplement 1), S61–S71 (2015)
3. P. Ammann, D. Wijesekera, S. Kaushik, Scalable, graph-based network vulnerability analysis, in *Proceedings of ACM CCS'02* (2002)
4. H.A. Basit, S. Jarzabek, Efficient token based clone detection with flexible tokenization, in *Proceedings of the 6th joint meeting of the European software engineering conference and the ACM SIGSOFT symposium on The foundations of software engineering* (ACM, New York, 2007), pp. 513–516
5. S. Bhatkar, D.C. DuVarney, R. Sekar, Address obfuscation: an efficient approach to combat a broad range of memory error exploits, in *Proceedings of the 12th USENIX security symposium*, Washington, DC, vol. 120 (2003)
6. S. Bhatkar, R. Sekar, Data space randomization, in *Proceedings of the 5th International Conference on Detection of Intrusions and Malware, and Vulnerability Assessment*, DIMVA '08 (Springer, Berlin/Heidelberg, 2008), pp. 1–22
7. R. Brixtel, M. Fontaine, B. Lesner, C. Bazin, R. Robbes, Language-independent clone detection applied to plagiarism detection, in *2010 10th IEEE Working Conference on Source Code Analysis and Manipulation (SCAM)* (IEEE, Los Alamitos, 2010), pp. 77–86
8. J. Caballero, T. Kampouris, D. Song, J. Wang, Would diversity really increase the robustness of the routing infrastructure against software defects? in *Proceedings of the Network and Distributed System Security Symposium* (2008)
9. B.G. Chun, P. Maniatis, S. Shenker, Diverse replication for single-machine byzantine-fault tolerance, in *USENIX Annual Technical Conference* (2008), pp. 287–292
10. B. Cox, D. Evans, A. Filipi, J. Rowanhill, W. Hu, J. Davidson, J. Knight, A. Nguyen-Tuong, J. Hiser, *N-variant systems: a secretless framework for security through diversity*. Defense Technical Information Center (2006)
11. CVE for ubuntu 11.04. http://www.cvedetails.com/vulnerability-list/vendor_id-4781/product_id-20550/version_id-104819/Canonical-Ubuntu-Linux-11.04.html, Sep, 2015.
12. T. Dullien, E. Carrera, S.M. Eppler, S. Porst, Automated attacker correlation for malicious code. Technical report, DTIC Document (2010)

13. C. Elton, *The Ecology of Invasion by Animals and Plants* (University of Chicago Press, Chicago, 1958)
14. W.S. Evans, C.W. Fraser, F. Ma, Clone detection via structural abstraction. Softw. Qual. J. **17**(4), 309–330 (2009)
15. N. Falliere, L.O. Murchu, E. Chien, W32.stuxnet dossier. Symantec Security Response (2011)
16. M. Frigault, L. Wang, A. Singhal, S. Jajodia, Measuring network security using dynamic Bayesian network, in *Proceedings of 4th ACM QoP* (2008)
17. K. Gaitanis, E. Cohen, Open bayes 0.1.0. https://pypi.python.org/pypi/OpenBayes (2013)
18. D. Gao, M. Reiter, D. Song, Behavioral distance measurement using hidden Markov models, in *Recent Advances in Intrusion Detection* (Springer, Berlin, 2006), pp. 19–40
19. M. Garcia, A. Bessani, I. Gashi, N. Neves, R. Obelheiro, OS diversity for intrusion tolerance: myth or reality? in *2011 IEEE/IFIP 41st International Conference on Dependable Systems & Networks (DSN)* (2011), pp. 383–394
20. M.O. Hill, Diversity and evenness: a unifying notation and its consequences. Ecology **54**(2), 427–432 (1973)
21. S. Jajodia, S. Noel, B. O'Berry, Topological analysis of network attack vulnerability, in *Managing Cyber Threats: Issues, Approaches and Challenges*, ed. by V. Kumar, J. Srivastava, A. Lazarevic (Kluwer Academic Publisher, Dordrecht, 2003)
22. S. Jajodia, A.K. Ghosh, V. Swarup, C. Wang, X.S. Wang, *Moving Target Defense: Creating Asymmetric Uncertainty for Cyber Threats*, 1st edn. (Springer, New York, 2011)
23. J. Jang, D. Brumley, S. Venkataraman, Bitshred: fast, scalable malware triage. *Cylab, Carnegie Mellon University, Pittsburgh, PA, Technical Report CMU-Cylab-10, 22* (2010)
24. J.H. Johnson, Identifying redundancy in source code using fingerprints, in *Proceedings of the 1993 conference of the Centre for Advanced Studies on Collaborative research: software engineering*, vol. 1 (IBM Press, 1993), pp. 171–183
25. G.S. Kc, A.D. Keromytis, V. Prevelakis, Countering code-injection attacks with instruction-set randomization, in *Proceedings of the 10th ACM conference on Computer and communications security* (ACM, New York, 2003), pp. 272–280
26. W.M. Khoo, A. Mycroft, R. Anderson, Rendezvous: a search engine for binary code, in *Proceedings of the 10th Working Conference on Mining Software Repositories*, MSR '13 (2013), pp. 329–338
27. T. Leinster, C.A. Cobbold, Measuring diversity: the importance of species similarity. Ecology **93**(3), 477–489 (2012)
28. B. Littlewood, L. Strigini, Redundancy and diversity in security. *Computer Security–ESORICS 2004* (2004), pp. 423–438
29. K.S. McCann, The diversity-stability debate. Nature **405**, 228–233 (2000)
30. M.A. McQueen, W.F. Boyer, M.A. Flynn, G.A. Beitel, Time-to-compromise model for cyber risk reduction estimation, in *Quality of Protection* (Springer, Berlin, 2006), pp. 49–64
31. P. Mell, K. Scarfone, S. Romanosky, Common vulnerability scoring system. IEEE Secur. Priv. **4**(6), 85–89 (2006)
32. National vulnerability database. Available at: http://www.nvd.org, May 9, 2008.
33. X. Ou, W.F. Boyer, M.A. McQueen, A scalable approach to attack graph generation, in *Proceedings of the 13th ACM conference on Computer and communications security*, CCS'06 (ACM, New York, 2006), pp. 336–345
34. E.C. Pielou, *Ecological Diversity* (Wiley, New York, 1975)
35. Penetration testing virtual labs. https://www.offensive-security.com/offensive-security-solutions/virtual-penetration-testing-labs/, Sep, 2015.
36. K. Ren, C. Wang, Q. Wang, Security challenges for the public cloud. IEEE Internet Comput. **16**(1), 69–73 (2012)
37. A. Sæbjørnsen, J. Willcock, T. Panas, D. Quinlan, Z. Su, Detecting code clones in binary executables, in *Proceedings of the eighteenth international symposium on Software testing and analysis* (ACM, New York, 2009), pp. 117–128
38. O. Sheyner, J. Haines, S. Jha, R. Lippmann, J.M. Wing, Automated generation and analysis of attack graphs, in *Proceedings of the 2002 IEEE Symposium on Security and Privacy* (2002)

39. L. Wang, M. Zhang, S. Jajodia, A. Singhal, M. Albanese, Modeling network diversity for evaluating the robustness of networks against zero-day attacks, in *Proceedings of ESORICS'14* (2014), pp. 494–511
40. Y. Yang, S. Zhu, G. Cao, Improving sensor network immunity under worm attacks: a software diversity approach, in *Proceedings of the 9th ACM international symposium on Mobile ad hoc networking and computing* (ACM, New York, 2008), pp. 149–158

A Suite of Metrics for Network Attack Graph Analytics

Steven Noel and Sushil Jajodia

Abstract This chapter describes a suite of metrics for measuring enterprise-wide cybersecurity risk based on a model of multi-step attack vulnerability (attack graphs). The attack graphs are computed through topological vulnerability analysis, which considers the interactions of network topology, firewall effects, and host vulnerabilities. Our metrics are normalized so that metric values can be compared meaningfully across enterprises. To support evaluations at higher levels of abstraction, we define family groups of related metrics, combining individual scores into family scores, and combining family scores into an overall enterprise network score. The *Victimization* metrics family measures key attributes of inherent risk (existence, exploitability, and impact) over all network vulnerabilities. The *Size* family is an indication of the relative size of the vulnerability attack graph. The *Containment* family measures risk in terms of minimizing vulnerability exposure across security protection boundaries. The *Topology* family measures risk through graph theoretic properties (connectivity, cycles, and depth) of the attack graph. We display these metrics (at the individual, family, and overall levels) in interactive visualizations, showing multiple metrics trends over time.

1 Introduction

Modeling and analysis of network attack graphs has reached a fair level of maturity. A variety of tools are able to merge network data from various sources to build graphs of attack vulnerability through networks [1–7]. Such vulnerability-based attack graphs provide a rich framework for new kinds of metrics for network attack risk. There is a critical need for such metrics, to summarize operational status at a glance, to compare security options, and to understand network health over time.

S. Noel (✉)
The MITRE Corporation, McLean, VA, USA
e-mail: snoel@mitre.org

S. Jajodia
Center for Secure Information Systems, George Mason University, Fairfax,
VA 22030-4444, USA

© Springer International Publishing AG 2017
L. Wang et al., *Network Security Metrics*,
https://doi.org/10.1007/978-3-319-66505-4_7

This chapter describes a suite of metrics for measuring overall network security risk, based on a comprehensive model of multi-step attack vulnerability. Our metrics span different complementary dimensions of enterprise security. These metrics are grouped into families, which are combined into an overall risk metric for the network at a point in time, based on vulnerabilities and policies.

Section 2 describes system architecture for computing our suite of attack graph metrics. In Sect. 3, we describe these metrics in detail. Section 4 shows how we portray our metrics as they evolve over time, through interactive visualizations. Section 5 examines our metrics suite through a case study that tracks the metrics over time as they are applied to a network that is progressively hardened. Section 6 describes related work in this area, and Sect. 7 summarizes our results and concludes this chapter.

2 System Architecture

Figure 1 depicts our system for computing security metrics from vulnerability-based network attack graphs. This system imports data from sources that are commonly deployed within enterprise networks, such as vulnerability scanners and firewall configuration files. The system then maps all the exposed vulnerabilities between pairs of hosts, which it organizes as an attack graph.

In this architecture, one option for computing such vulnerability-based attack graphs is the Cauldron tool [6]. Cauldron applies Topological Vulnerability Analysis (TVA) [8], analyzing network attack vulnerability from scan tools and other data sources. It correlates cyber vulnerabilities and environmental metadata, and applies network access policy (firewall) rules.

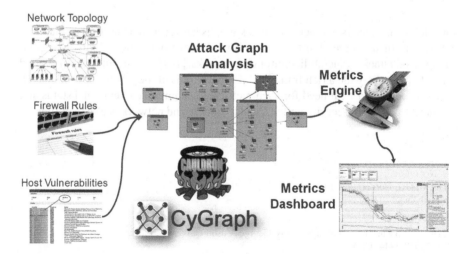

Fig. 1 Attack graph metrics suite

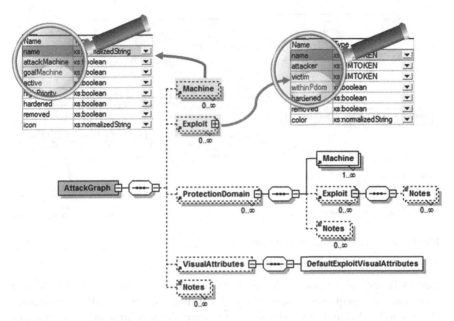

Fig. 2 Structure of attack graph model

By considering all source and destination host pairs, and testing reachability to other host vulnerabilities through the network topology and firewall rules, Cauldron finds each exposed host-to-host vulnerability vector, which it combines into an overall vulnerability attack graph. Vulnerability-based attack graphs computed in this way have quadratic complexity, i.e., $O(n^2)$ for n network hosts. For scaling to larger networks, we can apply the CyGraph tool [1, 2], which leverages big-data architecture.

In the architecture of Fig. 1, the attack graph engine (e.g., Cauldron or CyGraph) produces an attack graph representing attack reachability at a given time. Each attack graph instance is logged as input to the metrics computational engine, for the analysis of the metrics values over time.

Figure 2 shows the structure of an attack graph passed to the metrics engine. An attack graph is composed of a set of security protection domains, which contain host machines and exploits.

In the TVA attack graph model, protection domains are sets of machines that implicitly have reachability to each other's vulnerabilities. Optionally, machines (and exploits between them) can exist outside of protection domains. There other model elements for visual attributes (e.g., marking intrusion alerts). Figure 2 shows the model attributes for machines, including flags for attack start/goal, priority, and hardening state, as well as attributes for exploits, e.g., attacker and victim machines and indication of being within a protection domain (versus across domains).

Figure 3 shows the structure of the log produced by the metrics engine and consumed by the metrics dashboard. A metrics log begins with a definition of each

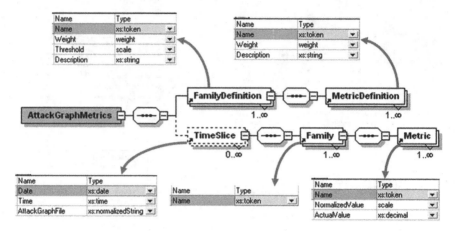

Fig. 3 Structure of attack graph metrics over time

metrics family, along with a definition of each metric within a family. The log then contains a sequence of time slices. Each time slice is the full set of metrics (family and individual) for a single point in time, derived from an attack graph of vulnerability paths through a network at that time.

Figure 3 includes the model attributes for a metrics family definition, including family name, relative weight (across families), threshold, and description. It also includes the attributes for an individual metric within a family, including metric name, relative weight (within the family), and description. The attributes for a metrics time slice include date/time and the corresponding attack graph file. For a metric family at a time slice, the attribute is the family name. The attributes for an individual metric are metric name and the normalized and actual metric values.

3   Attack Graph Metrics

The metrics engine computes individual metrics that each capture different aspects of overall security. We group related metrics into families, as shown in Fig. 4.

We combine individual metrics into family scores, and then combine those into an overall network score. The metrics are mapped to a common scale of zero to ten (least risk to most risk), as for the Common Vulnerability Scoring System (CVSS) [9].

We treat the individual metrics asindependent (orthogonal) components of a multi-dimensional vector. We then compute the Euclidean norm (magnitude) of the k-vector as the combined effect of k metrics (either individual or family).

The following subsections describe each of our metrics families and the individual metrics within them, i.e., the Victimization family (Sect. 3.1), the Size family (Sect. 3.2), the Containment family (Sect. 3.3) and the Topology family (Sect. 3.4).

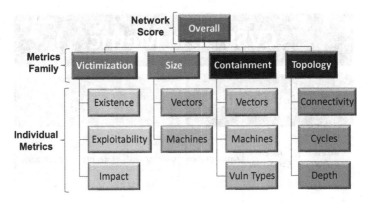

Fig. 4 Attack graph metrics families

3.1 Victimization Family

Individual vulnerabilities and exposed services each have elements of risk, independent of network topology and firewall access policy. These are risk dimensions inherent to the vulnerabilities themselves, in the sense of how they can be victimized by attackers. The *Victimization* metric family scores the entire enterprise network, as a summary of all vulnerabilities across these victimization dimensions.

The following subsections describe each of the individual metrics within the Victimization family, i.e., Existence (Sect. 3.1.1), and the two CVSS-based metrics (Exploitability and Impact) in Sect. 3.1.2. In Sect. 3.1.3, we describe how we combine these individual metrics into an overall metric score for the Victimization family.

3.1.1 Existence Metric

The Victimization family includes a direct measurement of the relative number of vulnerable network services. In particular, the *Existence* metric is the relative number of network services that are vulnerable, on the standard scale of [0,10]. In particular, for s_v vulnerable and s_n non-vulnerable services across the network, the Existence metric $m_{\text{existence}}$ is simply the number of vulnerable network services (that have one or more vulnerabilities), relative to the total number of services:

$$m_{\text{existence}} = \frac{10s_v}{s_v + s_n}.$$

3.1.2 CVSS-Based Metrics

The Victimization family also includes average scores (over all network vulnerabilities) of the two major components of CVSS Base Metrics—Exploitability and

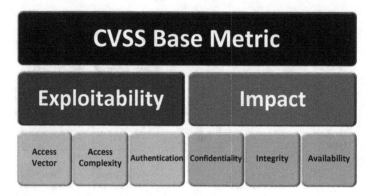

Fig. 5 Components of CVSS (Version 2) base metric

Impact. These components account for the two elements of risk, i.e., likelihood and impact. Figure 5 shows the components and sub-components of the CVSS Base Metric (for CVSS Version 2).

The following subsections these two CVSS-based metrics in more detail, i.e., Exploitability (Sect. 3.1.2.1) and Impact (Sect. 3.1.2.2).

Exploitability Metric

CVSS Exploitability measures the relative difficulty of exploiting a vulnerability. It includes the Access Vector (network, adjacent network, local, or physical) required for exploitation, Access Complexity (high or low) indicating level of attacker effort required, and Authentication (none, single, multiple) for the number of times the attacker must authenticate to a target. Our enterprise-wide *Exploitability* metric is the average value of the CVSS Exploitability score, averaged over all host vulnerabilities, on the scale of [0,10]. Given a vulnerability u_i, we denote its CVSS Exploitability as $\text{CVSS}_{\text{Exploitability}}(u_i)$. Then, for $|U|$ total vulnerabilities over all hosts in the network, the Exploitability metric $m_{\text{exploitability}}$ for the entire network is

$$m_{\text{exploitability}} = \frac{\sum_i^{|U|} \text{CVSS}_{\text{Exploitability}}(u_i)}{|U|}.$$

Impact Metric

The Impact component of CVSS measures the severity of impact upon exploitation of a vulnerability. It includes impact on data confidentiality, system integrity, and system availability, with each type denoted either complete, partial, or no impact. Our enterprise-wide *Impact* metric is the average value of the CVSS Impact score, taken over all vulnerabilities over all hosts, on the scale of [0,10]. Given a vulnerability u_i, we denote its CVSS Impact as $\mathrm{CVSS}_{\mathrm{Impact}}(u_i)$. Then, for $|U|$ total vulnerabilities over all hosts in the network, the Impact metric m_{impact} for the entire network is

$$m_{\mathrm{impact}} = \frac{\sum_i^{|U|} \mathrm{CVSS}_{\mathrm{Impact}}(u_i)}{|U|}.$$

3.1.3 Victimization Family Metric

Finally, we compute the metric $m_{\mathrm{victimization}}$ for the entire Victimization family as the weighted Euclidean norm of the Victimization components:

$$m_{\mathrm{victimization}} = \sqrt{\frac{\left(w_{\mathrm{existence}}\, m_{\mathrm{existence}}\right)^2 + \left(w_{\mathrm{exploitability}}\, m_{\mathrm{exploitability}}\right)^2 + \left(w_{\mathrm{impact}}\, m_{\mathrm{impact}}\right)^2}{w_{\mathrm{existence}}^2 + w_{\mathrm{exploitability}}^2 + w_{\mathrm{impact}}^2}}.$$

This treats the three individual Victimization metrics as components of a three-dimensional Euclidean space. The overall Victimization metric is then the norm (magnitude) of the vector with weighted Victimization components. Here, the weights $w_{\mathrm{[existence,exploitability,impact]}}$ are (optional) user-defined weights for assigning relative strengths of the Victimization family components.

3.2 Size Family

The size of an attack graph is a prime indication of risk. Intuitively, the larger the graph, the more ways you can be compromised (in the sense of attack surface [10]). The *Size* metric family measures enterprise network risk in terms of the attack graph size.

The following subsections describe each of the individual metrics within the Size family, i.e., Attack Vectors (Sect. 3.2.1) and Reachable Machines (Sect. 3.2.2). In in Sect. 3.2.3, we describe how we combine these individual metrics into an overall metric score for the Size family.

3.2.1 Attack Vectors Metric

Within the Size family, we define the *Attack Vectors* metric as the number of single-step attack vectors, relative to the total possible number for the network, on the scale of [0,10]. As shown in Fig. 6, we must consider two kinds of attack vectors: implicit (within protection domains) and explicit (across domains). Here, as defined in TVA, a *protection domain* (shaded box in the figure) is a set of network machines that have unrestricted access to one another's vulnerabilities.The total number of attack vectors is the sum of the implicit and explicit attack vectors. That is, for

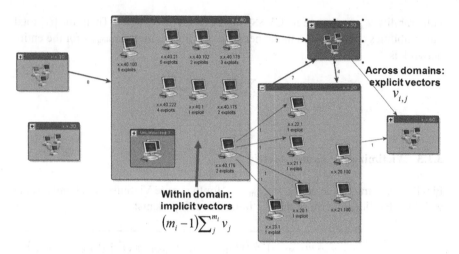

Fig. 6 Counting the single-step attack vectors

m_i vulnerable machines in protection domain i, v_j vulnerabilities on machine j, $v_{i,j}$ vulnerable (explicit) vectors domain i to domain j, and d domains, the total number of attack vectors v_a is

$$v_a = \sum_i^d (m_i - 1) \sum_j^{m_i} v_j + \sum_{i,j}^d v_{i,j}.$$

To map this raw number of attack vectors to the scale [0,10], we must normalize by the total possible number of attack vectors, i.e., in terms of all network services (both vulnerable and not vulnerable) across all machines. So, given m machines and s_i services on machine i, the total possible number of attack vectors v_p is then

$$v_p = (m - 1) \sum_i^m s_i.$$

The Attack Vectors metric, mapped to the scale [0,10] is then

$$v_{\text{attackVectors}} = 10 \sqrt{\frac{v_a}{v_p}}.$$

Here, we apply the square root as a nonlinear compression that reduces dynamic range of the typically large difference between the number of possible and actual attack vectors.

3.2.2 Reachable Machines Metric

Also in the Size family is the *Reachable Machines* metric. This is the number of machines in the attack graph, relative to the total number of machines in the network, on the scale of [0,10]. As shown in Fig. 7, we must consider the machines that are in the attack graph (reachable by an attacker through some number of attack steps) as

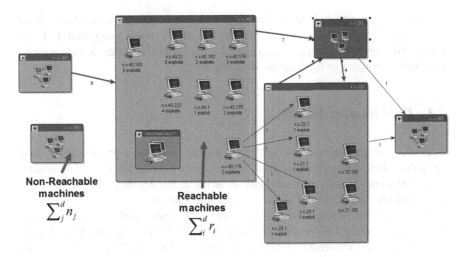

Fig. 7 Counting the number of attacker reachable machines

well as machines that are in the network but not in the attack graph. For r_i reachable machines in protection domain i, with d domains, the total number of reachable machines is

$$r = \sum_i^d r_i.$$

For n_i non-reachable machines (i.e., in the network but not in the attack graph), the total number n of non-reachable machines is

$$n = \sum_i^d n_i.$$

The Reachable Machines metric $m_{\text{reachableMachines}}$, mapped to the scale $[0,10]$ is then

$$m_{\text{reachableMachines}} = 10\frac{r}{r+n}.$$

3.2.3 Metric for Size Family

The overall metric for the Size family m_{size} is then the weighted Euclidean norm of the Size metric components:

$$m_{\text{size}} = \sqrt{\frac{\left(w_{\text{attackVectors}} \ m_{\text{attackVectors}}\right)^2 + \left(w_{\text{reachableMachines}} \ m_{\text{reachableMachines}}\right)^2}{w_{\text{attackVectors}}^2 + w_{\text{reachableMachines}}^2}}.$$

This treats the two individual Size metrics as components of a two-dimensional Euclidean space, with the overall Size metric as the norm (magnitude) of this vector. The weights $w_{[\text{attackVectors,reachableMachines}]}$ are (optional) user-defined weights for relative strengths of the Size family components.

3.3 Containment Family

Networks are generally administered in pieces (subnets, domains, etc.). Risk mitigation should aim to reduce attacks across such boundaries, to contain attacks. The *Containment* family measures risk in terms of the degree to which the attack graph contains attacks across security protection domains.

The following subsections describe each of the individual metrics within the Containment family, i.e., Vectors Containment (Sect. 3.3.1), Machines Containment (Sect. 3.3.2), and Vulnerability Types Containment (Sect. 3.3.3). In Sect. 3.3.4, we describe how we combine these individual metrics into an overall metric score for the Containment family.

3.3.1 Vectors Containment Metric

The *Vectors Containment* metric is the number of attack vectors across protection domains, relative to the total number of attack vectors, on the scale of [0,10]. As shown in Fig. 6, the attack vectors across domains are explicit, and are simply counted across all domain pairs. The attack vectors within protection domains are implicit, i.e., all machine vulnerabilities are directly reachable within the domain. That is, the number of attack vectors across domains v_c is

$$v_C = \sum_{i,j}^{d} v_{i,j}.$$

The total number of attack vectors v_a, both across and (implicit) within domains is

$$v_a = \sum_{i}^{d} (m_i - 1) \sum_{i}^{d} v_i + \sum_{i,j}^{d} v_{i,j}.$$

The Vectors Containment metric m_{vecsC} is then

$$m_{\text{vecsC}} = 10 \cdot \frac{v_c}{v_a}.$$

3.3.2 Machines Containment Metric

Next, the *Machines Containment* metric is the number of machines in the attack graph that are victims of attacks from other domains, relative to the total number of attack graph machines, on the scale of [0,10]. As shown in Fig. 8, the victim

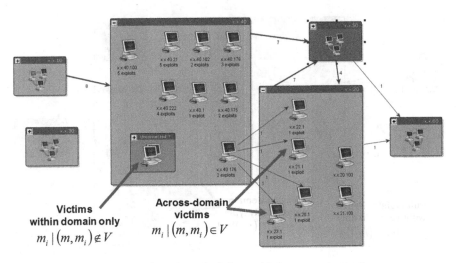

Fig. 8 Counting the number of attack graph victim machines

machines across domains are those machines that have no incoming incident edge in the domain-to-domain attack graph. The remaining machines are within-domain victims only. That is, the total number of across-domain victim machines m_a is

$$m_a = \sum_i^d \{m_i \,|\, (m, m_i) \in V\}.$$

The total number of within-domain victim machines m_w is

$$m_w = \sum_i^d \{m_i \,|\, (m, m_i) \notin V\}.$$

The Machines Containment metric m_{machsC} is then

$$m_{\mathrm{machsC}} = 10 \cdot \frac{m_a}{m_a + m_w}.$$

3.3.3 Vulnerability Types Metric

The *Vulnerability Types* metric is the number of unique vulnerability types in the attack graph that are victims of attacks from other domains, relative to the total number of vulnerability types across the entire attack graph, on the scale of [0,10]. As shown in Fig. 9, the across-domain vulnerability types are on hosts victimized across domains. The remaining vulnerability types are victimized within domains only. The idea is that multiple instances of the same vulnerability type are less costly to mitigate compared to the same number of instances of differing vulnerability types. That is, the total number of across-domain victim machines t_a is

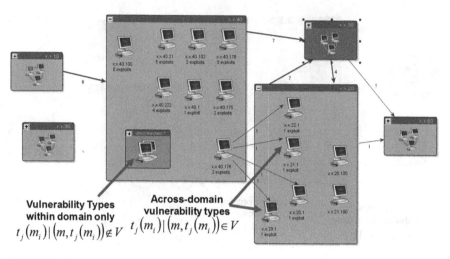

Fig. 9 Counting the number of attack graph vulnerability types

$$t_a = \sum_i^d \{t_i(m_i) \mid (m, t_i(m_i)) \in V\}.$$

The total number of within-domain victim machines t_w is

$$t_w = \sum_i^d \{t_i(m_i) \mid (m, t_i(m_i)) \notin V\}.$$

The Vulnerability Types metric m_{typesC} is then

$$m_{\text{typesC}} = 10 \cdot \frac{t_a}{t_a + t_w}.$$

3.3.4 Metric for Containment Family

The overall metric for the Containment family $m_{\text{containment}}$ is then the weighted Euclidean norm of the Containment metric components:

$$m_{\text{containment}} = \sqrt{\frac{(w_{\text{vecs C}} m_{\text{vecs C}})^2 + (w_{\text{machs C}} m_{\text{machs C}})^2 + (w_{\text{types C}} m_{\text{types C}})^2}{w_{\text{vecs C}}^2 + w_{\text{machs C}}^2 + w_{\text{types C}}^2}}.$$

This treats the three Containment metrics as components of a Euclidean space, with the overall Containment metric as the norm (magnitude) of this vector. The weights $w_{[\text{vecsC,machsC,typesC}]}$ are (optional) user-defined weights for relative strengths of the Containment family components.

3.4 Topology Family

Certain graph theoretic properties (i.e., connectivity, cycles, and depth) of an attack graph reflect how graph relationships enable network penetration. The Topology family measures enterprise network risk in terms of these properties, at the level of security protection domains.

The following subsections describe each of the individual metrics within the Topology family, i.e., Connectivity (Sect. 3.4.1), Cycles (Sect. 3.4.2), and Depth (Sect. 3.4.3). In Sect. 3.4.4, we describe how we combine these individual metrics into an overall metric score for the Topology family.

3.4.1 Connectivity Metric

The *Connectivity* metric is the number of weakly connected components in the domain-level attack graph, relative to the best (most secure) and worst (least secure) cases possible, on the scale of $[0,10]$. As shown in Fig. 10, the intuition is that it is better to have an attack graph that is disconnected parts versus a connected whole.

To map the Connectivity metric to the standard $[0,10]$ scale, we need the largest and smallest possible values for weak connectivity (at the protection domain level). This is shown in Fig. 11. The worst case (least secure) is a single weakly connected component. The best case (most secure) is completely disconnected, i.e., d weakly connected components for d domains. These ranges of possible numbers of components need to be mapped to the $[0,10]$ scale, consistent with the definition of zero as best case (most secure) and ten as best case (least secure).

As suggested by Fig. 12, to map to the $[0,10]$ scale, we need to define a function that linearly maps the best case (d components) to the number zero (most secure), and the worst case (one component) to the number ten (least secure). This function is the following sequence of linear transformations:

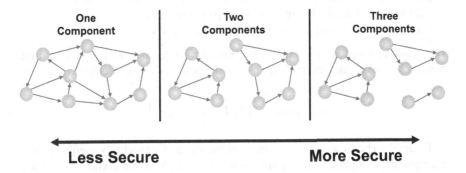

Fig. 10 Motivation for Connectivity metric

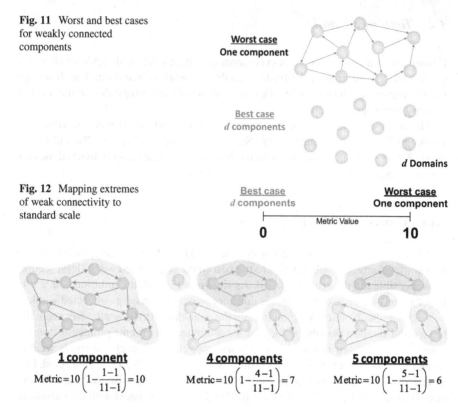

Fig. 11 Worst and best cases for weakly connected components

Fig. 12 Mapping extremes of weak connectivity to standard scale

1 component
$$\mathrm{Metric} = 10\left(1 - \frac{1-1}{11-1}\right) = 10$$

4 components
$$\mathrm{Metric} = 10\left(1 - \frac{4-1}{11-1}\right) = 7$$

5 components
$$\mathrm{Metric} = 10\left(1 - \frac{5-1}{11-1}\right) = 6$$

Fig. 13 Example Connectivity metric scores

1. Subtract the number of (weakly) connected components w_{weak} by unity, shifting them to the left by one
2. Divide by the range $d - 1$, normalizing the values to [0,1] (worst to best)
3. Multiply by negative unity, reversing the order to [-1,0] (best to worst)
4. Add unity, shifting to the right by one to [0,1] (best to worst)
5. Multiply by 10, yielding the scale [0,10] (best to worst)

The resulting transformation maps the best case (d components) to zero and the worst case (one component) to 10. This yields the Connectivity metric $m_{\mathrm{connectivity}}$:

$$m_{\mathrm{connectivity}} = 10\left(1 - \frac{w_{\mathrm{weak}} - 1}{d - 1}\right).$$

Figure 13 shows an example computation of the Connectivity metric. In this example, there are three attack graphs, shown at the protection-domain level. Each attack graph has the same set of domains, but different sets of domain-to-domain edges, resulting in different numbers of weakly connected components.

Fig. 14 Motivation for
Cycles metric

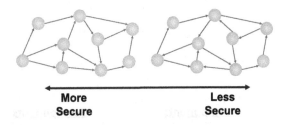

As shown in this example, an attack graph comprised of a single weakly connected component has the highest (riskiest) Connectivity score. The Connectivity
score decreases (is less risky) as the number of weakly connected components
increases.

3.4.2 Cycles Metric

The *Cycles* metric is the number of strongly connected components in the domain-
level attack graph, relative to the best (most secure) and worst (least secure) cases
possible, on the scale of [0,10]. As shown in Fig. 14, the intuition is that for a
(weakly) connected attack graph, it is better to avoid cycles within it (i.e., strongly
connected components).

Comparing the two attack graphs in Fig. 14, they both have the same number
of domains and domain-to-domain edges, and each graph has a single weakly
connected component. However, the upper graph is more secure in the sense that
all edges generally flow from left to right, so that attacker reachability is limited to
that directional flow. On the other hand, the lower graph is less secure because the
flow is cyclic. In fact, each domain is reachable from all other domains (i.e., cycle
connecting all domains).

To map the Cycles metric to the [0,10] scale, we need the largest and smallest
possible values for strong connectivity (at the protection domain level). The
extremes for strong connectivity are the same as for weak connectivity in Fig. 11.
That is, the worst case is a single strongly connected component, and the best case is
d strongly connected components for d domains. As before, these ranges of possible
numbers of components need to be mapped to the [0,10] scale, consistent with the
definition of zero as best case (most secure) and 10 as best case (least secure). Thus,
for computing the Cycles metric, we apply the same formulas as for computing the
Connectivity metric $m_{\text{connectivity}}$. The difference is that we count strongly connected
components w_{strong} (attack sub-graphs that are all reachable from each other), versus
weakly connected components w_{weak} as for $m_{\text{connectivity}}$. We thus have the Cycles
metric m_{cycles}:

$$m_{\text{cycles}} = 10 \left(1 - \frac{w_{\text{strong}} - 1}{d - 1} \right).$$

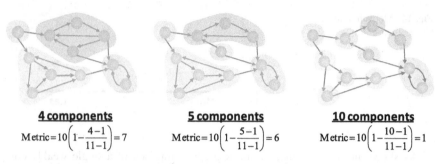

4 components

$$\text{Metric} = 10\left(1 - \frac{4-1}{11-1}\right) = 7$$

5 components

$$\text{Metric} = 10\left(1 - \frac{5-1}{11-1}\right) = 6$$

10 components

$$\text{Metric} = 10\left(1 - \frac{10-1}{11-1}\right) = 1$$

Fig. 15 Example Cycles metric scores

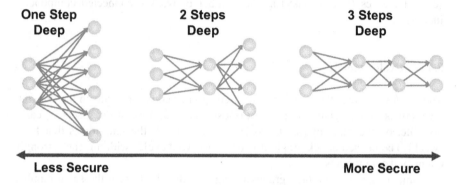

Fig. 16 Motivation for Depth metric

Figure 15 shows an example computation of the Cycles metric. In this example, there are three attack graphs, shown at the protection domain level. Each attack graph has the same set of domains, but different sets of domain-to-domain edges, resulting in different numbers of strongly connected components. As shown in the example, an attack graph with fewer components (cyclic reachability within each component) has higher (riskier) Cycles score. The Cycles score decreases (is less risky) as the number of strongly connected components increases.

3.4.3 Depth Metric

The *Depth* metric is the length of the maximum shortest path in the domain-level attack graph, relative to the best (most secure) and worst (least secure) cases possible, on the scale of $[0,10]$. In particular, this is the maximum shortest path over all possible attack graph vertex pairs, also known as the graph diameter. As shown in Fig. 16, the intuition is that it is better to have attack graph that is deeper versus shallower, i.e., requiring more attack steps to penetrate the entire network.

Comparing the attack graphs in Fig. 16, they all have the same number of protection domains (graph nodes). In addition, each graph has a single weakly

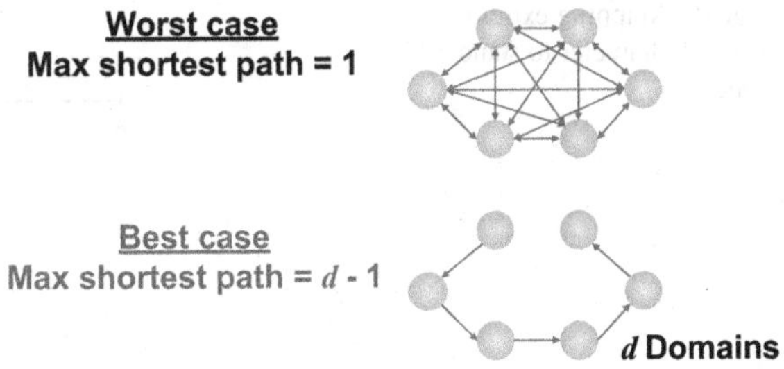

Fig. 17 Worst and best cases for graph diameter

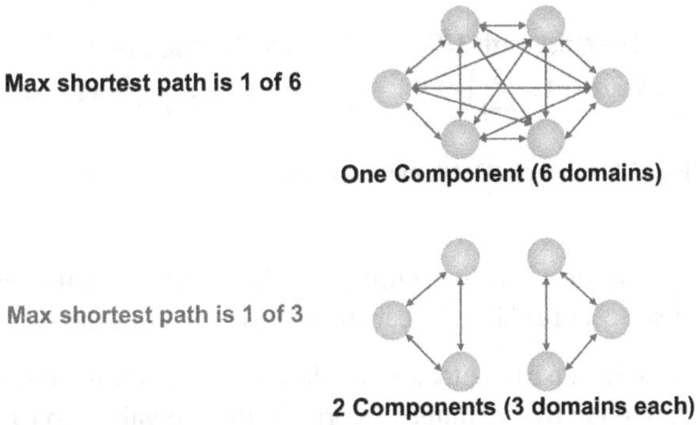

Worst case
Max shortest path = 1

Best case
Max shortest path = d - 1

d **Domains**

Fig. 18 Depth is relative to the size of connected components

Max shortest path is 1 of 6

One Component (6 domains)

Max shortest path is 1 of 3

2 Components (3 domains each)

connected component, and the maximum possible number of strongly connected components. However, the graph on the left side is less secure, in the sense that all domains are reachable in one attack step. On the other hand, the other graphs are more secure in the sense that more attack steps are needed before all domains are reached.

To map the Depth metric to the [0,10] scale, we need the largest and smallest possible values for the attack graph diameter (at the protection-domain level). This is shown in Fig. 17. The worst case (least secure) is a diameter (maximum shortest path) of one. The best case (most secure) is a diameter that is one less than the number of domains d. These ranges of possible diameters need to be mapped to the [0,10] scale, consistent with the definition of zero as best case (most secure) and ten as best case (least secure).

As shown in Fig. 18, the Depth metric needs to consider the potential impact of connectivity on graph diameter. In particular, if a graph is not (weakly) connected, then the graph diameter applies to each (weakly) connected component separately.

For example, the upper attack graph in Fig. 18 has a single connected component, while the lower attack graph has two connected components. In each case, the graph diameter is one. However, a diameter of one is a different relative score compared to the maximum possible of five (upper graph) versus three (lower graph). We must compute diameter for each connected component, map to standard scale, then combine scores for each component according to relative component size.

As suggested by Fig. 19, we need a function that linearly maps the best case (diameter of one less than the full size c of the domain-level component) to the

Fig. 19 Mapping extremes
of graph diameter to standard
scale

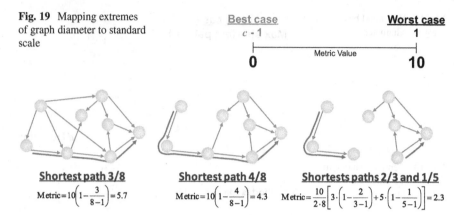

Fig. 20 Example Depth metric scores

number zero (most secure), and the worst case (diameter of one) to the number ten
(least secure). This linear transformation does the following:

1. Shift the diameter s to the left by one (subtract unity)
2. Divide by the range c, normalizing the values to [0,1] (worst to best)
3. Multiply by negative unity, reversing the order to [-1,0] (best to worst)
4. Add unity, shifting to the right by one to [0,1] (best to worst)
5. Multiply by 10, yielding the scale [0,10] (best to worst)

The resulting transformation maps the best case (diameter $c - 1$ for component size
c) to zero and the worst case (diameter one) to ten. This needs to be done for all
n connected components of the domain-level attack graph, for d domains, with the
diameter s_i for component i having size c_i. This yields the Depth metric m_{depth}:

$$m_{\text{depth}} = \frac{10}{nd} \sum_{i}^{n} c_i \left(1 - \frac{s_i - 1}{c_i} \right).$$

Figure 20 shows an example computation of the Depth metric. In this example,
there are three attack graphs, shown at the protection domain level. As shown
in the example, an attack graph with larger diameter(s) relative to its connected
component(s) has a lower (less risky) Depth score.

3.4.4 Metric for Topology Family

The overall metric for the Topology family m_{topology} is then the weighted Euclidean
norm of the Topology metric components:

$$m_{\text{topology}} = \sqrt{\frac{\left(w_{\text{connectivity}} \; m_{\text{connectivity}}\right)^2 + \left(w_{\text{cycles}} \; m_{\text{cycles}}\right)^2 + \left(w_{\text{depth}} \; m_{\text{depth}}\right)^2}{w_{\text{connectivity}}^2 + w_{\text{cycles}}^2 + w_{\text{depth}}^2}}.$$

This treats the three Topology metrics as components of a Euclidean space, with the overall Topology metric as the norm (magnitude) of this vector. The weights $w_{\text{[connectivity,cycles,depth]}}$ are (optional) user-defined weights for relative strengths of the Topology family components.

4 Metrics Visualization

We visualize our enterprise network security risk metrics in a dashboard for tracking and analyzing metrics values over time. The dashboard design presents the overall enterprise risk metric as the primary view, with drilldown into the details of the component metrics families.

Figure 21 shows the initial screen for the metrics dashboard visualization. In this view, the quick look for Overall is pressed; this causes the overall metric to be highlighted in the timeline (the individual families are diminished). The dashboard shows the initial and most recent date/time for the selected timeline. The overall and family quick looks show current (most recent) values, and changes with respect to the initial values. The quick looks also show how the current values compare to the threshold acceptable value. They also show the relative weights for each metrics family.

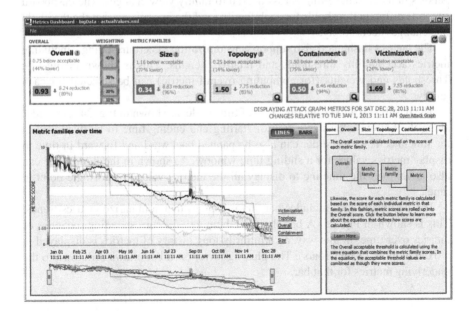

Fig. 21 Overall timeline for metrics dashboard

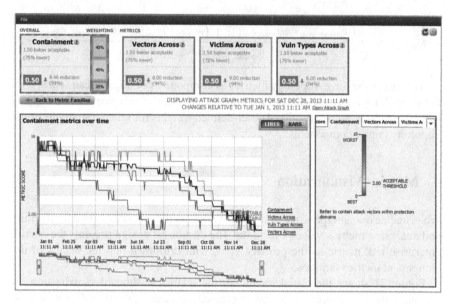

Fig. 22 Dashboard details for selected metrics family (Containment)

In Fig. 21, clicking on a magnifying glass on one of the family quick looks causes the display to show the details for the selected family. This is shown in Fig. 22, for the Containment family. The quick looks and timeline now show the overall family metric, as well as the individual metrics within the family. The selected time range persists in its current setting across overall to family view changes. The dashboard supports different thresholds for each family (and the overall), so that the threshold line changes accordingly.

The metrics dashboard also supports customization of certain settings, including metrics acceptability thresholds and relative weights. This is shown in Fig. 23. Thresholds and weights (for computing overall metric) can be selected for each family.

The dashboard allows the selection of time scale, as shown in Fig. 24. The slider along the bottom allows selection of starting and ending time to be displayed in the timeline. The time slider can also be panned backward and forward in time to display metrics values for a sliding time window. As shown in the figure, one can also hover over the timeline to display all the metrics values for a single point in time.

The dashboard also includes bar chart displays that summarize metrics trends. This is shown in Fig. 25. A bar chart is a binning of a corresponding sequence of metrics over time. In this way, an arbitrarily long history of metrics is displayed in a fixed number of bins (bars). The plus sign over each bar allows drilldown to the underlying metrics for that bar.

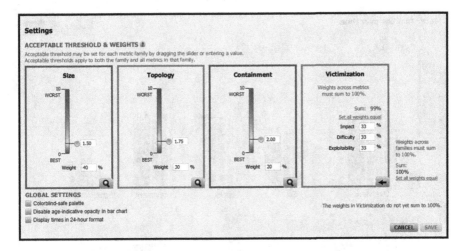

Fig. 23 Dashboard user-adjustable settings

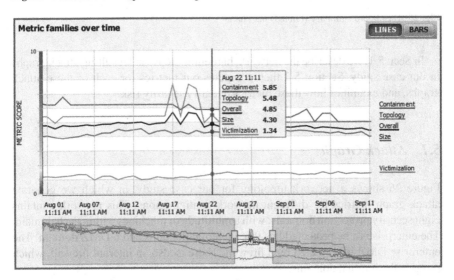

Fig. 24 Dashboard selection of time scale

5 Case Study

As a case study of our enterprise network security risk metrics, we consider a sequence of attack graphs representing the exposed vulnerabilities for a network, for a sequence of network hardening operations (software patches and firewall rule changes). We apply our metrics to track changes in enterprise risk over time.

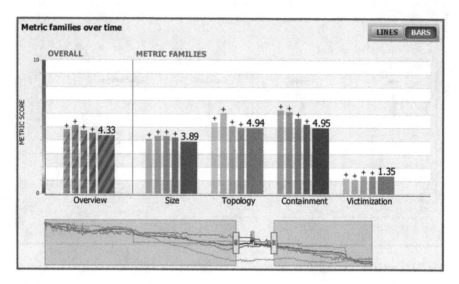

Fig. 25 Dashboard summary (binned) bar charts

In Sect. 5.1, we describe the network, hardening steps, and resulting attack graphs in our case study. Section 5.2 then computes our metrics for each of these attack graphs, and examines how these metrics quantify security risk.

5.1 Attack Graphs

Figure 26 shows a network topology for our case study, in which we generate attack graph metrics for different network configurations. This network contains eight security protection domains, with a multitude of machines within each domain. The enterprise to be protected has three internal domains and a DMZ domain. The enterprise DMZ is protected by a firewall. There is also an internal firewall, which protects the internal domains.

The enterprise allows some access from a partner organization, which has four domains. The primary defensive goal is to protect the internal domains against vulnerable exposures from either the partner domains or the DMZ.

In this case study, a Cauldron attack graph is generated for a baseline network configuration. The attack graph analysis identifies the critical exposures of vulnerable machines across domains. Mapping of vulnerable exposures to corresponding firewall rules leads to tightened policy based on mission requirements, which eliminate many of the vulnerable exposures.

Subsequent analysis indicates that the remaining exposed vulnerabilities are all among the internal enterprise domains. In that case, software patches are applied to

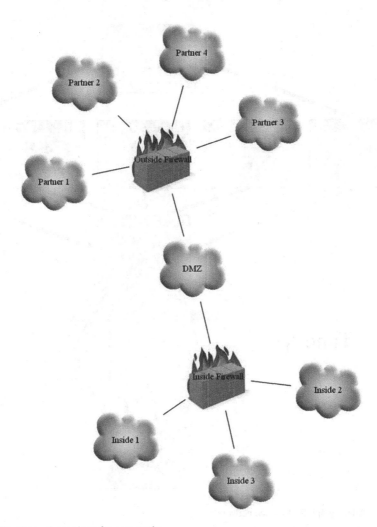

Fig. 26 Network topology for case study

remove the vulnerabilities, so that additional firewall blocking within the internal network is not needed to reduce risk.

Figure 27 shows the attack graph for the baseline network configuration, before any firewall rule changes or software patches have been applied. This attack graph shows that there are exposed vulnerabilities from the partner protection domains into the internal network, i.e., to the *Inside 3* domain. There are also exposed vulnerabilities from *Partner 4* to *DMZ*, and from *DMZ* to *Inside 3*.

An examination of the firewalls for rules permitting access into *Inside 3* reveals that there is a rule in both firewalls that allow access to all ports of certain machines. These machines are web servers that need to be accessed by the partners. However,

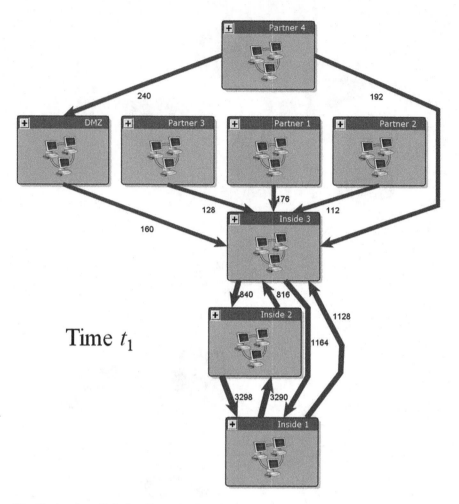

Fig. 27 Attack graph for baseline network

the vulnerabilities are actually on ports other than the HTTP port (80) needed by the mission. We therefore change the firewalls to allow access to port 80 only on these *Inside 3* machines. Figure 28 shows the resulting attack graph.

Figure 28 shows that there are still exposed vulnerabilities from *Partner 4* to *DMZ*. Examining the rules on the outside firewall for rules permitting access into *DMZ*, we see that there is a rule that allows access to all ports of the web servers in the *DMZ*. Again, the vulnerabilities are actually on ports other than the HTTP port (80) needed by the mission. We therefore change the outside firewall to allow access to port 80 only on these DMZ machines. No rule change is needed for the inside firewall, since it does not filter traffic from *Partner 4* to *DMZ*. Figure 29 shows the resulting attack graph.

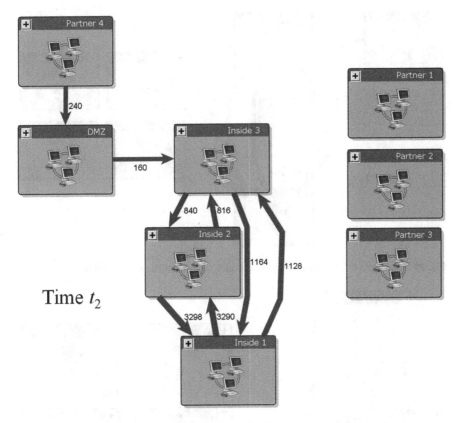

Fig. 28 Attack graph for restricting access to port 80 only from partners to *Inside 3*

Figure 29 shows there are still exposed vulnerabilities from *DMZ* to *Inside 3*. Examining the rules on the inside firewall, we see that there is a rule that allows access to all ports of web servers in *Inside 3*. Yet again, the vulnerabilities are on ports other than the HTTP port (80) needed by the mission. We therefore change the inside firewall to allow access to port 80 only on these *Inside 3* machines. No rule change is needed for the outside firewall, since it does not filter traffic from *DMZ* to *Inside 3*. Figure 30 shows the resulting attack graph.

Figure 30 shows that there are still exposed vulnerabilities among the inside protection domains. Under the assumption that further restriction of access within the inside domains will affect the mission, we consider the possibility of applying software patches.

Figure 31 shows the network vulnerabilities ranked (in Cauldron) by frequency of across-domain exposure for the attack graph in Fig. 30. This shows that two vulnerabilities are actually responsible for a large portion of the exposure instances. Figure 32 shows the resulting attack graph after all instances of those two vulnerabilities are patched.

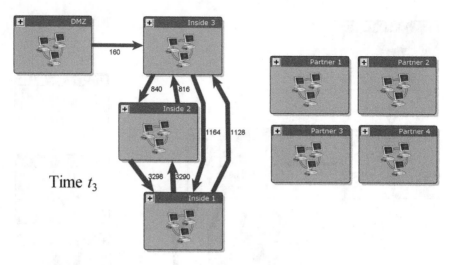

Fig. 29 Attack graph for restricting access to port 80 only from *Partner 4* to *DMZ*

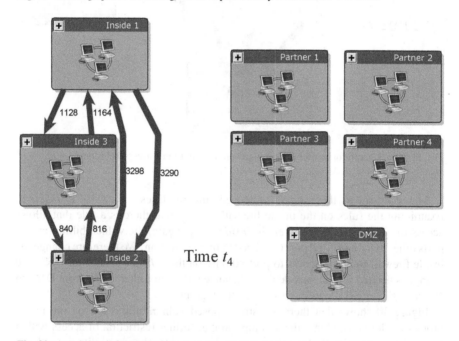

Fig. 30 Attack graph for restricting access to port 80 only from *DMZ* to *Inside 3*

In the next section, we compute metrics for each of these attack graph instances (Figs. 27, 28, 29, 30, and 31). Each attack graph represents the vulnerability exposures across the network at a given point in time, as steps were taken to incrementally reduce security risk (Fig. 33).

Vulnerability	CVSS Vector	CVSS Score	Hosts	Connections	Name	Summary	Description	Include
nessus.10940	No CVSS	-1	141	5140	Windows Te...	The remote ...	Synopsis :\n...	
nessus.42871	CVSS2#AV:...	5	140	5081	McAfee Com...	A remote ag...	Synopsis :\n...	
nessus.18405	CVSS2#AV:...	5.1	3	92	Microsoft Wi...	It may be po...	Synopsis :\n...	✓
nessus.11213	CVSS2#AV:...	4.3	1	59	HTTP TRACE...	Debugging f...	Synopsis :\n...	✓
nessus.11042	CVSS2#AV:...	4.3	1	59	Apache Tom...	The remote ...	Synopsis :\n...	✓
nessus.11041	CVSS2#AV:...	4.3	1	59	Apache Tom...	The remote ...	Synopsis :\n...	✓
nessus.10297	CVSS2#AV:...	5	1	46	Web Server ...	The remote ...	Synopsis :\n...	✓
nessus.25702	CVSS2#AV:...	7.6	1	0	McAfee Com...	The remote ...	Synopsis :\n...	✓

Fig. 31 Two vulnerabilities responsible for most risk exposures

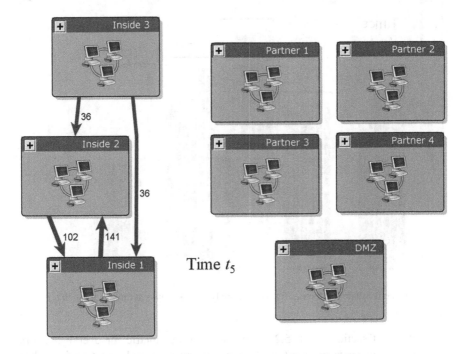

Fig. 32 Attack graph for the patching of two frequently exposed vulnerabilities

5.2 Security Risk Metrics

We now compute security risk metrics for the attack graphs in our case study (described in the previous section). By tracking these metrics over time, we assess the effectiveness of the network hardening measures taken at each step. For each attack graph representing the state of network security risk at time t_i, we compute the full suite of metrics (overall risk metric, four family-level metrics, and 11 individual metrics) for time t_i. We then plot these metrics values over time, at user-selected levels of detail. All metrics are calibrated from zero (least risk) to ten (most risk).

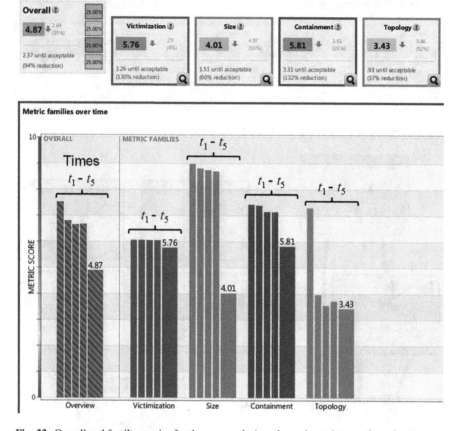

Fig. 33 Overall and family metrics for the case study (attack graphs at times t_1 through t_5)

In the next section (Sect. 5.2.1), we compute our metric for overall network risk for each instance in time (attack graph) in our case study. Section 5.2.2 then examines each of the family-level metrics in more detail.

5.2.1 Metric for Overall Network Risk

Figure 33 shows the initial metrics dashboard view for this case study. Because of the relatively small number of time values (five), the dashboard shows a bar chart rather than a line chart. The top row of the display is a quick view showing the current (most recent) values for the overall metric score and each of the four family-level scores. The left side of the main display shows scores for the overall network risk metric (for times t_1 through t_5). To the right are the scores (t_1 through t_5) for each of the metric families.

The overall risk score generally gets lower (at one point very slightly increasing), from an initial value of about 7.5 down to a final value of 4.87 (on the [0,10] scale). The family-level metrics follow this general trend, though with some differences.

The Victimization family metric is unchanged as a result of the firewall rule changes (times $t_1 - t_4$), decreasing only when vulnerability patches are applied at time t_5. This is consistent with the fact that the Victimization metrics depend on the state of endpoint hosts and their services/vulnerabilities, independent of attack reachability from other hosts. In that sense, the Victimization metrics are not actually based on attack graph analysis. Instead, they are summary statistics that one might find in more traditional vulnerability analysis (rather than TVA).

The metric for the Size family progressively decreases for each change in the network attack graph. The changes are relatively small for times $t_1 - t_4$, then there is a strong decrease for time t_5. The application of vulnerability patches at time t_5 causes the relatively large reduction in attack graph size, e.g., through the reduction of within-domain implicit attack vectors.

There is a similar pattern for the Containment metric, i.e., the number of vulnerabilities exposed across protection domains is significantly reduced (versus earlier network changes that do disconnect the attack graph, but only through relatively few across-domain vulnerabilities). On the other hand, the sharp drop in the Topology metric between t_1 and t_2 reflects the greater degree of topological changes (e.g., number of components increasing from one to four) between those times.

5.2.2 Family-Level Metrics

This section examines the metrics families for the five attack graphs in this case study. This includes the Victimization family (Sect. 5.2.2.1), the Size family (Sect. 5.2.2.2), the Containment family (Sect. 5.2.2.3), and the Topology family (Sect. 5.2.2.4). We show the individual metrics scores in each family, and how they combine into an overall metric for the family itself.

Victimization Family

Figure 34 shows the metrics within the Victimization family for the times $t_1 - t_5$. In this dashboard view, a user-defined threshold line of acceptable metric value (of 2.5 out of 10) is visible. The Existence metric is nearly constant just above the acceptable threshold for times $t_1 - t_4$, and then drops to nearly zero for time t_1. This reflects the number of vulnerable ports dropping to a relatively negligible number.

In Fig. 34, the Impact metric is low for times $t_1 - t_4$, then increases significantly for the last attack graph at t_5. This indicates that the patched vulnerabilities have relatively low impact (i.e., the remaining ones have higher impact). The Exploitability metric has the opposite trend; it is high for times $t_1 - t_4$, and then

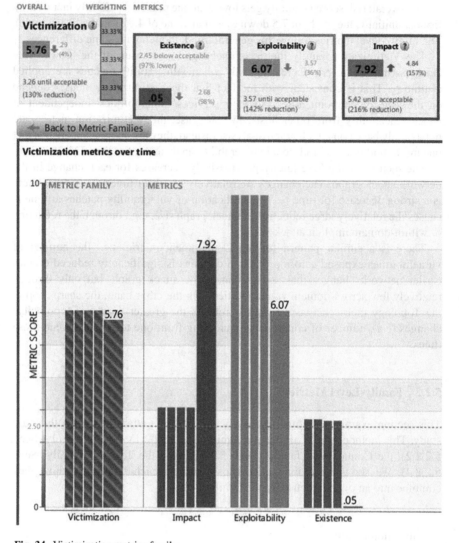

Fig. 34 Victimization metrics family

drops for t_5. This indicates that the patched vulnerabilities have relatively high exploitability (i.e., the remaining ones have lower exploitability).

The overall Victimization family metric changes little for these attack graphs. This is a result of the opposing trends for Impact versus Exploitability and Existence.

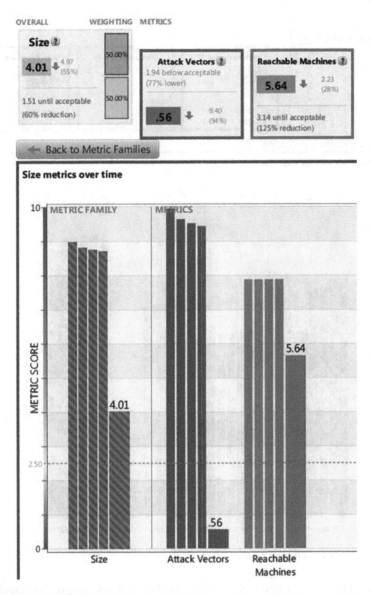

Fig. 35 Size metrics family

Size Family

Figure 35 shows the Size family for the times $t_1 - t_5$. The Attack Vectors metric decreases slightly for $t_1 - t_4$, and then sharply decreases to nearly zero for time t_5. This is consistent with the decrease from tens of thousands of across-domainattack

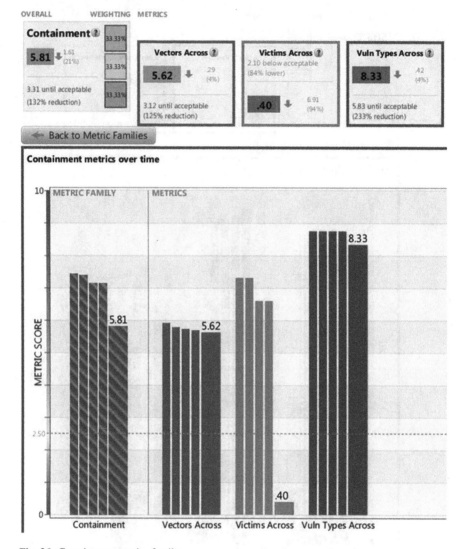

Fig. 36 Containment metrics family

vectors (Fig. 30) to a few hundred (Fig. 32) in the attack graphs. The number of attacker reachable machines is unchanged, until patches are applied that remove some of them.

Containment Family

Figure 36 shows the Containment family for the times $t_1 - t_5$. The Victims Across metric decreases slightly for the times $t_1 - t_4$, and then sharply decreases for time t_5.

This measures victim machines across domains, versus the Reachable Machines metric (Size family), which measures all reachable in the attack graph.

Similarly, the Vectors Across metric measures relative numbers of attack vectors across protection domains, versus the Attack Vectors (Size family), which measures all attack vectors (within and across domains). The Vulnerability Types Across measures distinct vulnerability types that are exposed across domains. In this case, it only changes for the last attack graph, since applied patches removed some vulnerability types.

Topology Family

Figure 37 shows the Topology family for the times $t_1 - t_5$. The Connectivity metric decreases from the highest possible risk (10) to nearly the threshold of acceptance (2.5). This reflects the subsequent decomposition of the attack graph into isolated components as hardening measures are applied.

The Cycles metric is relatively low, but remains unchanged except for the last attack graph at time t_5. This indicates that there are relatively few cycles in the attack graph, i.e., it has generally unidirectional flow.

The Depth metric is high for the baseline network at time t_1, then decreases to the threshold value for the first hardened attack graph at time t_2. This is because the direct access from *Partner 4* to *Inside 3* is removed, increasing the attack graph depth. In subsequent attack graphs (times), the Depth metric decreases as the attack graph has fewer steps.

6 Related Work

Cybersecurity metrics have been proposed based on a wide range of criteria, including intrusion detection, security policy, security incidents, game theory, dependability theory, and statistical methods [11–13]. There are many similarities between measuring cyber risk, cyber resilience [14–16], and cyber situational awareness [17]; particularly relevant current research at The MITRE Corporation seeks to measure the expected effectiveness of cyber resiliency.

Security metrics standardization efforts such as CVSS [9] and the NIST guidelines for security metrics [18] consider the relative severity of individual vulnerabilities in isolation, and do not consider the overall impact of combined vulnerabilities.

A number of proposed security metrics employ attack graph models, including those based on statistical properties of graph paths [19, 20], distances between attack graphs [21], percentage of compromised hosts [22], the weakest adversary required to compromise a network [23], attack success likelihood [24, 25], resilience to zero-day attacks [26], and scores along the dimensions of vulnerability, exploitability, and attackability [27]. Attack graph metrics have been applied for intrusion alert

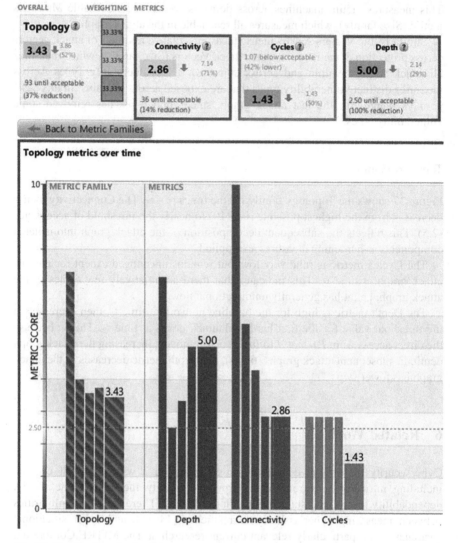

Fig. 37 Topology metrics family

correlation [28] and prioritization [29]. Aspects of our attack graph metrics are previously described [30, 31].

7 Summary and Conclusions

This chapter describes a suite of metrics for measuring enterprise cybersecurity risk. These metrics measure risk based on a comprehensive network-wide model of multi-step attack vulnerability. Our metrics span different complementary dimensions of enterprise security, including elements of the CVSS standard. We provide rich interactive visualizations of multiple metrics, including timelines over multiple temporal scales, to understand how network security evolves over time.

We group our metrics into families, and combine individual scores into overall metric scores at the family level. We then combine family metric scores into an overall metric score for the network. We display these metrics (at the individual, family, and overall levels) in interactive visualizations, showing multiple metrics trends over time at user-selected temporal resolutions.

Our attack graph metrics suite has a number of distinct advantages. It incorporates a straightforward model with clear semantics, which helps lower barriers for acceptance. The grouping of metrics into families and an overall score helps reduce the cognitive burden of dealing with multiple scores. Experimental results suggest that our metrics are consistent with intuitive notions of attack risk across a network.

Acknowledgments The work of Steven Noel was funded in part by the MITRE Innovation Program (MIP) project *CyGraph: Graph-Based Analytics and Visualization for Cybersecurity* (project number EPF-14-00341), with George Roelke as MIP Cybersecurity Innovation Area Lead. The work of Sushil Jajodia was supported in part by the Army Research Office under grant numbers W911NF-13-1-0421 and W911NF-15-1-0576, by the Office of Naval Research under grant number N00014-15-1-2007, and by the National Science Foundation under grant number IIP-1266147.

References

1. S. Noel, E. Harley, K.H. Tam, M. Limiero, M. Share, CyGraph: graph-based analytics and visualization for cybersecurity, in *Cognitive Computing: Theory and Applications*, Handbook of Statistics, vol. 35, ed. by V. Raghavan, V. Gudivada, V. Govindaraju, C.R. Rao (Elsevier, New York, 2016)
2. S. Noel, E. Harley, K.H. Tam, G. Gyor, Big-data architecture for cyber attack graphs: representing security relationships in NoSQL Graph Databases, in *IEEE Symposium on Technologies for Homeland Security*, Boston, Massachusetts, April, 2015
3. Skybox Security, https://www.skyboxsecurity.com/
4. RedSeal Cybersecurity Analytics Platform, https://www.redseal.net/
5. M. Artz, *NetSPA: A Network Security Planning Architecture*, master's thesis, Massachusetts Institute of Technology (2002)
6. S. Jajodia, S. Noel, P. Kalapa, M. Albanese, J. Williams, Cauldron: mission-centric cyber situational awareness with defense in depth, in *30th Military Communications Conference (MILCOM)*, November 2011
7. X. Ou, W. Boyer, M. McQueen, A scalable approach to attack graph generation, in *13th ACM Conference on Computer and Communications Security*, New York, NY (2006)
8. S. Jajodia, S. Noel, Topological vulnerability analysis, in *Cyber Situational Awareness: Issues and Research, Advances in Information Security*, vol. 46, ed. by S. Jajodia, P. Liu, V. Swarup, C. Wang (Springer, Heidelberg, 2010)

9. NIST, NVD Common Vulnerability Scoring System (CVSS), http://nvd.nist.gov/cvss.cfm
10. P. Manadhata, *An Attack Surface Metric*, doctoral dissertation, Carnegie Mellon University, CMU-CS-08-152 (2008)
11. A. Jaquith, *Security Metrics: Replacing Fear, Uncertainty, and Doubt* (Addison-Wesley Professional, Reading, MA, 2007)
12. V. Verendel, Quantified security is a weak hypothesis: a critical survey of results and assumptions, in *ACM New Security Paradigms Workshop* (2009)
13. M. Pendleton, R. Garcia-Lebron, J.-H. Cho, S. Xu, A survey on systems security metrics. ACM Comput. Surv. **49**(4), 62 (2017)
14. D. Bodeau, R. Graubart, *Cyber Resilience Metrics: Key Observations*, The MITRE Corporation, https://www.mitre.org/sites/default/files/publications/pr-16-0779-cyber-resilience-metrics-key-observations.pdf (2016)
15. S. Musman, S. Agbolosu-Amison, *A Measurable Definition of Resiliency Using "Mission Risk" as a Metric*, The MITRE Corporation, https://www.mitre.org/sites/default/files/publications/resiliency-mission-risk-14-0500.pdf (2014)
16. D. Bodeau, R. Graubart, L. LaPadula, P. Kertzner, A. Rosenthal, J. Brennan, *Cyber Resiliency Metrics*, The MITRE Corporation, https://registerdev1.mitre.org/sr/12_2226.pdf (2012)
17. S. Noel, W. Heinbockel, An overview of MITRE cyber situational awareness solutions, in *NATO Cyber Defence Situational Awareness Solutions Conference*, Bucharest, Romania, August, 2015
18. M. Swanson, N. Bartol, J. Sabato, J. Hash, J. Graffo, *Security Metrics Guide for Information Technology Systems*, NIST Technical Report 800-55, July 2003
19. C. Phillips, L.P. Swiler, A graph-based system for network vulnerability analysis, in *ACM Workshop on New Security Paradigms*, New York, NY, USA, 1998
20. N. Idika, B. Bhargava, Extending attack graph-based security metrics and aggregating their application. IEEE Trans. Dependable Secure Comput. **9**(1), 75–85 (2012)
21. G. Bopche, B. Mehtre, Graph similarity metrics for assessing temporal changes in attack surface of dynamic networks. Comput. Secur. **64**, 16–43 (2017)
22. R. Lippmann, K. Ingols, C. Scott, K. Piwowarski, K. Kratkiewicz, M. Artz, R. Cunningham, Validating and restoring defense in depth using attack graphs, in *IEEE Conference on Military Communications (MILCOM)* (2006)
23. J. Pamula, S. Jajodia, P. Ammann, V. Swarup, A weakest-adversary security metric for network configuration security analysis, in *2nd ACM Workshop on Quality of Protection* (2006)
24. S. Noel, S. Jajodia, L. Wang, A. Singhal, Measuring security risk of networks using attack graphs. Int. J. Next-Gener. Comput. **1**, 135–147 (2010)
25. Z. Huang, *Human-Centric Training and Assessment for Cyber Situation Awareness*, doctoral dissertation, University of Delaware, ProQuest 10014764 (2015)
26. L. Wang, S. Jajodia, A. Singhal, P. Cheng, S. Noel, k-Zero day safety: a network security metric for measuring the risk of unknown vulnerabilities. IEEE Trans. Dependable Secure Comput. **11**, 30–44 (2013)
27. M. Tupper, A.N. Zincir-Heywood, VEA-bility security metric: a network security analysis tool, in *3rd International Conference on Availability, Reliability and Security* (2008)
28. S. Noel, E. Robertson, S. Jajodia, Correlating intrusion events and building attack scenarios through attack graph distances, in *20th Annual Computer Security Applications Conference (ACSAC)*, Tucson, Arizona, December 2004
29. S. Noel, S. Jajodia, Attack graphs for sensor placement, alert prioritization, and attack response, in *Cyberspace Research Workshop, Air Force Cyberspace Symposium*, Shreveport, Louisiana, November 2007
30. S. Noel, Metrics suite for network attack graphs, in *65th Meeting of IFIP Working Group 10.4 on Dependable Computing and Fault Tolerance*, Sorrento, Italy, January 2014
31. S. Noel, S. Jajodia, Metrics suite for network attack graph analytics, in *9th Annual Cyber and Information Security Research Conference*, Oak Ridge National Laboratory, Tennessee, April 2014

A Novel Metric for Measuring Operational Effectiveness of a Cybersecurity Operations Center

Rajesh Ganesan, Ankit Shah, Sushil Jajodia, and Hasan Cam

Abstract Cybersecurity threats are on the rise with evermore digitization of the information that many day-to-day systems depend upon. The demand for cybersecurity analysts outpaces supply, which calls for optimal management of the analyst resource. In this chapter, a new notion of cybersecurity risk is defined, which arises when alerts from intrusion detection systems remain unanalyzed at the end of a work-shift. The above risk poses a security threat to the organization, which in turn impacts the operational effectiveness of the cybersecurity operations center (CSOC). The chapter considers four primary analyst resource parameters that influence risk. For a given risk threshold, the parameters include (1) number of analysts in a work-shift, and in turn within the organization, (2) expertise mix of analysts in a work-shift to investigate a wide range of alerts, (3) optimal sensor to analyst allocation, and (4) optimal scheduling of analysts that guarantees both number and expertise mix of analysts in every work-shift. The chapter presents a thorough treatment of risk and the role it plays in analyst resource management within a CSOC under varying alert generation rates from sensors. A simulation framework to measure risk under various model parameter settings is developed, which can also be used in conjunction with an optimization model to empirically validate the optimal settings of the above model parameters. The empirical results, sensitivity study, and validation study confirms the viability of the framework for determining the optimal management of the analyst resource that minimizes risk under the uncertainty of alert generation and model constraints.

R. Ganesan (✉) • A. Shah • S. Jajodia
Center for Secure Information Systems, George Mason University, Mail Stop 5B5, Fairfax, VA 22030-4422, USA
e-mail: rganesan@gmu.edu; ashah20@gmu.edu; jajodia@gmu.edu

H. Cam
Army Research Laboratory, 2800 Powder Mill Road, Adelphi, MD 20783-1138, USA
e-mail: hasan.cam.civ@mail.mil

© Springer International Publishing AG 2017
L. Wang et al., *Network Security Metrics*,
https://doi.org/10.1007/978-3-319-66505-4_8

1 Introduction

Sensors monitor the traffic flow in the network, and sensor data is analyzed by intrusion detection systems (IDSs) for malicious activities, which issues an alert when such an activity is detected. Several such alerts are received for further investigation by cyber security analysts at a Cyber Security Operations Center (CSOC) who is a service provider. An efficient CSOC requires that all intrusion alerts must be analyzed in a timely manner. The efficiency of a CSOC can be measured in terms of the number of unanalyzed alerts at the end of every work-shift (constitutes risk), which is a new notion of cybersecurity risk that is defined in this chapter. The chapter summarizes the main findings in [16, 17], that has focused on optimally scheduling the cybersecurity analysts and their allocations to sensors such that the total number of unanalyzed alerts that remain at the end of the shift is minimized. The goal of the CSOC is to minimize the above risk, and maintain the risk under a pre-determined threshold. In this chapter, the number of unanalyzed alerts at the end of every work-shift (risk) directly depends on four primary analyst resource parameters: (1) number of analysts in a work-shift, and in turn within the organization, (2) expertise mix of analysts in a work-shift to investigate a wide range of alerts, (3) optimal sensor to analyst allocation, and (4) optimal scheduling of analysts that guarantees both number and expertise mix of analysts in every work-shift. A CSOC has a limited number of regular analysts that are far fewer than the number of sensors being monitored, which calls for optimal management of the analyst resource. Also, it is required that the CSOC adapt to changing alert generation rates by hiring on-call analysts in order to maintain the risk under the pre-determined threshold in every shift. Furthermore, it is well-known that the CSOCs have been in existence since the Morris Internet Worm incident in 1988, but they are largely managed in an ad hoc way. Hence, the objective of this research is to develop a framework to study the influence of the above analyst resource parameters on the new notion of risk, and determine the optimal settings for the number of regular and on-call analysts in a work-shift, analyst's expertise mix levels in a work-shift, sensor to analyst allocation, and shift schedules for the analysts over a 14-day work-cycle such that the risk is maintained under the pre-determined threshold value for every work-shift of the CSOC. In what follows the current alert analysis process and the definition of the new notion of risk are presented next.

1.1 Current Alert Analysis Process

Alerts are generated and analyzed by cyber security analysts as shown in Fig. 1. In the current system, the number of analysts that report to work remains fixed, and sensors are pre-assigned to analysts. A 12 h shift cycle is used, and analysts work 6 days on 12 h shift and 1 day on 8 h shift, thus working a total of 80 h during a 2-week period. There is a very small overlap between shifts to handover any notes and the

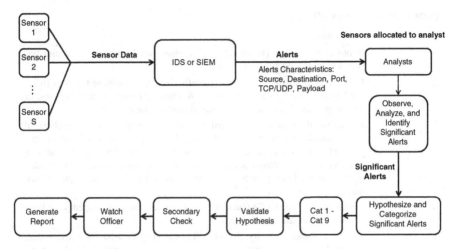

Fig. 1 Alert analysis process [17]

work terminal or workstation to the analyst from the following shift. The type and the number of sensors allocated to an analyst depend upon the experience level of the analysts. The experience level of an analyst further determines the amount of workload that they can handle in an operating shift. The workload for an analyst is captured in terms of the number of alerts/h that can be analyzed based on the average time taken to analyze an alert. In this chapter, three types of analysts are considered (senior L3, intermediate L2, and junior L1 level analysts), and their workload value is proportional to their level of expertise.

A cybersecurity analyst must do the following: (1) observe all alerts from the IDS such as SNORT or a Security Information and Event Management (SIEM) tool such as ArcSight [5], (2) thoroughly analyze the alerts that are identified as significant alerts that are pertinent to their pre-assigned sensors, and (3) hypothesize the severity of threat posed by a significant alert and categorize the significant alert under Category 1–9. The description of the categories are given in Table 1 [8]. If an alert is hypothesized as a very severe threat and categorized under Cat 1, 2, 4, or 7 (incidents) then the watch officer for the shift is alerted and a report is generated (see Fig. 1).

1.2 Definition of Risk

From an alert investigation point of view, there are two metrics that impact a cybersecurity organization—one of them is a quantity metric that measures the number of alerts thoroughly investigated among those generated, which highlights the capacity of the organization, and the other is the quality metric that measures the accuracy of investigation, which highlights the true/false positive and true/false negative rates of the alert investigation process. The scope of the chapter is focused

Table 1 Alert categories [8]

Category	Description
1	Root Level Intrusion (Incident): Unauthorized privileged access (administrative or root access) to a DoD system
2	User Level Intrusion (Incident): Unauthorized non-privileged access (user-level permissions) to a DoD system. Automated tools, targeted exploits, or self-propagating malicious logic may also attain these privileges
3	Unsuccessful Activity Attempted (Event): Attempt to gain unauthorized access to the system, which is defeated by normal defensive mechanisms. Attempt fails to gain access to the system (i.e., attacker attempts valid or potentially valid username and password combinations) and the activity cannot be characterized as exploratory scanning. Can include reporting of quarantined malicious code
4	Denial of Service (DOS) (Incident): Activity that impairs, impedes, or halts normal functionality of a system or network
5	Non-Compliance Activity (Event): This category is used for activity that, due to DoD actions (either configuration or usage) makes DoD systems potentially vulnerable (e.g., missing security patches, connections across security domains, installation of vulnerable applications, etc.). In all cases, this category is not used if an actual compromise has occurred. Information that fits this category is the result of non-compliant or improper configuration changes or handling by authorized users
6	Reconnaissance (Event): An activity (scan/probe) that seeks to identify a computer, an open port, an open service, or any combination for later exploit. This activity does not directly result in a compromise
7	Malicious Logic (Incident): Installation of malicious software (e.g., trojan, backdoor, virus, or worm)
8	Investigating (Event): Events that are potentially malicious or anomalous activity deemed suspicious and warrants, or is undergoing, further review. No event will be closed out as a Category 8. Category 8 will be re-categorized to appropriate Category 1–7 or 9 prior to closure
9	Explained Anomaly (Event): Events that are initially suspected as being malicious but after investigation are determined not to fit the criteria for any of the other categories (e.g., system malfunction or false positive)

on the first metric (quantity) of determining whether or not an organization has the capacity to analyze all the alerts and the significant alerts within them based on available resources, time constraints, manpower constraints, and shift scheduling constraints. The premise of the chapter is that an organization must have the capacity to investigate all the alerts generated in a work-shift or day, otherwise the unanalyzed alerts will pose a threat to the organization. In this chapter, a new and precise notion of risk is used, which is defined as the percentage of the significant alerts that were not thoroughly or properly analyzed. This insufficient analysis of alerts could happen due to the following reasons such as sub-optimal scheduling of analysts, not enough personnel to analyze, lack of time to analyze a significant alert, and/or not having the right mix of expertise in the shift in which the alert occurs. Risk can be stated as follows:

$$Risk\% = 100 - Alert\ Coverage\% \tag{1}$$

It is true that unless an alert is thoroughly analyzed, its category or severity is unknown. Also, the time taken to analyze an alert depends on its category or severity, whether or not it is a known or a new pattern of alert, and the expertise level of the analyst. Therefore, at the time of drawing an alert from the queue for investigation, since its category or severity is unknown, the time to analyze an alert in this chapter is based upon an average time from a probability distribution, which can be obtained from historical real world data. The total time needed to thoroughly analyze all the alerts and significant alerts can be compared to the total time available, which is based on the current capacity of the organization (number and expertise mix of analysts), their sensor-to-analyst allocation rules, and shift-schedules, in order to determine the % of significant alerts that would remain unanalyzed (risk). Such a risk metric could be used to initiate actions to build analyst capacity for the organization with optimal number of analysts, expertise mix in a work-shift, sensor-to-analyst allocation, and optimal shift schedules. Hence, the scope of the chapter is focused on capacity building for a cyber-defense organization through the optimal allocation and scheduling of its analysts, regardless of the type of alert (category or severity), using the notion that some alerts will need more time than the others. Several parameters are considered in this chapter to calculate the alert investigating capacity of the organization, which includes number of sensors, an average alert generation rate for the sensors, number of analysts, their expertise level, sensor-to-analyst allocation, analyst time to investigate an alert, and their work-shift schedule. The chapter assumes that all the alerts that were thoroughly investigated were also accurately categorized. It should be noted that as a second metric (quality), once a significant alert has been detected by thorough alert analysis, a different definition of risk can be used to measure the quality of work performed by capturing the true positive and false negative rates. Furthermore, the severity of the threat that an alert poses to the organization, and actions to mitigate the threat can be taken. However, such a definition of risk and the actions to mitigate are beyond the scope of this chapter and are mentioned as part of future work.

1.2.1 Risk as an Upper Bound

In the following section, the chapter explains that for the optimization model, risk is used as a constraint with an upper bound instead of being a direct objective of the optimization algorithm. In this research, risk is proportional to a combination of factors, including the number of analysts, their experience mix, analyst's shift and days-off scheduling, and their sensor assignment in a work shift. Hence, scheduling cybersecurity analysts is a critical part of cybersecurity defense. For the cybersecurity alert analysis process described above, it is imperative to have an efficient cybersecurity analyst scheduling system, which in turn will minimize risk. The requirements of such a system can be broadly described as follows. The cybersecurity analyst scheduling system,

Fig. 2 Risk vs available resource [17]

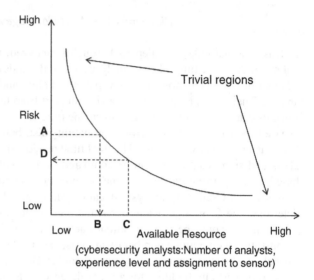

(cybersecurity analysts:Number of analysts, experience level and assignment to sensor)

1. Shall ensure that risks due to threats are maintained at the minimum,
2. Shall ensure that an optimal number of staff is available and are optimally allocated to sensors to meet the demand to analyze alerts,
3. Shall ensure that a right mix of analysts are staffed at any given point in time, and
4. Shall ensure that weekday, weekend, and holiday schedules are drawn such that it conforms to the working hours/leave policy of the organization.

The relationship between risk and available resource (cybersecurity analysts) can be understood from Fig. 2. The trivial regions are those where either there is too much resource (very low risk) or too little resource (very high risk) wherein any amount of optimal scheduling will not significantly affect the risk levels. Optimal scheduling gains importance only when there is just enough resource that must be managed well for reaching the lowest possible risk. Two types of models can be studied from Fig. 2. First, given a certain available cybersecurity analyst resource (i.e. number of analysts, experience mix, and sensor-to-analyst allocation), a *simulation* model can be constructed to evaluate the risk for a given significant alert generation rate. This is depicted from $C \rightarrow D$. However, several simulations will be needed to measure the risk associated with different combinations of the available cybersecurity analyst resource by varying the number of analysts, experience mix, and sensor-to-analyst allocation. Such simulations are computationally impractical to implement on a large-scale to determine the best sensor-to-analyst allocation and the right analyst expertise mix. The second model is an *optimization* model in which an optimal cybersecurity analyst schedule is obtained after determining the optimal number of analyst, right experience mix, and optimal sensor-to analyst allocation for a given upper bound on the risk level and for a given significant alert generation rate. This is depicted from $A \rightarrow B$ in Fig. 2. The output of the optimization model can then be used to generate the shift and days-off schedule for the analysts.

One of the main contributions is that the chapter presents a thorough treatment of risk and the role it plays in analyst resource allocation within a CSOC under varying alert generation rates from sensors. The chapter summarizes the risk related contributions in [16, 17]. A simulation framework to measure risk under various model parameter settings is developed, which can also be used in conjunction with an optimization model to empirically validate the outputs of the model. The risk minimization capability of the optimization model is a direct measure of the goodness of the analyst resource allocation system. It should be noted that the optimization algorithms are generic and is independent of the number of sensors, however, the algorithm's output adapts to the estimated workload from the varying alert traffic per sensor and the number of sensors in the system. The other contributions include a set of meta-principles that provide the general guidelines for developing and implementing an efficient CSOC.

The chapter is organized as follows. Section 2 presents the related literature on cybersecurity analyst resource allocation. In Sect. 3, the model parameters are presented. Section 4 presents the optimization, scheduling, and simulation framework in which risk is measured under different CSOC conditions. Section 5 presents the results from testing the above framework along with sensitivity study of the model parameters. Finally, in Sect. 6, the conclusions and future research directions are presented.

2 Related Literature

Intrusion detection has been studied for over three decades beginning with the pioneering works by Anderson [2] and Denning [10, 11]. Much of the work has focused on developing automated techniques for detecting malicious behavior [1, 12, 22, 29]. Some of the early research focused on misuse detection models (developing signatures of known attacks; any matched activity is flagged as an attack) or anomaly detection models (characterizing normal behaviors of all users and programs; any significant deviation from the normal profile is considered suspicious).

Alert correlation is an important topic and pertains to a collection of IDS or SIEM alerts [31]. Correlation is done by SIEM, or automatically by analyst tools, or manually by analysts. Alert correlation logic is built over the output from disparate log sources. Similarity based clustering or causal relationship based reasoning is often used for alert correlation, and uncertainty is captured via Bayesian networks. Yet, the task of alert correlation is made challenging by the ever changing threat environment and by the need for scalability to handle large complex coordinated attacks. For example, alert correlation can use various security events such as unusual port activities in firewall (malicious scanning), Apache server exploit, suspicious DNS requests, logs from web application firewall, threats recognized from antivirus, transmission of sensitive data in plain text, and resource access outside business hours to detect a potential threat. Correlation can capture a high level view of the attack activity on the target network without losing security-relevant information. The output of alert correlation is the grouping of alerts, which are then investigated [13] by analysts. A more detailed example of alert correlation can be found in [27].

Recently, there has been some work that has focused on the need to improve efficiency of cybersecurity analysts [9, 14, 35]. As the volume of alerts generated by intrusion detection sensors became overwhelming, a great deal of later research work focused on developing techniques (based on machine learning [28] or data mining [4], for example) for reducing false positives by developing automated alert reduction techniques. Indeed, there are open source [24] and commercially available Security Information and Event Management (SIEM) [5, 33, 35] tools that take the raw sensor data as input, aggregate and correlate them, and produce alerts that require remediation by cybersecurity analysts. Understanding the human and organizational problems faced by a CSOC has been studied in [6, 15]. Improving efficiency of analysts by building trust has been studied in [30]. The chapter differs from the above literature by focusing on the cybersecurity analysts who are viewed as a critical resource. It develops a generic optimization and simulation framework that provides the flexibility to optimally schedule the cybersecurity analysts, by splitting the workforce into two components—static and dynamic (on-call) workforce as presented in [16, 17].

The dynamic scheduling in this chapter in comparison with extensive work in the fields of reactive scheduling, real-time scheduling, online scheduling, dynamic scheduling for parallel machines and multi-agents, would apparently appear to be similar in terms of the overall goal where in scheduling decisions are done under uncertainty, however, dynamic scheduling in the cybersecurity field poses several new challenges and to our knowledge this is the first time where it has been applied to cyber security area. One of the first differences with current literature is the severity aspect of sub-optimal scheduling of cybersecurity analysts that has the potential for devastating consequences, ranging from an organization level to a national and world level, to their security, financial integrity, and economic stability. Unlike any other published literature on scheduling, the cybersecurity scheduling problem is unique in terms of the factors that affect its implementation, namely, the sensor deployment, alert generation rates, 24/7 work time, shift periods, occurrence of unexpected events affecting analysts' workload, broad scope of cybersecurity vulnerabilities and exploits, and analyst experience. Another important difference with existing scheduling literature is that the chapter's objective is to minimize risk whereas the literature is focused on minimizing cost or tardiness or completion time.

Some of the literature pertaining to dynamic scheduling include the work by [19], where the authors discuss a heuristic dynamic scheduler to generate long-term schedules in the field of network technicians with the objective to minimize cost. Examples of dynamic scheduling from freight handling, and airline fleet and crew scheduling are also geared toward reducing operational costs to improve customer satisfaction [21]. In comparison to the dynamic scheduling work in manufacturing, distribution, and supply chain management that uses multi-agents, the chapter's dynamic aspects are very different [26, 34]. For example, in the multi-agent environment, the coordination and communication mechanism is essential for autonomic decisions by the agents, whereas in cybersecurity the factors given earlier such as the broad scope of cybersecurity vulnerabilities and exploits, and analyst experience are critical in making dynamic scheduling decisions. In job-shop and parallel machine scheduling, a reinforcement learning based dynamic scheduler optimizes a cost function which is related to the weighted tardiness or completion time in the presence of uncertainty arising from future job arrivals [3, 23]. It is clear from the above that the practice of dynamic scheduling must be adapted to a new context of cybersecurity with the objective to minimize risk under several system and operational constraints, which is novel and complements existing literature.

3 Model Parameters

This section presents the details of the model parameters of the cybersecurity analyst resource allocation model, which is presented in the next section. In the following, the fixed input parameters, system-requirement parameters, decision parameters, and underlying assumptions of the resource allocation model are presented.

3.1 Fixed Parameters

Several input parameters are maintained fixed for the optimization model. The number of sensors, average alert generation rate from the sensors, which follows a Poisson or uniform distribution, and analyst characteristics are kept fixed during the execution of the optimization model. The analyst characteristics consists of the following components: analyst availability (binary indicator variable), analyst experience level, number of sensors allocated to an analyst, which depends on their experience, and time taken to analyze an alert for a given level of analyst experience. The chapter uses three levels of analyst experience as given below.

1. L3—senior analyst. L3 analysts are assigned 4–5 sensors and they and can handle on average 12 alerts per hour (5 min/alert).
2. L2—intermediate analyst. L2 analysts are assigned 2–3 sensors and they can handle on average 7–8 alerts per hour (8 min/alert).
3. L1—junior analyst. L1 analysts are assigned 1–2 sensors and they and can handle on average 5 alerts per hour (12 min/alert).

3.2 System-Requirement Parameters

The cybersecurity analyst allocation model must meet the following system requirements.

1. The system must minimize risk (maximize alert coverage by analysts). For the optimization model, an upper bound on risk is specified as a constraint.
2. Analyst utilization must exceed 95%, which is added as a constraint to the optimization model. This is computed based on the amount of time an analyst is idle during the shift. This allows the optimization algorithm to allocate enough sensors to analysts based on their experience level (L1, L2, or L3) and alert generation rates, such that they are all highly utilized.
3. The desired mix of expertise level among analysts for an organization must be specified such as 20–40% L1, 30–50% L2, and 30–40% L3 level analysts to facilitate training of juniors and providing career opportunities such as promotions within an organization. This will prevent the optimization model to pick all L3 level analysts who are the most efficient in examining the alerts.

3.3 Decision Parameters

The decision parameter of the optimization model is the sensor-to-analyst allocation that satisfies the system-requirement and adheres to the characteristics set by the fixed parameters of the model. The assignment can be envisioned as a matrix of 0's and 1's where the rows represent analyst identity and columns represent sensor identity. Also, '1' means that a sensor has been assigned to an analyst, and '0' otherwise. From this allocation matrix, the number of analysts at each level of expertise that are needed per day can be derived.

3.4 Model Assumptions

The assumptions of the optimization model are as follows.

1. All alerts that were thoroughly investigated were also accurately categorized. Hence, false positives and false negatives are not modeled in this chapter.
2. An analyst's average service time to investigate an alert can either remain fixed as given under the fixed parameters above or be allowed to change by drawing from a distribution such as Poisson or Uniform.
3. Analysts work in two 12-h shifts, 7AM–7PM and 7PM–7AM. However, the optimization model can be adapted to 8 h shifts as well.
4. Each analyst on regular (static) schedule works for 80 h in 2 weeks (6 days in 12-h shift and 1 day in 8-h shift)
5. At the end of the shift all analysts must complete the last alert that they are investigating even if there is a small spillover of their time into the next shift. This could result in analyst utilization to exceed 100%. However, no new alert will be taken up by an analyst once their shift time is completed.
6. When a group of analysts are allocated to a group of sensors by the optimization algorithm, the alerts generated by that group of sensors are arranged in a single

queue based on their arrival time-stamp, and the next available analyst within that group will draw the alerts from the queue based on a first-in-first-out rule.

7. Based on experience, an analyst spends, on average, about the same amount of time to investigate alerts from the different sensors that are allocated, which can be kept fixed or drawn from a probability distribution.

8. Analysts of different experience levels can be paired to work on a sensor.

9. Significant alerts are generated from a distribution such as Poisson or Uniform. The chapter uses an average alert generation rate, and on some days the alert rate will be above average and on others below average. The average number of alerts generated per sensor is kept equal and fixed throughout the day for all sensors. However, the model can be adapted easily to the situation where the average number of alerts generated per sensor is unequal but fixed throughout the day. It should be noted that as alert rates increase beyond the analyzing capacity of the work shift then the risk will also increase for that shift. For a dynamic alert generation rate that changes by the hour, a control-theoretic approach to optimization with future workload prediction is required, which is one of the future works of this research.

10. The optimization model is run for 24-h to determine the sensor-to-analyst allocation for that day. Simulation statistics on risk and analyst utilization are calculated at the end of the 24-h day.

11. Writing reports of incidents and events during shifts is considered as part of alert examining work, and the average time to examine the alert includes the time to write the report.

12. The time taken to analyze the significant alert also factors in the time taken to observe all the alerts (99% of which are insignificant) that the IDS or SIEM generates.

13. L1 analysts are not scheduled on-call because the purpose of on-call workforce is to schedule the most efficient workforce to handle the additional alerts above the historical daily-average that are generated.

4 Analyst Resource Management Model Framework

This section presents the details of the cybersecurity analyst resource management model to minimize risk, and maintain risk under a pre-determined threshold. The framework of the model is provided in Fig. 3. The framework combines the model framework presented in [16, 17] into a single framework that explains the role of static and dynamic optimization, scheduling, and simulation. The analyst resource management model consists of three modules: the optimization, the scheduler and the simulation module. The optimization module determines the (1) number of analysts in a work-shift, and in turn within the organization, (2) expertise mix of analysts in a work-shift to investigate a wide range of alerts, and (3) optimal sensor to analyst level allocation, and the scheduling module for analysts guarantees that both number and expertise level of analysts in every work-shift are met.

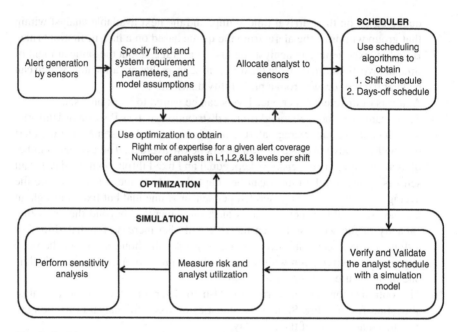

Fig. 3 Analyst resource management model

The simulation module takes the input from the optimization and scheduler, and determines the risk and analyst utilization by simulating different alert arrival rates. Feedback about risk and analyst utilization is provided to the optimization module to dynamically adjust the analyst workforce, both number and expertise mix, using on-call analysts. The simulation module can also be used a s a stand-alone module to perform sensitivity analysis of the model parameters. The details of the above framework are presented next.

4.1 Optimization Module

The optimization model consists of three models, which are executed in the following order—(1) a static mixed-integer programming model for obtaining the minimum number of analysts (static or regular workforce) for a historical daily-average alert generation rate calculated over the past 2-week period, (2) a dynamic model based on stochastic dynamic programming to obtain the minimum number of additional workforce and their expertise level that is needed (dynamic or on-call workforce) based on the estimated additional alerts per sensor for the next day, and (3) a genetic algorithm heuristic model that allocates sensors to analysts (both static and dynamic combined) subject to the constraints on analyst utilization, upper bound on risk, system constraints on analyst workload, and the desired experience level mix that is specified by the organization. The mathematical details of the models, algorithms, and implementation guidelines are available in [16, 17].

4.1.1 Static Workforce Optimization

The main input to the static optimization model is the number of sensors and a historical daily-average alert generation rate calculated over the past 2-week period. All sensors are treated equally and the historical daily-average alert generation rate is assumed to be the same for all sensors over the next 14-day period. The static optimization algorithm begins with the assumption that a large number of analysts are available at each experience level, among which the minimum number will be selected such that the model constraints are met. It should be noted that all calculations are done per day (24-h period) in the optimization model, whose output is now the input to the static scheduling model. Since regular (static) analysts work in 12- and 8-h shifts as per the model assumptions, the static scheduling model will determine the final workforce size of the organization and a feasible long-term days-off schedule for the analysts. The above optimization formulation is modeled and solved as a mixed-integer programming algorithm [7, 20, 32].

4.1.2 Dynamic Workforce Optimization

Stochastic Dynamic Programming (SDP) models for dynamic resource allocation problems exploit the fact that for complex systems with no well-defined analytical models and no closed form solutions, their *evolving properties can be studied through their interactions with the environment*. For the cybersecurity analyst dynamic scheduling problem, the availability of analysts is the dynamic (on-call) resource, and uncertainty is modeled by interacting with the dynamic alert generating environment. The three main inputs to the dynamic optimization model are the estimated additional number of alerts per sensor per hour for the following day, the available on-call analyst resource that must be optimally allocated, and the state value function, which is derived from the error in alert estimation. The additional number of alerts per sensor per hour is the number that is over and above the historical daily-average per sensor per hour that was used in the above static optimization. Also, alert rates for a sensor could drop below the average per hour. All sensors are not treated equally and the alert generation rate is assumed to be different for all sensors both within a day and between days over the next 14-day period. The above estimation is provided by the alert estimator model on a daily basis, however such a model was not developed in this chapter. Instead of an alert estimator model, the chapter assumes distributions for alert prediction, which could be replaced with the outputs of an alert estimator model. The dynamic optimization algorithm uses the information on next-day alert estimation, available on-call resource, the number of days left in a 14-day cycle, and its own state-value functions to determine the optimal number of dynamic (on-call) workforce needed along with their expertise level. The state value function plays a very important role by avoiding a myopic decision of reacting to completely fulfill all immediate analyst needs and running out of on-call analysts in the future when the estimated alert is high. Instead, the state value function guides the decision making process to be optimal overall by taking a long-term view that effectively manages the limited on-call resource.

4.1.3 Sensor to Analyst Allocation Using Heuristics

The sensor-to-analyst allocation for the following day is done by a genetic algorithm heuristic that considers the total workforce (static and dynamic) that reports to work and allocates them to sensors such that the model constraints are met under the 1-day look-ahead allocation block. If the allocation is not feasible then the constraints could be relaxed and/or the size and expertise mix of the on-call workforce could be overridden by a watch officer until an acceptable and feasible solution is found. In the long-run, it is expected that the alert estimation would improve and the dynamic programming model would have learnt to find the optimal actions (optimal number of on-call workforce per day) so that the genetic algorithm would also find a feasible sensor-to-analyst allocation that meets the constraints of the model. Also, it is very important to note as a word of caution that (1) allowing the heuristic to perform the job of dynamic programming in selecting the size of on-call workforce and their expertise level would make the decision making process myopic, which results in the risk of running out of on-call analysts in the future, and (2) excessive human intervention that changes the available on-call workforce will curtail the ability of the dynamic programming algorithm to learn action policies that makes the overall system optimal in the long-run. Decoupling the on-call decision making process by dynamic programming and the allocation process by heuristic has a computational advantage because the dynamic programming model is driven by the need to minimize and balance risk over the 14-day period, and the computational complexity of finding a feasible sensor-to-analyst allocation subject to the constraints will not slow down the dynamic programming's decision making process. Besides, another advantage is that human intervention can be modeled separately whose decision to override the dynamic programming's on-call workforce size decision will only affect the available on-call resource for the next day but not the current optimal decision of the dynamic programming model.

Once a feasible sensor to analyst allocation is implemented for the following day based on estimated alert generation, the on call-schedule is appended to the static 14-day schedule. At the end of that day, the performance metrics on risk and analyst utilization are obtained using the actual alert generated and investigated by the analysts through simulation.

4.2 Scheduler Module

The input to the 14-day static scheduling module is the number of personnel needed per level per day, which is derived from the integer programming optimization module. An optimal schedule for the static workforce can be derived based on the following constraints.

1. Each analyst gets at least 2 days off in a week and every other weekend off.
2. An analyst works no more than 5 consecutive days.
3. An analyst works 80 h per 2 weeks counted over 14 consecutive days between a Sunday and a Saturday. Both 12 and 8 h shift patterns are allowed.

The objective of the static workforce scheduling algorithm is to find the best days-off schedule and days-on schedule for both 12 and 8 h shifts for all analysts in the organization subject to the above scheduling constraints. A mixed integer programming scheduling model is used to obtain the 14-day static schedule.

During the 14-day schedule, the dynamic programming algorithm would assign on-call status to those analysts who have the day-off. The number of on-call analysts that actually report to work in a day is drawn from those who have been designated with the on-call status.

4.3 Simulation Module

The simulation module is used to validate the output of the optimization and the scheduler module. The simulation algorithm is presented under Algorithm 1. It is also used as a stand-alone module to perform initial risk analysis and sensitivity analysis of model parameters. The inputs to the simulation module are as follows.

1. Number of sensors, alert characteristics such as alert generation rate for the sensors,
2. Analyst characteristics such as time taken to analyze an alert based on the experience,
3. Number of analyst and sensor-to-analyst allocation for a given day, which are the outputs of the optimization model,
4. The shift and days-off schedule for analysts, which are the outputs of the scheduling model,
5. The assumptions of the optimization model that are also valid for the simulation model as well.

The outputs of the simulation model measure the utilization of each analyst per shift per day and the goodness of the cybersecurity analyst allocation model in terms of the risk. The alert generation is done using a probability distribution such as Poisson or uniform for the arrival of the alerts. The simulation module is run several times to obtain 95% confidence intervals on the overall utilization and the risk level that can be attained for a given sensor-to-analyst allocation that was determined by the optimization module.

Algorithm 1: Simulation algorithm to calculate risk and analyst utilization

---

Input: Number of sensors S, the number of analysts of L1, L2, and L3 type,
  sensor-to-analyst allocation for L1, L2, and L3 type analyst, total number of
  significant alerts generated M, the average time (in hours) taken by an analyst with
  L1, L2, and L3 level experience.

Output: 95% confidence intervals on risk, analyst utilization in % the number of significant
  alerts analyzed by analyst, and the total time spent by an analyst while engaged in
  alert investigation during a shift.

Step 1: Simulate a day's alert investigation by analysts
timeindex = 0;

repeat

  for *a given sensor-to-analyst allocation* **do**
    Generate alerts using a probability distribution and queue them based on arrival
    time;
    Analyze alerts using a first-in-first-out rule;
    Calculate total time that an analyst was engaged;
    timeindex ++ (1 hr time steps);

  end

until *timeindex* = 24;
Calculate Risk;
Calculate analyst utilization ;
Step 2: Replicate the simulation to calculate confidence intervals on risk and analyst
utilization

repeat

  Step 1 using newly generated alerts from the probability distribution;
  Continue calculating and storing the risk and analyst utilization for each simulation run;
  until *the number of simulation replications have been completed*;
  return *Confidence interval on risk and analyst utilization*

---

5   Results

The following section presents the results of the simulation studies that were
performed to obtain several useful insights about the cybersecurity analyst resource
management problem to mitigate risk and maintain risk under a pre-determined risk
threshold. First, the results of the initial stand-alone simulation study is provided,
including a separate section that provides the results from the design of experiments
study that analyses the sensitivity of the modeling parameters. Second, some results
of the static and dynamic optimization model is provided that shows the behavior
of risk under varying alert generation rates, and the adaptation of the optimization
model to meet the changes in workload demand for alert investigation. Finally,
the outputs of optimization are also validated through simulation. All the initial
simulation experiments to understand risk behavior were conducted with both
uniform and Poisson distribution for the average alert generation rate per sensor.

Table 2 Risk and analyst utilization for 10 sensors and 10 analysts [17]

	Case 1	Case 2	Case 3
Risk in %			
10-L3 level analysts only	2.2	60.9	82.4
4-L1, 3-L2, 3-L3	15.3	2.4	2.2
Analyst utilization in %			
10-L3 level analysts only	76.1	102.7	103.0
4-L1, 3-L2, 3-L3	89.5	98.4	99.4

Case 1: one-on-one sensor assignment. Case 2: multiple sensors to analyst. Case 3: all analysts can work on all sensors.

5.1 Results from Simulation Studies

The first stand-alone simulation study to measure risk was conducted with 10 sensors. Two types of analyst experience-level mix were studied—(1) all employees are highly trained (L3 level) before they are assigned to the 10 sensor(s), and (2) the analyst group has a mix of 40% L1, 30% L2 and 30% L3 level analyst who work on the 10 sensors. Three types of sensor-to-analyst allocation strategies were studied: (1) one-on-one allocation, (2) multiple sensors to analysts (L1 analyses 1–2 sensors, L2 analyses 2–3 sensors and L3 analyses 4–5 sensors), and (3) all analysts were assigned all sensors. The final variation was in the total number of analysts in which two levels were studied—with 10 (10 L3 vs 4-L1, 3-L2, 3-L3) and 5 (5 L3 vs 2-L1, 1-L2, 2-L3) analysts respectively.

The sensor-to-analyst allocation for the three cases were as follows—Case 1: one-on-one allocation, Case 2: multiple sensors to analysts (L1 analyses 1–2 sensors, L2 analyses 2–3 sensors and L3 analyses 4–5 sensors), and Case 3: all analysts were assigned all sensors. The time taken in hours by the analyst to investigate an alert from a given sensor based on their training was also provided. This data was obtained based on the information on analyst workload given under the fixed parameters section of the chapter. A similar set of tables were created for the five analyst scenario.

The significant alert generation rate was 1% of the entire alerts generated. Each sensor is said to generate about 15,000 alerts per day and 1% (approx. 150) are deemed to be significant, which must be analyzed by a cybersecurity analyst. The remaining alerts are considered insignificant. Therefore, the average significant alert generation per hour was taken to be 6.5. A uniform distribution ($U(0,13)$) and a Poisson distribution ($P(6.5)$), was used to generate the significant alerts per hour for this study. The results below are presented for the uniform distribution.

Table 2 presents the results of the first simulation study with 10 sensors and 10 analysts with varying proportions of experience and allocation strategy. The average values of overall risk and analyst utilization are presented from 50 simulation runs. First, the observations when all 10 analysts are at L3 level are presented. It is observed from Table 2 that the one-on-one sensor-to-analyst allocation (Case 1) with all L3 level analysts is ideal to achieve the lowest risk of 2.2%, however, the average analyst utilization is about 76.1%. This allocation strategy is certainly inefficient because the analysts are not being fully utilized, but more importantly, it is impractical to have as many analysts as the number of sensors. In Case 3, the risk level is very high (82.4%) when analysts are allowed to work on all sensors because analysts take more time to analyze alerts from sensors that they are not trained on. It is also impossible to train all analysts on all sensors. In Case 2, highly trained analysts work on multiple sensors but they are trained on only one of them. The strategy helps to increase their utilization but the risk level was high at 60.9%. The utilization was very high with numbers around 100%. Some of the utilization numbers are above 100%. This is because the analyst would finish the alert investigation that is on-going even if their shift time has ended. So they tend to stay a few minutes longer. Hence, the ratio of the time the analyst was utilized to the total length of their shift time could exceed 1. At the moment it is assumed that analysts immediately pick up the next alert in the queue as and when an on-going alert has been investigated. If no alert is available then the analyst would be idle. Personal break times are not modeled although a few breaks can be easily introduced in the simulation by adding scheduled analyst down-time.

Second, results from Table 2 when there is a mix of analysts experience such as 4-L1, 3-L2, 3-L3 are presented. It can be observed that the one-on-one allocation (Case 1) is a poor strategy because allocating a dedicated sensor to a junior analyst will result is many unanalyzed alerts due to the slow pace of work. This resulted in a risk of 15.3%. Having everyone work on all sensors (Case 3) was found to be the best strategy but it is impractical to train everyone on every sensor. Hence, the strategy that is viable and makes the most sense is to have a mix of analyst experience (Case 2) and train them on a set of multiple sensors by following the rule in which L1 analyses 1–2 sensors, L2 analyses 2–3 sensors and L3 analyses 4–5 sensors. The average risk level is 2.4% and the overall average analyst utilization is about 98.4%.

It is observed that Case 2 in Table 2 still has equal number of analysts and sensors, which is a very expensive strategy, hence, not very realistic to implement. In the following simulation study, all the parameters of the above simulation were held constant with the only change in the number of analysts from 10 to 5. Table 3 presents the results of the second simulation study with 10 sensors and 5

Table 3 Risk and analyst utilization for 10 sensors and 5 analysts [17]

	Case 1	Case 2	Case 3
Risk in %			
5-L3 level analysts only	NA	30.9	30.6
2-L1, 1-L2, 2-L3	NA	46.2	48.4
Analyst utilization in %			
5-L3 level analysts only	NA	99.6	99.7
2-L1, 1-L2, 2-L3	NA	99.7	100.0

Case 1: one-on-one sensor assignment. Case 2: multiple sensors to analyst. Case 3: all analysts can work on all sensors. NA: not applicable.

analysts. The one-on-one allocation strategy is not applicable for this study. The ideal strategy, given 5 analysts, was to have all five L3 analysts (senior level), which yielded an average risk of 30%. Since the queue length of the alerts were long due to fewer analysts, there was not a statistically significant difference between allocating multiple sensors (4–5 sensors to L3 level analysts) as in Case 2 and all sensors to all L3 analysts as in Case 3. The utilization in both cases was found to be almost 100%.

Since an organization tends to have a mix of analysts with various levels of expertise, a mix of 2-L1, 1-L2, 2-L3 level analysts was chosen for the 10 sensor and 5 analyst simulation study. Since L1 and L2 tend to work slower than L3, the risk increased from an average of 30% with all L3 level analysts to about an average of 47% with the analyst mix for both Case 2 and Case 3. There was no statistically significant difference between Case 2 and Case 3 in mitigating risk and in analyst utilization. The only way to minimize risk in a situation with a mix of analysts with different experience would be to increase the number of personnel. For a given risk, one of the ways to study the tradeoff between having a few L3 level analysts and a larger group of analysts with a mix of experience is to study the cost of hiring, which is one of the future works of this research. The utilization in both cases was found to be almost 100%.

5.2 Design of Experiments

The above simulation studies provided the basis for conducting further simulations of cybersecurity analyst resource management scenarios to measure risk. A design of experiment (DOE) test was conducted with the alert generation rate fixed at $(U(0,13))$ to study the impact of (1) increasing the number of sensors, and (2) varying the analyst/sensor ratio on the risk measure of the system. The analyst mix was maintained at 40% L1, 30% L2 and 30% L3 levels. Since the number of sensors is scaled up, all analysts were allowed to work on all sensors because there are several possible combinations of sensor-to-analyst allocation if one were to choose only a few sensors for each analyst. The main assumption of this study is that all analysts are also trained on all sensors. The time taken by analysts to investigate the alerts is the same as the previous studies, and the details on the time to investigate are the same as those provided under the fixed parameters section of this chapter. The DOE treatment combinations are as follows.

1. Vary the number of sensors. The DOE treatment levels are 10, 25, 50, 75, and 100.
2. Vary the analyst/sensor ratio. The DOE treatment levels are 0.5, 0.6, 0.75, 0.9, and 1.

Both risk and analyst utilization were observed in all the simulations and the average values of 50 simulations per treatment combination is presented for risk in Table 4. It can be observed from Table 4 that as the number of sensors is increased

Table 4 Risk in % [17]

| | Number of sensors | | | | |
Analyst/sensor ratio	10	25	50	75	100
0.5	48.4	46.6	47.5	46.8	48.1
0.6	25.4	26.2	26.4	25.8	26.4
0.75	10.8	10.5	11.2	10.9	10.3
0.9	4.5	4.1	4.2	4.1	3.9
1	2.2	2.2	2.8	2.6	2.5

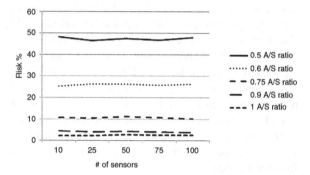

Fig. 4 Risk % vs number of sensors for varying analyst/sensor ratios [17]

there is no significant change in the Risk %. This is also shown in Fig. 4. This can be explained as follows. With the increase in the number of sensors and proportionally the number of analysts, both the arrival rate of alerts and the service rate of analysts are proportionally increased. If we assume that both arrival rate of alert from a sensor and service rate of an analyst to be Poisson distributed then the sum of several Poisson distributions is also Poisson distributed. From queueing theory, for a M/M/1 queue with Markovian arrival rate (total arrival rate of the system of several sensors), Markovian service rate (total service rate of the system with several analysts), and 1 service personnel (represents the combined service of all service personnel), the queue length and waiting time in the queue are dependent on the arrival and service rates [18]. The ratio of the arrival to service rate ρ remains the same when the number of sensors and analysts are increased proportionally. Hence, the risk % will remain the same. The only way to reduce the risk is to increase the service rate by holding the arrival rate fixed (increase the number of analysts). Also, in the above experiment, all analysts were trained on all sensors, which is neither cost-effective nor is practical to implement.

In summary, both from the above DOE study and the simulations done earlier, it is clear that a mix of analysts is required for an organization of cybersecurity analysts, and realistically only a few sensors can be allocated to an analyst based on their level of expertise. Hence, it is imperative to have a model that can assign sensors to analysts such that minimum number of analyst with the right experience mix are hired for a given upper bound on risk%, number of sensors, and alert generation rate.

5.3   Results from Static Workforce Optimization

The following section presents the results in terms of risk for a static workforce with no estimation of future alerts (hence cannot adapt to varying alert generation), which serves as a baseline for comparison with the learning-based stochastic dynamic programming model that includes the estimation of future alert rates. The mixed integer programming model determines the optimal number of static analysts at each expertise level per 12 h shift and optimally allocates the sensors to analysts. The objective is to minimize the total number of analysts in the organization. The mathematical details of the models, algorithms, and implementation guidelines are available in [17].

The following input parameters and constraints were provided.

1. Number of sensors = 10.
2. An organization that aims to have a mix of personnel with L1, L2 and L3 level experience should aim to find the right mix of expertise for a given upper bound on risk level that it wishes to maintain. The required analyst proportion in the organization was set to 20–40% L1, 30–50% L2 and 30–40% L3 level.
3. Number of days to optimize per run of the algorithm—2 weeks (14 days). The 2-week run is used to obtain $12 * 6 + 8 * 1 = 80$ h of work in a 14-day period.
4. Risk upper bound = 5%.
5. Analyst utilization = 95–100%.
6. Number of sensors to be allocated per analyst 1–2 for L1, 3–4 for L2, and 4–5 for L3.
7. Alert generation rate per sensor per h. The significant alert generation rate was 1% of the entire alerts generated per day. The remaining alerts are considered insignificant. Due to lack of real-world data (highly sensitive), an alert estimator model was not developed. Instead, the alert predictions were generated for 14 days using a combined Uniform distribution $U(0,13)$ and Poisson(2) distribution with a mean value of $\lambda = 2$ alerts per h/sensor (referred as baseline for this research). The Poisson distribution provided a wide range of variability for the uncertainty model. After combining the above distributions, the actual alert generation was approximately 9 alerts per hour per sensor and was drawn from $(U(0,18))$ per hour per sensor, with each sensor having a different rate of alert generation. The above process for predicted and actual alert generation was repeated for each 14-day run of the integer programming model. In the real-world the actual rate will come from the process itself and the predicted rate from the statistical model developed by the organization, which is part of the future work of this research.
8. Average alert analysis rate for each level of analyst is specified in time units— 12 min/alert for L1, 7.5 min/alert for L2, and 5 min/alert for L3.

Table 5 shows a sample output of the actual number of alerts generated, actual number analyzed, risk % for a sensor to analyst allocation as determined by the genetic algorithm heuristic. It can be observed that the risk was ≤5% on days (5, 7,

Table 5 Number of alerts investigated and risk % for a sample 14-day run using a static sensor-analyst allocation [17]

Day	1	2	3	4	5	6	7	8	9	10	11	12	13	14	Average
Total # actual alerts	2275	2064	2256	2066	2125	2250	2165	2230	2110	2165	2089	2225	2165	2105	2164
# of alerts investigated	2088	2077	2088	2053	2088	2088	2088	2088	2088	2088	2077	2088	2088	2088	2084
Risk %	8.0	0.0	8.0	0.0	2.8	7.0	3.9	7.0	0.6	2.8	0.0	6.0	3.9	0.6	3.6

10, and 13) when the number of actual alerts were statistically indifferent to the 14-day historical daily-average alert generation rate reported in the last column of the table (14-day average = 2164). The above outcome is because the mixed integer programming model was run with a 5% risk upper bound and a fixed 14-day historical daily-average alert generation rate as input. On days (1, 3, 6, 8, and 12) when the actual number of alerts exceeded the historical daily-average (statistically significant), the risk % was higher because the integer programming model has a static sensor to analyst allocation and could not adapt the workforce size to match the increase in alert generation. Similarly, on days (2, 4, 9, 11, and 14) with alert generation being significantly below the historical daily-average alert generation rate, the risk was closer to the ideal value of 0%, because the mixed integer programming optimization model for determining the minimum number of analysts and their sensor to analyst allocation was run with a 5% upper bound on risk. Also, it must be noted that the utilization requirement of all analysts was kept between 95% and 100% during the run of the optimization model. However, in a rare occurrence, if the actual number of alerts falls far below the historical daily-average alert generation per day then one can expect some underutilization of analysts.

Clearly, the above sample result indicates that the static mixed integer programming model cannot adapt to the uncertainty in alert generation rate, and at best can provide a static workforce requirement for a 14-day period that is based on historical daily-average alert generation rate. Consequently, on days when the alert generation is higher than the historical daily-average, the risk will be higher than the 5% upper bound. Therefore, a dynamic workforce scheduling model is needed, which estimates the 1-day look-ahead uncertainty in workload and schedules the analysts to meet the workload demand. The results of the dynamic model are presented next.

5.4 Results from Dynamic Workforce Optimization

The dynamic model is run in three stages—exploration, exploitation (learning), and learnt (implementation or validation). All of the inputs as specified above in the mixed integer programming model are valid for the dynamic model except there is a change in how the alert generation is processed by the model. Unlike the integer programming model which uses only historical average alert generation rate, the dynamic model estimates the 1-day look-ahead alert generation rate at the end of the current day. If the estimate exceeds the historical daily-average then analysts from the dynamic (on-call) workforce is called in to work for the next day. The historical daily-average alert generation is handled by the daily scheduled workforce, who is referred as static work force in both the stochastic dynamic programming model and the static mixed-integer programming model. The results of the learnt phase of the dynamic programming model are given below. The mathematical details of the models, algorithms, and implementation guidelines are available in [16].

Table 6 Risk % over a 14-day period with both static and dynamic (on-call) workforce [16]

Day of week	Sun	Mon	Tue	Wed	Thu	Fri	Sat	Sun	Mon	Tue	Wed	Thu	Fri	Sat
Day	1	2	3	4	5	6	7	8	9	10	11	12	13	14
Total # actual alerts	2275	2064	2256	2066	2125	2250	2165	2230	2110	2165	2089	2225	2165	2105
Total # of alerts investigated	2218	2057	2218	2057	2057	2218	2057	2218	2057	2057	2057	2218	2057	2057
Risk %	2.5	0.3	1.7	0.4	3.2	1.4	5.0	0.5	2.5	5.0	1.5	0.3	5.0	2.3
Analyst mix	3L1	3L1	3L1	3L1	3L1	3L1	3L1	3L1	3L1	3L1	3L1	3L1	3L1	3L1
	3L2	3L2	3L2	3L2	3L2	3L2	3L2	3L2	3L2	3L2	3L2	3L2	3L2	3L2
	5L3	4L3	5L3	4L3	4L3	5L3	4L3	5L3	4L3	4L3	4L3	5L3	4L3	4L3

5.4.1 Alert Processing by Dynamic Programming

In order to compare the dynamic programming results with the mixed integer programming results, the predicted alert generation rate was maintained at $U(0,13)$ + Poisson(2)/h/sensor, which is also the number of alerts for the static model that has no prediction. Myopically, the decision of a shift manager would have been to determine the required number of additional analysts at each level of expertise that are needed to investigate fully the predicted additional demand in the workload due to the alerts that are over and above the historical daily-average number of alerts. Thus, a long-term view is not taken, and there is a potential danger to run-out of on-call workforce toward the later part of the 14-day work cycle. Since the dynamic workforce is limited, the dynamic programming decision obtained may not necessarily provide all of the required number of analysts to meet the next-day's additional workload demand fully. Instead, the dynamic programming algorithm will aim to balance risk between the 14 days by taking a long-term view (includes the value of the next system state), which in turn avoids the situation of running out of on-call resources when there is a critical need.

Finally, the actual number of alerts per sensor per hour was obtained using $U(0, 18)$, and the total number of actual alerts per day from all sensors is shown in Table 6. Using a pair-wise student t-test, it was observed with a 95% confidence level that there was no statistical significant difference between the total predicted and the total actual number of alerts generated per day. In the real-world, the alert prediction model per sensor must be constructed from historical actual alert patterns, and actual alerts per sensor must be obtained directly from the intrusion detection system. The risk % is shown in Table 6, which is obtained by comparing the number of alerts investigated to the actual number of alerts generated. Since the risk % was kept below 5%, it can be concluded that the optimization decision to bring in the additional analysts (dynamic workforce) was optimal subject to the constraints in the model.

Table 7 Sensitivity analysis [16]

Estimated number of alerts	Static workforce per 12 h shift	Additional dynamic workforce needed per 12 h shift	Risk %
Number of alerts below average	3L1,3L2,4L3	No dynamic workforce	Less than 5%
Average number of alerts	3L1,3L2,4L3	No dynamic workforce	5
2.5% increase in alerts above average	3L1,3L2,4L3	1L3	0
9.3% increase in alerts above average	3L1,3L2,4L3	1L3	5
9.3% increase in alerts above average	3L1,3L2,4L3	1L3 and 1L2	0
18.4% increase in alerts above average	3L1,3L2,4L3	1L3 and 1L2	5
18.4% increase in alerts above average	3L1,3L2,4L3	2L3	0
24.8% increase in alerts above average	3L1,3L2,4L3	2L3	5
24.8% increase in alerts above average	3L1,3L2,4L3	2L3 and 1 L2	0
28.7% increase in alerts above average	3L1,3L2,4L3	2L3 and 1 L2	5
28.7% increase in alerts above average	3L1,3L2,4L3	2L3 and 2L2	0
33% increase in alerts above average	3L1,3L2,4L3	2L3 and 2L2	5

5.5 Sensitivity Analysis

One of the main sensitivity analyses is to test the efficacy and adaptability of the stochastic dynamic programming model to minimize risk subject to the variations in the prediction of alert generation. The total number of actual alerts is calculated from the sum of alerts generated at U(0,13)/sensor/h and the additional alerts generated from Poisson(λ)/sensor/h for capturing the uncertainty in alerts. Again, the sum of $U(0, 13)$ *and Poisson*(2) was used as the baseline historical daily-average alert generation rate. To perform the sensitivity analysis, the value of λ is increased very gradually (instead of steps of 1 for inducing spikes as shown earlier). The predicted value of alerts, the available workforce, and the number of days left in the 14-day cycle were used to trigger a decision of how many additional dynamic (on-call) workforce was needed and at what level of expertise. As performance metrics, the changes in the risk %, and workforce mix were observed. Table 7 provides the outcome of the above study. As the alert generation was increased in steps (measured in percentage increase over the historical daily-average alert generation rate per day), there are certain intervals when the risk would increase from 0% towards 5%

Fig. 5 Risk % vs
analyst/sensor ratio [17]

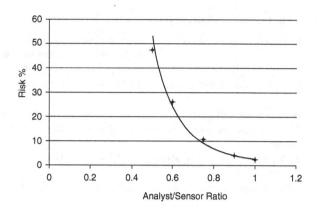

for a constant analyst mix. Any further increase in predicted alert generation would
then increase the risk above 5%, however, by adding an analyst from the dynamic
workforce, the risk is reduced to 0%. For example, between 2.5% and 9.3% increase
in alert generation over the above historical daily-average, one additional L3 analyst
is enough to maintain the risk below 5%, however, any increase above 9.3% in
alert generation over the historical daily-average would require an additional L2
analyst to keep the risk under 5%. The combined effort of 1 additional L3 and
1 additional L2 analyst can keep the risk under 5% until the additional alerts
generated increase above 18.4% of the historical daily-average alert generation rate.
The above observations show that the stochastic dynamic programming algorithm is
adaptable to increases in historical daily-average alert generation rates by drawing
upon a dynamic workforce (on-call analysts) to meet the uncertain demands in alert
investigation such that the risk remains below the pre-set upper bound of 5%.

5.6   Validation of Optimization Using Simulation

The sensor-to-analyst allocation results that were obtained from the optimization
model were run 50 times each using the simulation model, and the 95% confidence
intervals on risk and analyst utilization are presented in Table 8. The simulation
followed Algorithm 1. For each simulation, the number of sensors, and the number
of analysts at L1, L2, and L3 levels were fixed for 5% and 25% risk respectively.
Alerts were generated using both U(0,13) and Poisson(6.5) distributions, and
results from the uniform distribution are presented here. The alert allocation and
investigation continued for a 24 h period and the 95% confidence intervals on risk
and analyst utilization were determined. Several simulation scenarios were studied
and the results from a sample of four cases is presented in Table 8. It can be observed
that the average values of the risk and analyst utilizations match those that were set
for the optimization algorithm. Thus, the optimization results were validated using
the simulation model.

Figure 5 summarizes the plot between risk and analyst/sensor (A/S) ratio. It should be noted from Fig. 4 that for a given A/S ratio, there is no significant change in risk as the number sensors increases. This means that as long as the rate of arrival of alerts and the rate of service by analysts remain the same regardless of the number of sensors, the queue length and the time that an alert awaits investigation will remain the same as proved by the queueing theory model for M/M/1 queues [18]. Figure 5 is an important chart that explains the relationship between risk and number of personnel to hire per day for a given number of sensors, which is expressed as A/S ratio. It should be noted that the plot holds good only for a given analyst mix that the organization desires, fixed average alert generation rate per sensor, fixed value of number of sensors that can be allocated to an analyst, fixed analyst mix in a work shift which depends on scheduling constraints, and fixed value of the service time to investigate an alert which depends on the analyst experience level. Clearly, risk depends on several factors. Hence, Fig. 5 is a simplified plot of risk vs. A/S ratio in which the ratio of analysts to sensors determines the risk level when all other factors given above are kept constant. Therefore, it should not be construed that the optimization model can be simplified merely by adjusting the A/S ratio to build a certain capacity that can maintain a certain upper-bound on risk. The figure shows a non-linear relationship between risk and analyst/sensor ratio. As the A/S ratio drops, the risk increases dramatically. The above figure can guide the personnel hiring decision making process of an organization provided the other factors given above are maintained fixed at a pre-determined level. The total cost of personnel can be easily derived using personnel pay-scale, once the number personnel and their expertise level is known.

In summary, the simulation studies indicated the following:

1. One-on-one allocation of sensor to analyst is the best strategy for minimizing risk, however, the strategy is impractical to implement.

Table 8 Confidence interval on risk and analyst utilization for four sample sensor-to-analyst allocations [17]

Number of sensors	50	75	25	100
Analysts with experience mix L1	10	15	3	10
Analysts with experience mix L2	15	23	6	30
Analysts with experience mix L3	16	24	6	20
Average risk in %	5.8	6.2	26.8	26.2
95% confidence internal on risk in %	4.9–6.7	5.1–7.3	25.2–28.4	24.8–27.6
Analyst utilization in %	99.9	99.5	99.6	99.4
95% confidence internal on utilization in %	99.8–100	99.3–99.7	99.5–99.7	99.3–99.5

2. Do not allocate a dedicated sensor to a junior analyst. Junior analysts are slower in investigating alerts and many significant alerts will remain unanalyzed.
3. When there are fewer analysts in comparison to the number of sensors (analyst to sensor ratio = 0.5), having all L3 level senior analysts is the best strategy than having a mix of experience among the analysts.
4. A single queue for alerts waiting for investigation is used. When multiple sensors are assigned to an analyst and multiple analysts are assigned to sensors, the sensors are grouped and allocated to the analyst group. A single queue of alerts is formed within this group based on the time of arrival. Alerts are drawn from the queue on a first-in-first-out basis.
5. An organization that aims to have a mix of personnel with L1, L2 and L3 level experience should aim to find the right mix of expertise for a given upper bound on risk level that it wishes to maintain.

6 Conclusion

The chapter presents operations research and simulation methods to an important operational security problem on how to manage analyst resources better to minimize security threats. A new notion of risk is defined that measures the number of unanalyzed alerts at the end of every work-shift. The goal of the CSOC is to minimize the risk and maintain it under a pre-determined threshold. In order to achieve the above, the chapter determines the primary parameters that affect risk such as (1) the number of analysts in a work-shift, and in turn within the organization, (2) expertise mix of analysts in a work-shift to investigate a wide range of alerts, (3) optimal sensor to analyst allocation, and (4) optimal scheduling of analysts that guarantees both number and expertise mix of analysts in every work-shift.

The chapter then presents an optimization model for setting the optimal values of the above parameters in a dynamic environment that has variations in alert generation rates. The framework to measure risk is modeled in three modules: (1) optimization, (2) scheduler, and (3) simulation. The framework is very generic and can be used with any number of sensors with various alert generation rates. The model parameters are adaptable to increasing alert generation rates by drawing from a pool of available dynamic analyst workforce (on-call). Risk as defined in this chapter can be further mitigated with the above dynamic workforce that complements the static workforce to meet the increase in the workload demand for alert investigation. A combination uniform and Poisson distributions is used as the 1-day look-ahead prediction of alert generation per sensor. The empirical results, sensitivity study, and validation study confirms the viability of the framework to optimally manage the analyst resource to minimize and maintain risk within a pre-determined threshold under the uncertainty of alert generation and model constraints.

There are several future extensions to the research chapter. Uncertainty modeling (alert estimation or prediction) is a key component that drives the dynamic workforce scheduling. Hence, accurate estimate of the uncertainty is very critical. The chapter used an uncertainty model by combining two distributions to test the concept of dynamic scheduling, however, sophisticated models of uncertainty (alert prediction models) could be built that identifies patterns on a time-frequency scale and in space (location of sensor). Also, major world events, sporting events, and national holidays could be used as triggers for scheduling additional analysts. Shift scheduling was not performed, and analysts were assumed to have non-overlapping shifts. However, alert generation rate can change from time-to-time. Consequently, more analysts are needed at certain hours of the day. In such a case, over-lapping shifts with different shift lengths can provide the required number of analysts to meet the hourly demand using shift-scheduling algorithms [25]. The sensor-to-analyst allocation model in this chapter is dynamic to the extent that it is based on an estimated workload for the next day. Consequently, a dynamic workforce may or may not be called. Once fixed at the end of the day, the sensor-to-analyst allocation model is static for the rest of the next day and does not adapt to changes in alert generation rates within a shift due to unforeseen reasons such as absenteeism of analysts or excessive workload from an intrusion in one or many sensors. A new model for within shift reallocation of sensors to analysts is required to address variations in alert generation between sensors in a shift. The model will adapt to changing demands and ensure that the optimal workforce is maintained from hour-to-hour on a daily basis. The above extensions combined with the chapter's dynamic (on-call) workforce component will further increase the efficiency of the cybersecurity workforce to minimize the overall risk from threats, which will provide the maximum readiness capability to the cyber defense organization.

Acknowledgements The authors would like to thank Dr. Cliff Wang of the Army Research Laboratory for suggesting this problem to us. Ganesan, Jajodia, and Shah were partially supported by the Army Research Office under grants W911NF-13-1-0421 and W911NF-15-1-0576 and by the Office of Naval Research grant N00014-15-1-2007.

References

1. M. Albanese, C. Molinaro, F. Persia, A. Picariello, V.S. Subrahmanian, Discovering the top-k unexplained sequences in time-stamped observation data. IEEE Trans. Knowl. Data Eng. **26**(3), 577–594 (2014)
2. J.P. Anderson, Computer security threat monitoring and surveillance. Tech. Rep. James P. Anderson Co., Fort Washington, PA (1980)
3. M.E. Aydin, E. Oztemel, Dynamic job-shop scheduling using reinforcement learning agents. Robot. Auton. Syst. **33**(2), 169–178 (2000)
4. D. Barbara, S. Jajodia (eds.), *Application of Data Mining in Computer Security*, vol. 6. Advances in Information Security (Springer, New York, 2002)
5. S. Bhatt, P.K. Manadhata, L. Zomlot, The operational role of security information and event management systems. IEEE Secur. Priv. **12**(5), 35–41 (2014)

6. D. Botta, K Muldner, K Hawkey, K Beznosov, Toward understanding distributed cognition in it security management: the role of cues and norms. Cogn. Tech. Work **13**(2), 121–134 (2011)
7. D.S. Chen, R.G. Batson, Y. Dang, *Applied Integer Programming* (Wiley, Hoboken, 2010)
8. CIO, DON Cyber Crime Handbook. Department of Navy, Washington, DC (2008)
9. A. D'Amico, K. Whitley, The real work of computer network defense analysts: the analysis roles and processes that transform network data into security situation awareness, in *Proceedings of the Workshop on Visualization for Computer Security*, pp. 19–37 (2008)
10. D.E. Denning, An intrusion-detection model, in *Proceedings of IEEE Symposium on Security and Privacy*, Oakland, CA, pp. 118–131 (1986)
11. D.E. Denning, An intrusion-detection model. IEEE Trans. Softw. Eng. **13**(2), 222–232 (1987)
12. R. Di Pietro, L.V. Mancini (eds.), *Intrusion Detection Systems*, vol. 38. Advances in Information Security (Springer, New York, 2008)
13. H. Du, S.J. Yang, Temporal and spatial analyses for large-scale cyber attacks, in *Handbook of Computational Approaches to Counterterrorism*, ed. by V.S. Subrahmanian (Springer, New York, 2013), pp. 559–576
14. R.F. Erbacher, S.E. Hutchinson, Extending case-based reasoning to network alert reporting, in *2012 ASE International Conference on Cyber Security*, pp. 187–194 (2012)
15. S.M. Furnell, N. Clarke, R. Werlinger, K. Muldner, K. Hawkey, K. Beznosov, Preparation, detection, and analysis: the diagnostic work of it security incident response. Inf. Manag. Comput. Secur. **18**(1), 26–42 (2010)
16. R. Ganesan, S. Jajodia, A. Shah, H. Cam, Dynamic scheduling of cybersecurity analysts for minimizing risk using reinforcement learning. ACM Trans. Intell. Syst. Technol. **8**(1), 4:1–4:21 (2016). https://doi.org/10.1145/2882969
17. R. Ganesan, S. Jajodia, H. Cam, Optimal scheduling of cybersecurity analyst for minimizing risk. ACM Trans. Intell. Syst. Technol. **8**(4), 52:1–52:33 (2017). http://dx.doi.org/10.1145/2914795
18. D. Gross, J. Shortle, J. Thompson, C. Harris, *Fundamentals of Queuing Theory* (Wiley-Interscience, New York, 2008)
19. D. Lesaint, C. Voudouris, N. Azarmi, I. Alletson, B. Laithwaite, Field workforce scheduling. BT Technol. J. **21**(4), 23–26 (2003)
20. G.L. Nemhauser, L.A. Wolsey, *Integer and Combinatorial Optimization* (Wiley-Interscience, New York, 1999)
21. Y. Nobert, J. Roy, Freight handling personnel scheduling at air cargo terminals. Transp. Sci. **32**(3), 295–301 (1998)
22. S. Northcutt, J. Novak, *Network Intrusion Detection*, 3rd edn. (New Riders Publishing, Thousand Oaks, CA, 2002)
23. C.D. Paternina-Arboleda, T.K. Das, A multi-agent reinforcement learning approach to obtaining dynamic control policies for stochastic lot scheduling problem. Simul. Model. Pract. Theory **13**(5), 389–406 (2005)
24. V. Paxson, Bro: a system for detecting network intruders in real-time. Comput. Netw. **31**(23–24), 2435–2463 (1999)
25. M. Pinedo, *Planning and Scheduling in Manufacturing and Services* (Springer, New York, 2009)
26. J. Reis, N. Mamede, *Multi-Agent Dynamic Scheduling and Re-Scheduling with Global Temporal Constraints* (Kluwer Academic Publishers, Boston, 2002)
27. R. Sadoddin, A. Ghorbani, Alert correlation survey: framework and techniques, in *Proceedings of the ACM International Conference on Privacy, Security and Trust* (ACM, New York, 2006), pp. 1–10
28. R. Sommer, V. Paxson, Outside the closed world: on using machine learning for network intrusion detection, in *Proceedings of IEEE Symposium on Security and Privacy*, pp. 305–316 (2010)
29. V.S. Subrahmanian, M. Ovelgonne, T. Dumitras, A. Prakash, *The Global Cyber-Vulnerability Report* (Springer, Cham, 2015)

30. S.C. Sundaramurthy, J. McHugh, X. Ou, M. Wesch, A.G. Bardas, S.R. Rajagopalan, Turning contradictions into innovations or: how we learned to stop whining and improve security operations, in *Twelfth Symposium on Usable Privacy and Security (SOUPS 2016)* (2016)
31. F. Valeur, G. Vigna, C. Kruegel, R.A. Kemmerer, A comprehensive approach to intrusion detection alert correlation. IEEE Trans. Dependable Secure Comput. **1**(3), 146–169 (2004)
32. W. Winston, *Operations Research* (Cengage Learning, New York, 2003)
33. S.J. Zaccaro, R.S. Dalal, L.E. Tetrick, J.A. Steinke, *Psychosocial Dynamics of Cyber Security* (Routledge, New York, 2016)
34. F. Zhou, J. Wang, J. Wang, J. Jonrinaldi, A dynamic rescheduling model with multi-agent system and its solution method. J. Mech. Eng. **58**(2), 81–92 (2012)
35. C. Zimmerman, *The Strategies of a World-Class Cybersecurity Operations Center* (The MITRE Corporation, McLean, VA, 2014)